The Not-Yet God

Other Orbis books from Ilia Delio

Christ in Evolution

The Emergent Christ:
Exploring the Meaning of Catholic in an
Evolutionary Universe

The Unbearable Wholeness of Being:
God, Evolution, and the Power of Love

From Teilhard to Omega:
Co-Creating an Unfinished Universe

Making All Things New:
Catholicity, Cosmology, Consciousness

Birth of a Dancing Star:
My Journey from Cradle Catholic to Cyborg Christian

Re-Enchanting the Earth:
Why AI Needs Religion

The Hours of the Universe:
Reflections on God, Science, and the Human Journey

The Not-Yet God

*Carl Jung, Teilhard de Chardin,
and the Relational Whole*

Ilia Delio, OSF

ORBIS BOOKS
Maryknoll, New York 10545

Second Printing, March 2024

Founded in 1970, Orbis Books endeavors to publish works that enlighten the mind, nourish the spirit, and challenge the conscience. The publishing arm of the Maryknoll Fathers and Brothers, Orbis seeks to explore the global dimensions of the Christian faith and mission, to invite dialogue with diverse cultures and religious traditions, and to serve the cause of reconciliation and peace. The books published reflect the views of their authors and do not represent the official position of the Maryknoll Society. To learn more about Maryknoll and Orbis Books, please visit our website at www.orbisbooks.com.

Library of Congress Cataloging-in-Publication Data

Names: Delio, Ilia, author.
Title: The Not-yet God : Carl Jung, Teilhard de Chardin, and the relational whole / Ilia Delio, OSF.
Description: Maryknoll, NY : Orbis Books, [2023] | Includes bibliographical references and index. | Summary: "A Christian theological engagement with evolutionary theory, quantum theory, and relational holism through the works of Teilhard de Chardin and Carl Jung" — Provided by publisher.
Identifiers: LCCN 2023007213 (print) | LCCN 2023007214 (ebook) | ISBN 9781626985353 | ISBN 9781608339921 (epub)
Subjects: LCSH: Jung, C. G. (Carl Gustav), 1875–1961—Religion. | Teilhard de Chardin, Pierre—Religion. | Religion and science—Philosophy. | Theology. | Philosophical theology. | Holism—Philosophy. | Christianity—Philosophy. | Cosmology. | Theology of religions (Christian theology) | God.
Classification: LCC BL240.3 .D453 2033 (print) | LCC BL240.3 (ebook) | DDC 150.19/54092—dc23/eng/20230628
LC record available at https://lccn.loc.gov/2023007213
LC ebook record available at https://lccn.loc.gov/2023007214

I am grateful for the work of my research assistant,
Robert Nicastro, whose keen eye for details
made footnotes look ready-made;
and for the excellent editorial work of
Dr. Thomas Hermans-Webster of Orbis Books,
whose expertise in Process theology was very helpful;
and for the Holy Child Sisters who graciously shared their
Motherhouse space while the hallway
outside my apartment underwent major repair.
The transcendent goodness of the human person
is evolution's best kept secret,
and the ultimate source of this goodness is God.
I dedicate this book
to all who seek the living God in a world of change.

"We are mothers when we carry Him in our heart and body through a divine love and a pure and sincere conscience and give birth to him through a holy activity which must shine as an example before others."

Saint Francis of Assisi, "Letter to the Faithful"

"My me is God, nor do I recognize any other me except my God Himself."

Saint Catherine of Genoa, "Life and Doctrine"

"May I be for him a new humanity in which he can renew all his mystery."

Saint Elizabeth of the Trinity, "Prayer to the Most Holy Trinity"

Contents

Introduction

Every five hundred years or so religion undergoes a significant paradigm shift.[1] The shift we are in today is so dramatic I thought about putting a warning label at the beginning of this book. *WARNING: This book may be hazardous to the stability of your soul and may cause undue anxiety or outright bursts of emotion.*

We are, indeed, in a major "God" shift. The old God of the starry heavens, the sky God, has been falling since the early twentieth century; at the same time, a new God has been rising up from the strange world of matter. This book tells the story of the new God emerging in a new paradigm. The title, *The Not-Yet God,* was inspired by John Haught's recent book, *God after Einstein,* where he brilliantly discusses how the new universe story evokes a new understanding of God.[2] What Haught describes on

---

1. See Phyllis Tickle's landmark work, *The Great Emergence* (Ada, MI: Baker Publishing Group, 2012), in which she focuses on the ways that Christianity has undergone paradign shifts every five hundred-or-so years. Others have since noticed similar patterns in other religious traditions.

2. John F. Haught, *God after Einstein: What's Really Going on in the Universe?* (New Haven: Yale University Press, 2022), 12.

the cosmic level, I describe on the personal level, for the human person not only recapitulates but also advances the universe on the level of self-consciousness.

I wish this could be a book of meditations rather than one with numerous footnotes and heavy philosophical ideas. But we are a complex people in a complex world, and philosophical insight is necessary for theology. So, please, be patient as you ponder the ideas put forth. Of course, I should be able to tell this story without having to rely on so many external sources, but if I were to do so, I doubt the new God story would be taken too seriously. Even now, with all the footnotes, many theologians and philosophers will undoubtedly dismiss my claims as sheer nonsense or, better yet, heretical (this is more likely the case). A woman theologian espousing a new theology is bound to be suspect. Yet, "God speaks in many and various ways" (Heb 1:1–4), and today God is speaking loudly through women. So, please, pay attention.

When Albert Einstein proposed the theory of relativity in 1905, the world of physics was shocked to its core. Isaac Newton's laws had reigned for more than three hundred years, and to overturn them seemed—well—scientifically heretical. Yet Einstein's mathematics pointed to the fact that the laws of relativity better fit reality than did Newton's laws of absolute space and time. Pondering a beam of light, Einstein came up with equations that upset Newtonian physics and gave birth to a new science of quantum physics. Both quantum physics and evolution turned the God question upside down by challenging religions to realize there is no "up" or "down." What we thought was beyond us is now within us. What we considered to be clear and logical is now dark and mysterious. The renowned physicists Max Planck, Werner Heisenberg, and Albert Einstein all agreed that the universe is filled with mystery. Planck's brilliant insight is integral to this book: "Science cannot solve the ultimate mystery of nature. And that is because, in the last analysis, we ourselves are a part of the mystery we are trying to solve."[3]

---

3. Max Planck, *Where Is Science Going?* (Quebec: Minkowski Institute Press, 1932), 217.

To appreciate the new God story, we have to enter into the greatest mystery of all: the human person. What are we humans, after all, but gods in the making, and making the wrong god makes the wrong kind of world in which to live. One sign that our God-compass is out of whack is the cultural entropy of our fragile world. Global warming, the power of greed, sexism and racism—all are wearing down the integrity of the earth. The development of artificial intelligence and the meteoric rise of cyberspace in the late twentieth century revealed the human person's desperate search for ultimate connections. Despite our well-honed Christian theology, there seems to be a cavernous God-hole in the human heart. The great Jesuit theologian Karl Rahner recognized this fact in the twentieth century, as did Steve Jobs, the founder of Apple Corporation. What Rahner sought in the development of his transcendental theology, Jobs sought in the development of the computer. Both Rahner and Jobs realized that the inmost center of the human person is nothing less than the infinite depth of desire.

Science has overturned our understanding of mind and matter, and religion is being uprooted as I write. We are not what we think we are, and we are not quite happy with what we are. The poet T. S. Elliot expresses human depth in its open mystery:

Love is most nearly itself.
When here and now cease to matter.
Old men ought to be explorers
Here or there does not matter
We must be still and still moving
Into another intensity
For a further union, a deeper communion
Through the dark cold and the empty desolation,
The wave cry, the wind cry, the vast waters
Of the petrel and the porpoise.
In my end is my beginning.[4]

---

4. T. S. Eliot, *The Complete Poems and Plays: 1909–1950* (London: Harcourt Brace and Company, 1950), 129.

We humans are always ending and beginning; this is the story of our evolution. We humans *are in* evolution, and evolution is fundamental to the new story of religion.

MYTH

We need a new story because we *Homo sapiens* are a story species. Myths are stories that help us make sense of our liminal existence. A myth is always a true story because it narrates a sacred history, not necessarily a factual history, but one that has meaning and value for human life. Myths are true in that they have the symbolic and imaginative power to make us aware of the unity of reality in its greatest depth and breadth. Myth begins in humanity's experience of the sacred which, Mircea Eliade states, is an element in the *structure of consciousness*, not a stage in the history of events. Eliade spoke of an irreducible sacred dimension of all reality, a cosmic axis around which everything, both literally and meta-phorically, revolves. He saw the motif of the separation of heaven and earth in creation myths pointing to a fundamental alienation from the primordial unity of spiritual being. Consequently, people could maintain their connection to the spiritual sources of meaning only through an imaginal conduit, an *axis mundi*, a bond between heaven and earth which became implicitly present in religious ritual and which was embodied architecturally in important temples and sacred sites. The *axis mundi* ("axis of the world") is an image of connection between the mundane, terrestrial plane and the transcendent home of the spirit(s) above.

Myths naturally evolve and change. Karl Jaspers noted a major shift in consciousness from about 800 BCE to 200 BCE, what he called the "axial age," in Europe and Asia. The axis of the world had shifted over time, and that shift corresponded to new understandings of cosmic order. During the "pre-axial age," early communities of the human species thought the world was flat and two-tiered, with spiritual and material realms. Religious consciousness manifested itself in communal rituals and animism —godly powers in nature—all woven together, linking nature and humanity. The pre-axial period was marked by a level of religious-mythic consciousness that was cosmic, collective, tribal, and ritualistic. Ancient civilizations looked at the physical and human worlds as interdependent. An imbalance in one sphere could result in an imbalance in the other. Ewert Cousins notes that the pre-axial consciousness of tribal cultures was rooted in the cosmos and in fertility cycles of nature.[5] These early humans, or "first earth persons," "mimed" and venerated nature in which nature appeared as a sacred reality determining one's destiny.

The axial age differed from pre-axial in that it was marked by the rise of the individual and of religious cultures. In the axial age, persons gained possession of their own identity, but they lost their organic relationship to nature and community, severing the harmony with nature and the tribe. Jaspers notes that the axial age gave rise to "a new departure within mankind," "a kind of critical, reflective questioning of the actual and a new vision of what lies beyond."[6] Describing human consciousness in the axial age, he writes: "Man becomes conscious of Being as a whole, of himself and his limitations. He experiences the terror of the world and his own powerlessness. He asks radical questions. Face to face with the void, he strives for liberation and redemption. . . . He experiences absoluteness in the depths of selfhood and in the lucidity of transcendence." [7]

Axial consciousness generated a new self-awareness, which included awareness of autonomy and a new sense of individuality.[8] The human person as subject emerged. The monotheistic faiths—Judaism, Christianity, and Islam—are axial religions.

---

5. Ewert H. Cousins, *Christ of the 21st Century* (Rockport, MA: Element Books, 1992), 5.

6. Benjamin I. Schwartz, "The Age of Transcendence," *Daedalus* 104 (1975): 3.

7. Karl Jaspers, "The Axial Period," *The Origin and Goal of History* (New Haven: Yale University Press, 1953), 2; cf. S. N. Eisenstadt, *The Origin and Diversity of Axial Age Civilizations* (Albany: State University of New York Press, 1986); Karen Armstrong, *The Great Transformation: The World in the Time of Buddha, Socrates, Confucius and Jeremiah* (London: Atlantic Books, 2006).

8. William M. Thompson, *Christ and Consciousness: Exploring Christ's Contribution to Human Consciousness* (New York: Paulist Press, 1977), 21.

Now, more than two thousand years later, we seem to be undergoing another paradigm shift. With the development of the theory of evolution and the rise of quantum physics and Big Bang cosmology, the twentieth century saw the dawning of a new axis of consciousness that has led to what Cousins called a "second axial age."[9] Like the first axial age, this new axial age has been developing for several centuries, beginning with the rise of modern science. And, also like the first, it is effecting a radical transformation of consciousness. While the first axial age produced the self-reflective individual, the second axial age is giving rise to the hyperpersonal or hyperconnected person. Technology has fundamentally altered our view of the world and of ourselves in the world. The tribe is no longer the local community but the global community, which can now be accessed immediately via television, internet, satellite communication, and travel. "For the first time since the appearance of human life on our planet," Cousins wrote, "all of the tribes, all of the nations, all of the religions are beginning to share a common history."[10] People are becoming more aware of belonging to humanity as a whole and not just to a specific group.

Today, we are religiously in the first axial period and culturally in the second axial period. We are a species "in between," and thus our religious myths are struggling to find new connections in a global, ecological order. The new myth of relational holism, which I will propose in this book, has to do with the search for a new connection to divinity in an age of quantum physics, evolution, and cultural pluralism. The idea of relational holism is one that is rooted in the God-world relationship, beginning with the Book of Genesis, but it finds its real meaning in quantum physics and the new understanding of the relationship between mind and matter. Our story, therefore, will traverse the

---

9. Cousins, *Christ of the 21st Century*, 7–8. Thomas Berry used the term "Second Axial Age" to refer to the convergence of world religions, which led to a new phase of human culture and civilization. See Mary Evelyn Tucker, John Grim, and Andrew Angyal, *Thomas Berry: A Biography* (New York: Columbia University Press, 2019), 93.

10. Cousins, *Christ of the 21st Century*, 7–10.

fields of science, scripture, theology, history, culture, and psychology. The complex human can no longer be reduced to one view or another. We must see our existence within the whole or we will not see the truth of our existence at all.

SCRIPTURAL HOLISM

The ancient Hebrews did not coin the word "God." Rather, the word "God," Raimon Panikkar states, has its origin in Sanskrit and means light or brilliance.[11] This root meaning of God is more helpful than the later scholastic definition, *ipsum esse subsistans*, or self-subsistent Being or simply Being itself. Scripture is not conceptual but experiential and relational. It is significant that the Book of Genesis begins with God bringing forth light out of darkness: "Darkness was over the surface of the deep, and the Spirit of God was hovering over the waters. And God said, 'Let there be light,' and there was light" (Gen 1:3). In the axial age people had an experience of God, a light-filled awareness of God, a sense of God's openness. God does not preserve Godself but goes forth into the openness of the creation, illuminating all life with life itself.

The Hebrew word for "create" is *bara*, which means "to bring into relationship." The author of Genesis used *bara* to denote a work of God altogether *sui generis*, a bringing forth into existence of what had not been here previously (Exod 34:10). The newness of creation gives us a glimpse into the myth of divine reality. If creation means being brought into relationship with the divine source of life, then to say "God creates" means that God shares God's life with us. God is the ungraspable *openness of life*. Divinity is not a projection of a supernatural being but the *excess of life* experienced as a personal invitation into the fullness of life. The divine mystery is the ultimate *AM* of everything. Creation exists because God exists and God exists because creation exists: God

---

11. Raimon Panikkar, *Mysticism and Spirituality: Part Two: Spirituality, The Way of Life* (Maryknoll, NY: Orbis Books, 2014), 7.

and creation mutually co-inhere. The divine is never alone or by itself, Panikkar states, because it has no "self"; it is a dimension of the Whole.

Relationship is fundamental to the God-world unity. Creation is not radically separate from God. Creation is not a mere external act of God, an object on the fringe of divine power; rather, it is rooted in the self-diffusive goodness of God's own life; it is God's action in the very actuality of action. We humans are part of God's own life and God is integral to our lives. The integral relationship of God and world is such that God and world form a complementary whole. Panikkar called this God-world unity "cosmotheandrism," indicating that *cosmos, theos,* and *anthropos* are three integral realities.[12] Traditionally, God and the universe have been understood as two realities over against each other, with God reaching into the world to act at particular moments. This common way of imaging the God-world relationship results in an interventionist view of divine action. God is imagined as intervening to create and to move creation in the right direction at certain times. However, God cannot transcend the world without first in some way being in it. The dual notion of God's nearness (immanence) and beyondness (transcendence) exists in both preaxial and axial religions. Divine immanence is the basis of divine transcendence. The God-world unity poetically expressed in the Old Testament reflects the integral relationship between the development of the human person and the awareness of divine reality. The Jewish scholar, Abraham Heschel, insightfully proclaimed that we are not simply related to God, we are part of God's own life. The human is in search of God because God is in search of the human. The God-human relationship is an irreducible wholeness that cannot be reduced to either God or human as separate and distinct entities. The earliest scripture writers were experiential, not philosophical, and the language of scripture symbolically conveys what is otherwise ineffable mystery. Reality is an inextricable whole.

---

12. See Raimon Panikkar, *The Trinity and the Religious Experience of Man* (Maryknoll, NY: Orbis Books, 1975).

LET THERE BE LIGHT

Light is a fundamental component of the universe. When medieval scholars were studying light, they believed they were studying God or the emanations of God. One of the major proponents of a light metaphysics was Robert Grosseteste, who taught at the University of Oxford in the thirteenth century. Grosseteste developed a metaphysics of light whereby the basis of all that exists, including the cosmos itself, is formed out of light. In describing the initiation of the process of creation from a single point of primordial light, Grosseteste used the image of an expanding sphere of light that diffuses in every direction instantaneously so long as no opaque matter stands in the way. The expansion of light replicating itself infinitely in all directions is the basis of the created world.[13]

Recent studies show that light is the most important factor in the first formation of the universe and is integral to matter.[14] Some scholars even argue that light and consciousness are correlated, and that consciousness may be light itself.[15] Revelation is the awakening to light or becoming "enlightened," conscious of a deep reality beyond the everyday world. The prophet Isaiah spoke of darkness and light as the meaning of revelation: "The people walking in darkness have seen a great light; on those walking in darkness a new light has dawned" (Isa 9:2). Early Christian writers spoke of the light-filled presence of God. For example, in the words of Saint Augustine:

> But what do I love when I love my God?...when my soul is bathed in light that is not bound by space; when it listens to sound that never dies away; when it breathes

---

13. Daniel Horan, "Light and Love: Robert Grosseteste and Duns Scotus on the How and Why of Creation," *Cord* 57, no. 3 (2007): 246–47.

14. See Eda Alemdar, "Consciousness: Look at the Light!" *Biomedical Journal of Scientific and Technical Research* 25, no. 4 (2020): 19, 284–19, 288.

15. See Peter Russell, *From Science to God: A Physicist's Journey into the Mystery of Consciousness* (Novato, CA: New World Library, 2002).

fragrance that is not borne away on the wind; when it tastes food that is never consumed by the eating; when it clings to an embrace from which it is not severed by fulfillment of desire. This is what I love when I love my God.[16]

Pseudo-Dionysius, writing in the fifth century, spoke of God as the super-luminous light, a blinding light that darkens vision by its sheer luminosity, like the flash of a camera aimed directly on the human eye, "the brilliant darkness of a hidden silence."[17] Light and consciousness: God and human. The ancient writers spoke of these realities as symbols, but modern science is beginning to explore light and consciousness as our most fundamental realities. God seems to be hardwired into the human brain because the brain is like a giant electronic grid in the field of consciousness.[18]

HOLISM

The ubiquity of light prompted early physicists to explore the nature of matter. Is light a wave or a particle? The well-known double-slit experiment led to the theory of wave-particle duality and the introduction of quantum physics. Niels Bohr's Copenhagen interpretation of quantum mechanics brought quantum physics to the level of philosophical discussion. Bohr rejected the notion of "things" as ontologically basic entities. He called into question the Cartesian belief in the inherent distinction between subject and object, knower and known, since nothing can be said apart from an act of *conscious* knowing. He rejected language and measurement as performing *mediating* functions. There is

---

16. Saint Augustine, *Confessions*, trans. R. Pine-Coffin (London: Penguin Books Limited, 2003), 88.

17. See Pseudo-Dionysius, "The Celestial Hierarchy," *Pseudo-Dionysius: The Complete Works*, trans. Colm Luibheid (New York: Paulist Press, 1987).

18. See Andrew Newberg, Eugene D'Aquili, and Vince Rause, *Why God Won't Go Away: Brain Science and the Biology of Belief* (New York: Ballantine Books, 2008).

no mediator between mind and matter, he claimed. Language has artificially carved up the world. In Bohr's view, the conceptual and the physical are intertwined. The inseparability of knower and known, subject and object, gives rise to a new God-human relationship—a holism. To enter into this new relationship of holism is to explore the fundamental mysteries of mind and matter.

Einstein had an intuitive sense of the whole when he wrote:

> A human being is a part of the whole called by us universe, a part limited in time and space. He experiences himself, his thoughts and feelings as something separated from the rest, a kind of optical delusion of his consciousness. This delusion is a kind of prison for us, restricting us to our personal desires and to affection for a few persons nearest to us. Our task must be to free ourselves from this prison by widening our circle of compassion to embrace all living creatures and the whole of nature in its beauty.[19]

The notion of wholeness at the quantum level corresponds to something recognized by systems biologists, namely, that living systems are networks within the so-called hierarchies of nature. The interconnected levels of networks constitute a web of life wherein systems interact with other systems, forming networks within networks. Because reality exists in systems, every system is a supersystem; systems exist within systems. Such insights led to the positing of *holons* or whole/parts. Arthur Koestler proposed the word *holon* to describe the hybrid nature of sub-wholes and parts within in-vivo systems. A *holon* is something that is simultaneously a whole and a part. From this perspective, holons exist simultaneously as self-contained wholes in relation to their subordinate parts and as dependent parts when considered from the inverse direction. Koestler defines a holarchy as a hierarchy of

---

19. Albert Einstein, cited in Walter Sullivan, "The Einstein Papers: A Man of Many Parts," *New York Times Archives* (March 29, 1972), https://www.nytimes.com/1972/03/29/archives/the-einstein-papers-a-man-of-many-parts-the-einstein-papers-man-of.html.

self-regulating holons that function first as autonomous wholes in supra-ordination to their parts; second, as dependent parts in sub-ordination to controls on higher levels; and third, in coordination with their local environment. Holarchy is the principle of holons or whole/parts whereby the number of levels in a holarchy describe its depth. David Spangler distinguishes hierarchy from holarchy in this way: "In a hierarchy participants can be compared and evaluated on the basis of position, rank, relative power, seniority and the like. But in a holarchy each person's value comes from his or her individuality and uniqueness and the capacity to engage and interact with others to make the fruits of that uniqueness available."[20] Ken Wilber notes that evolution produces greater depth and less span; as the individual *holon* acquires greater depth, the span or the collective gets smaller and smaller.[21] A whole atom is part of a whole molecule; a whole molecule is part of a whole cell; a whole cell is part of a whole organism. Similarly, the human person is a whole within oneself and yet is a part of a larger communal whole, which is a part within a whole society. Reality is composed of neither wholes nor parts but of whole/parts—holons—or what Wilber calls integral systems.[22]

MIND AND MATTER

Two principal positions on consciousness and matter have been at the heart of philosophical discussions in the twentieth century: the first, known as monism or *panpsychism*, claims that both the physical and mental are ontologically equal parts of reality and that one cannot be reduced to the other. Physicist Max Tegmark holds to a radical panpsychism whereby there is a fundamental realm of

---

20. David Spangler, "A Vision of Holarchy," https://lorian.org/community/from-the-archives-a-vision-of-holarchy-part-1-of-2.

21. Ken Wilber, *A Theory of Everything: An Integral Vision for Business, Politics, Science, and Spirituality* (Boston: Shambhala, 2001), 50.

22. See Ken Wilber, *Integral Consciousness and the Future of Evolution: How the Integral World Is Transforming Politics, Culture and Spirituality* (St. Paul, MN: Paragon House, 2007).

matter, which is consciousness.[23] Philosopher Phillip Goff, author of *Galileo's Error*, explains that panpsychism is the best explanation for our current understanding of physics. He writes:

> Physical science doesn't tell us what matter *is*, only what it *does*. The job of physics is to provide us with mathematical models that allow us to predict with great accuracy how matter will behave. This is incredibly useful information; it allows us to manipulate the world in extraordinary ways, leading to the technological advancements that have transformed our society beyond recognition. But it is one thing to know the *behavior* of an electron and quite another to know its *intrinsic nature*: how the electron is, in and of itself. Physical science gives us rich information about the behavior of matter but leaves us completely in the dark about its intrinsic nature. In fact, the only thing we know about the intrinsic nature of matter is that some of it—the stuff in brains—involves experience. We now face a theoretical choice. We either suppose that the intrinsic nature of fundamental particles involves experience or we suppose that they have some entirely unknown intrinsic nature. On the former supposition, the nature of macroscopic things is continuous with the nature of microscopic things. The latter supposition leads us to complexity, discontinuity and mystery. The theoretical imperative to form as simple and unified a view as is consistent with the data leads us quite straightforwardly in the direction of panpsychism.[24]

The second position, known as *dual-aspect monism*, states that the mental and the material are different aspects or attributes of a

---

23. Max Tegmark, "Consciousness as a State of Matter," *Chaos, Solitons & Fractals* 76 (July 2015): 238–70. Tegmark gives the name "perceptronium" to this fundamental state of matter which is consciousness.

24. Philip Goff, "Panpsychism is Crazy, but it's also most probably true," Aeon (March 1, 2017), https://aeon.co/ideas/panpsychism-is-crazy-but-its-also-most-probably-true.

unitary reality, which itself is neither mental nor material. They are both properties of one neutral substance x, which is neither physical nor mental. Harald Atmanspacher describes the phenomenon in this way: "In dual-aspect monism according to Pauli and Jung, the mental and the material are manifestations of an underlying, psychophysically neutral, holistic reality called *unus mundus,* whose symmetry must be broken to yield dual, complementary aspects. From the mental, the neutral reality is approached via Jung's collective unconscious; from the material, it is approached via quantum nonlocality."[25] Pierre Teilhard de Chardin was aware of the problem of consciousness and held to a dual-aspect monist position to explain evolution. Life, he wrote, is "a specific effect of matter turned complex; a property that is present in the entire cosmic stuff."[26] He considered matter and consciousness not as "two substances" or "two different modes of existence, but as two aspects of the same cosmic stuff."[27] Mind and matter form the reality of the whole.

CARL JUNG AND TEILHARD DE CHARDIN

Our guides for a new myth of relational holism are the psychoanalyst Carl Jung and the Jesuit scientist-theologian Pierre Teilhard de Chardin. Jung was a psychiatrist who came from a deeply religious background. His father was a devout Christian and an ordained pastor. Jung was to follow in his father's footsteps, but instead decided to study medicine and specialized in the field of psychiatry. He collaborated with Sigmund Freud for several years but differed with Freud largely over the latter's insistence on the sexual bases of neurosis. A serious disagreement came in 1912, with the publication of Jung's *Wandlungen und Symbole der Libido*

---

25. Harald Atmanspacher, "20th Century Variants of Dual-Aspect Thinking," *Mind and Matter* 12, no. 2 (2014): 253.

26. Pierre Teilhard de Chardin, *Man's Place in Nature,* trans. René Hague (New York: Harper and Row, 1966), 34.

27. Pierre Teilhard de Chardin, *The Phenomenon of Man,* trans. Bernard Wall (New York: Harper and Row, 1959), 56–64.

(*Psychology of the Unconscious*, 1916), which ran counter to many of Freud's ideas. Jung broke with Freud and developed his own ideas on the unconscious, especially because of his intense dream life, which gave him insight into the hidden levels of the mind. He became interested in the connection between psychology and religion and saw that the Christian religion was part of a historic process necessary for the development of consciousness. He also became interested in esoteric movements, such as Gnosticism and alchemy, and saw these movements as manifestations of unconscious archetypal elements not adequately expressed in mainstream Christianity. His view of alchemy was that it had constructed a kind of textbook of the collective unconscious. He developed an interest in older people who had lost meaning in their lives and had abandoned religious belief. He thought that if they could discover their own myth as expressed in dreams and imagination, they could develop more complete personalities. This process of personal myth-making he called "individuation."

Teilhard de Chardin was a scientist and mystic. Educated as a Jesuit priest, he studied at the Sorbonne and became a specialist in the Eocene era of evolutionary biology (about 56 million years ago). His writings focused on synthesizing science and religion into a new vision of the whole. He understood Christianity as a religion of evolution because of God's involvement in the material world, and he saw the direction of incarnation as moving toward the pleroma or the fullness of Christ Omega. For Teilhard, matter *is* the incarnating presence of divinity; God is present *in* matter and not merely *to* matter. Both Jung and Teilhard rejected the Thomistic view of divine creation and participation. God and matter, they said, form a relational whole.

The insights of Teilhard, like those of Jung, sprang from the type of inquisitive search that a scientist brings to the open book of nature. Teilhard thought of science as a process, and he found joy in exploring the unknown mysteries of matter. Science is a mystical quest; it is the pursuit of a discovery that can create a new truth. Truth is not a given; it is the unitive horizon of reality formed by the mind in its pursuit of knowledge. Teilhard spoke of scientific truth as "the supreme spiritual act by which the dust-cloud of experience takes on form and is kindled at the fire of knowledge."[28] As scientists struggle to make sense of their findings, they are searching for new truths, grasping for new horizons of insight. The fibers of the unifying universe are seeking to come together in the scientist's mind. "It is in these terms . . . that we must understand Teilhard's talk of loving God . . . 'with every fiber of the unifying universe.'"[29] Teilhard called the work of science, "dark adoration," because the mind is drawn to a power hidden in matter. To enter the world of matter disturbs the mind and affects our prayer and worship because we discover new insights never before imagined. He also spoke of scientific work as "troubled worship."[30] When the mind opens up to the heart of matter, we lose our sense of control, everything becomes disturbed, and rightly so. When we enter into the mysterious domains of matter, we find ourselves in a strange and wonderful land of the unknown, a place where we discover new worlds never even dreamed of before. The scientist, whether explicitly or implicitly, finds oneself in the midst of mystery — better yet — in the midst of God. Matter is the elusive playground of God.

A NEW PANTHEISM

Both Jung and Teilhard espoused a pantheism, not Spinoza's God but indeed an inseparable union of God and matter. The word "pantheism" undergirds a doctrine that essentially states, All (*pan*) is God and God (*theos*) is All. There are many different types of pantheism, as Dean Inge notes. For our purposes here, use of the word pantheism is distinct from monism which does not rec-

---

28. Pierre Teilhard de Chardin, *Activation of Energy*, trans. René Hague (New York: Harcourt Brace Jovanovich, 1963), 9.

29. Thomas King, "Scientific Research as Adoration," *The Way* 44, no. 3 (July 2005): 29.

30. King, "Scientific Research as Adoration," 31–34.

ognize distinct orders of being (God and All) but simply affirms the absolute Oneness of all that there is. The type of pantheism engaged here recognizes God as unique Being but is not simply content to accept God's functions (what God does) without recognizing God's essential existence (what God is). Christian theology has fallen into dualism partly out of fear of pantheism. The vehement opposition to pantheism is rooted in the need to preserve God's unique, divine Being which, in classical terms, cannot be reduced to created being.

A related term, "panentheism," has tried to preserve the integral relationship of God and world without collapsing them, like flour and eggs, into a pancake. The word "panentheism" consists of pan (all), en (in) and theos (God), or all is in God. Anthony Thiselton explains:

> The term stands in contrast to pantheism. If pantheism identifies God with the whole of reality, panentheism denotes the belief that the reality of the world and the whole created order does not exhaust the reality of God without remainder. Yet it also holds in common with pantheism that God's presence and active agency permeates the world, actively sustaining it in every part....Panentheism stresses first and foremost divine immanence, but without excluding divine transcendence.[31]

Marcus Borg states it this way:

> Panentheism as a way of thinking about God affirms both the transcendence of God and the immanence of God. For

---

31. Anthony Thiselton, *A Concise Encyclopedia of the Philosophy of Religion* (Grand Rapids, MI: Baker Academic, 2002), 221. Other thinkers have other terms for a similar set of convictions: John Macquarrie refers to it as "dialectical theism," and David Griffin calls it "naturalistic theism." Hartshorne sometimes calls it panentheism, and sometimes "dipolar theism." For more on this point, see Michael Brierley, "Naming a Quiet Revolution: The Panentheistic Turn in Modern Theology," *In Whom We Live and Move and Have Our Being: Panentheistic Reflections on God's Presence in a Scientific World*, ed. Philip Clayton and Arthur Peacocke (Grand Rapids, MI: William B. Eerdmans, 2004), 4.

Panentheism, God is not a being "out there." The Greek roots of the word point to its meaning: *pan* means "everything," *en* means "in," and *theos* means "God." God is more than everything (and thus transcendent), yet everything is in God (hence God is immanent). For Panentheism, God is "right here," even as God is also more than "right here."[32]

Whereas pantheism equates God and matter with no distinction (all pancakes are God), panentheism aims for a relationship that is like the mind-body relationship. God is in the world and the world is in God, but God is not the world and the world is not God. However, the God model of neither Jung nor Teilhard fits these descriptions. Teilhard was clear that a healthy dose of pantheism can heal God and earth, but his understanding of matter puts a whole new spin on this term. Quantum physics significantly affects the language of matter, which is why the classical terms of pantheism or panentheism are not helpful today. I will use the term "entanglement" throughout the book because it better expresses the inextricable relationship of mind and matter. Entanglement is a concept born from the strangeness of quantum physics and depends on non-local entities or reality constituting an unbroken whole. Entanglement refers to the inseparability of phenomena, so that relationship is primary to that which is related. However, I will retain use of the word "pantheism" when discussing the insights of Jung and Teilhard, in fidelity to their ideas.

OUTLINE OF CHAPTERS

Chapter 1 explores the quantum model of relational holism based on David Bohm's model of implicate order and is introduced as

---

32. Marcus Borg, *The God We Never Knew: Beyond Dogmatic Religion to a More Authentic Contempoary Faith* (San Francisco, CA: HarperCollins, 1997), 32.

a conceptual framework for a new understanding of the mind-matter relationship and of the God-matter relationship. I am using the word "matter" instead of "world" because the nature of matter is experiential in contrast with the notion of world, which is conceptual. As we will see, experience is everything in the new paradigm. The essential role of consciousness in the formation of matter and the notion of matter as a mirror of the mind are discussed. Hence, the fundamental order of unbroken wholeness as the integral unity of consciousness and matter is explored as a helpful model for a new theology.

Chapters 2 and 3 examine the insights of Teilhard de Chardin and Carl Jung, respectively, on the mind-matter relationship as expressed in the human person. While Teilhard situates the human person within the flow of evolution, Jung plunges into the depth dimension of personhood, from consciousness into unconsciousness. Between these two thinkers, we begin to appreciate the horizontal and vertical axes of human development. Jung's thought is particularly provocative and original. In a sense, Jung hacked the human brain long before artificial intelligence burst onto the scene. We will examine his understanding of the psyche as the field of the unconscious, the similarities between the psyche and quantum physics, and the implications of the psyche for God.

Chapters 4 and 5 take up theological concerns. Chapter 4 deals with the meaning of God in terms of transcendence and immanence. A brief history of the supernatural is discussed and reconsidered in view of quantum physics and evolution. The God-world is viewed as a relational whole and explored in terms of complexity and consciousness. Chapter 5 continues the exploration by considering the question of God in terms of the depth dimension of matter and looking to the insights of theologian Paul Tillich to support Jung's claims. Tillich was influenced by Freud's notion of the human depth dimension and interprets this Freudian idea in terms of God as ground. In this respect, Tillich approaches the type of pantheism espoused by Jung and Teilhard, although he is reticent about assuming such a position. Tillich, like Jung and Teilhard, realized that God-talk can be dangerous if it begins to rattle the cages of ancient and medieval doctrine. However, one cannot be attentive to the insights of modern science today without taking up the challenge of a new pantheism or God-ness (*theos*) throughout whole-ness (*pan*). One way into the new paradigm of holism is through the mystics, such as Meister Eckhart and Angela of Foligno, who broke through the wall of orthodoxy and expressed inspirational pantheistic ideas. In light of the mystics and relational holism, I coin a new term, "theohology" (from *theos* = God; and *holos* = whole). Theohology is experiential talk of the God-whole. This new theology or theohology is inspired by quantum physics and a renewed mysticism, in which the higher degrees of consciousness play a fundamental role in one's experience of the whole.

Chapter 6 focuses on the Trinity as a relational God and explores the Trinity as both the basis of psychosomatic unity and a dynamic process of trinitization. "Trinitization" is a word coined by Teilhard de Chardin to suggest that the Trinity unfolds throughout the evolution of complexified life. With the enfolding Trinity, complexified life on a higher level of consciousness comes into awareness of God. The new paradigm of relational holism, with its corresponding view of the complexity of God, radically overturns the classical attributes of divine simplicity and immutability. David Nikkel writes: "Classical theism, in affirming certain divine attributes stemming from ancient Greek philosophy—immutability (unchangeability), impassibility (to be unaffected by another), and eternity (in the sense of strict timelessness)—does not permit God to be in genuine relation to the world."[33] Trinitization is based on the Trinity of love. A God who is seeking completion in creation is one who is open to change and new relationships, which reflect the essence of God as love. Where there is real love, there is real relationship and the desire to grow more deeply in love.

The discussion on trinitization leads into chapter 7 and what Jung called the concept of "the individuation of God." God becomes God, assumes Godly life, in evolution through a process of increasing consciousness and development. Teilhard's position is

---

33. David Nikkel, "Panentheism," *Encyclopedia of Science and Religion*, ed. Nancy Howell, Niels Henrick Gregersen, Wesley Wildman, Ian Barbour, and Ryan Valentine (New York, Macmillan, 2003), 642.

similar to that of Jung and summed up in the words of Peter Todd: [I]t is precisely [an] expanded and higher consciousness which Jung [and Teilhard] believes God acquires through incarnation in humankind."[34] The inextricable relationship of God and human in evolution is the full meaning of the incarnation. Hence, the model of divine individuation is Christ.

Chapter 8 examines Jung's notion of Christ as archetype or model of human development; for Teilhard, Christ is the model of human evolution. Neither spoke of Christ as savior, and both emphasized human participation in the work of salvation. While Jung's ideas do not really contradict scripture, they challenge us to revisit the formula of Chalcedon and reconsider the significance of this formula for us today. His ideas call for a new understanding of salvation in an open and unfinished universe. In his view, every person has the capacity to be Christ because every person has the capacity for Christ consciousness, a position supported by Raimon Panikkar's notion of Christophany.

Chapter 9 builds on the Christ archetype by rethinking the topic of salvation. Jung rejected the doctrine of Christ as universal savior because he thought it significantly undermined theology. Teilhard is less explicit in dismissing Christ as universal savior, but nowhere does he explicitly support the doctrine of Christ as universal savior either. His emphasis on the human person as the spearhead of evolution and his ideas on the incarnate God as empowering evolution suggest that, in his view, salvation is a co-redemptive process of pleromization. As God is fulfilled in us and we are fulfilled in God, we are made whole together and thus "saved" by the energies of love. Like Jung, Teilhard places the onus of salvation on human choice and action.

The active and integral role of the human person in the redemptive process, which is integral to God's own completion, undergirds the rise of the cosmic Christ in evolution. This complex process leads to the notion of quaternity, or the fourth person of the Trinity, which I discuss in chapter 10. Jung regarded quaternity as the most important symbol, even more important than

---

34. Peter Todd, "Teilhard and Other Modern Thinkers on Evolution, Mind, and Matter," *Teilhard Studies* 66 (2013): 5.

Trinity, because quaternity is cosmic, an archetype of universal occurrence. He was influenced by the mystic Jacob Boehme who spoke of quaternity in his writings. However, I think Teilhard's ideas on trinitization and pleromization offer a new way to think of quaternity, not as a fourth member of the Trinity, but as the emergent New Person, the Christic, who complexifies Trinity (3) and the human person (1) into a new type of person—the ultra-human—who is neither God nor human but a mutation of both, a radically new God-human. For Teilhard, the unitive process is one in which God transforms Godself as God incorporates us. This is the ongoing development of the fullness of Christ or *pleroma*. This process of pleromization is one in which we complete God and God completes us.[35] Quaternity refers to the complexity of God in human evolution, which culminates in Omega. Hence, Omega is the symbol of quaternity.

My intention is to offer a new framework for thinking about God and salvation in an age of quantum physics and evolution. With a new model of Wholeness, we can consider new models of the Church and sacramental life. Building on the model of relational holism helps us realize the work needed for the healing of the earth and the process of cosmic personalization. Teilhard claimed that matter is the divine *milieu*, charged with creative power, "like the ocean stirred by the Spirit; matter is the clay molded and infused with life by the incarnate Word."[36] Something, or rather Someone, he says, is rising up in this world of chaos through the sufferings and struggles of the world. The universe is a transpersonal and cosmic formative process—the rise of the cosmic Christ. God is being born from within.

Chapter 11 anticipates what religion might look like in the future as we move beyond the axial religions. Religion will not go away, because religion emerges from the "inside" of matter, that is, the spiritual side of evolution. God is the name of unlim-

---

35. Pierre Teilhard de Chardin, *Human Energy*, trans. J. M. Cohen (New York: Harcourt Brace Jovanovich, 1969), 52–53.

36. Pierre Teilhard de Chardin, *Hymn of the Universe*, trans. Gerald Vann, OP (New York: Harper and Row, 1965), 65.

ited life undergirding all reality. How we find meaning today depends on how we experience the reality of God and the many names of God that speak to us. In this chapter I discuss the insights of media specialist Marshall McLuhan, who prophetically identified computer technology and artificial intelligence with the next stage of evolution, reflecting Teilhard's notion of Christogenesis (the birthing of Christ) on the level of noogenesis (the new level of mind). If God is the depth of matter, and matter is a reflection of mind, then cyberspace not only extends the psyche but makes it more accessible to the conscious person. Cyberspace, in a sense, is the digitized psyche. Hence, the process of individuation and, even more so, divinization, is ideally enhanced on the level of computer technology. McLuhan understood the implications of computer technology in terms of the Body of Christ and thought that it could bring about a new level of holism and world unity. The religion of tomorrow will have no final claim on reality, no final revelation; heaven will find a new relationship with earth.

TOWARD A NEW MYTH

We humans are in transition but unsure of where we are going. We have built a world of extraordinary complexity, but it is a world too large for our small brains to handle. Axial religions arose in a different age and are no longer helpful in guiding us collectively on this earth journey in an expanding universe. Religious myths abound, but they are tribal and conflicting and stifle the whole we desperately seek. Jung thought that true religion was yet to be born. In his view, Christianity established the right direction for growth in consciousness, but Christianity was not meant to be a new religion, much less an institution. We hesitate to confront this question: Did the Church cut off the root meaning of the New Testament as the path to Christ consciousness, forging the Christ experience into philosophical doctrine shaped by Greek metaphysics? Both Jung and Teilhard said "yes." While the New Testament put an end to tribal gods and warring religions, narrowly defined doctrine has stifled the New Testament. Both Jung and Teilhard attempted to relocate the God question on the level of human experience and growth, understood in terms of modern science. God is the name of the transcendent psyche, the collective unconscious, the depth and ground of matter. If matter is the mirror of mind, as Teilhard claimed, then God is integral to matter and matter is integral to God, without collapsing or blending matter and God into a vague wisp of thought. Any type of supernatural God is an abstraction and unhelpful, diverting our attention away from our divine depth toward a projected otherworldly realm. Jesus of Nazareth entered into unitive Christ consciousness and lived from the center of his own divine reality. Jesus is the model of Christ consciousness, according to Jung, because Jesus was fully human like us. Jung summed up the root reality of incarnation this way: the many gods become one God, the one God becomes human, and the human is to become God. Every human person has the capacity to be divine, holy, and sacred. God is seeking fulfillment in human life, as human life seeks fulfillment in God. Teilhard fully agreed and saw the ongoing event of incarnation as the impulse of evolution. Augustine was right when he said: "[O]ur hearts are restless until they rest in You."[37] We are seeking God because God is seeking us. Without God, we do not really exist, and without humans, God is an abstraction.

A culture without God is sheer cosmic information, in which the human person becomes part of the information that can be deleted or changed. Faith tells us otherwise. We are here because we are the thinking portion of the universe, part of a cosmic wholeness that is grounded in divine reality. God is the Whole of the whole in evolution, distinct yet inseparable from everything else that exists. Relational holism means that everything is connected. There are no separate parts; rather, each distinct entity is determined by its relationships. The works of Jung and Teilhard impel us to rethink the Christian story as a relational whole—a "theohology." Holism calls for a new type of logic, one defined not by causality but by relationality. The logic of love is the logic

---

37. Augustine, *Confessions*, 5.

of the whole; the energy of love is the energy of the whole. Love sees the whole, while the partial intellect sees fragments. We humans have a capacity to actualize the whole by personalizing divine love.

Actualization is part of the process of individuation, coming home to ourselves as irreducible fractals of divine light. Both Jung and Teilhard de Chardin made this journey. They were mystics who thought from their own inner depths and felt the pulse of life, unafraid of power and authority or of small gods who distort the truth. If we are seeking logical and causal explanations to govern our lives, institutions to save us, we will fail as an earth community. The Godliness of matter must be reborn in the human seeker, one who can face the familiar and see it with new eyes. The quantum world evokes the new mystic, one who dreams from a deeper center and loves from an unknown spring of life, for the mystic already lives in the world of tomorrow.

1

Consciousness and the Unbroken Whole

Evolution and quantum physics have fundamentally changed how we understand the world. Significantly different from past understandings, each of these discoveries caused major paradigm shifts in the twentieth century. A paradigm is a distinct set of concepts or theories that characterize a particular entity or field within which ideas are generated, such as biology or religion. Philosopher of science Thomas Kuhn, proposed that paradigms can change or shift when the paradigm no longer explains the phenomena sufficiently. In other words, a paradigm can shift in light of new data. As new insights arise that no longer fit the prevailing paradigm, they give birth to a new paradigm, which emerges over time. The new paradigm is not just an extension of the old, but a completely new worldview.

Although paradigm shifts occur when scientific theories offer better explanations of reality than previous ones, such shifts occur funeral by funeral. The nineteenth-century philosopher Arthur Schopenhauer once quipped: "Every truth passes through three stages before it is recognized. First, it is ridiculed. Second, it is opposed. Third, it is regarded as self-evident."[1] Max Planck added his own perspective: "A new scientific truth does not triumph by convincing its opponent and making them see the light, but rather because its opponents eventually die."[2] The West has lived with two prominent paradigms for the last several hundred years: the mechanistic worldview and the medieval worldview. The mechanistic worldview has governed culture while the medieval worldview has governed monotheistic religion. The new sciences of physics and evolution have ushered in a new paradigm of relational holism; however, the transition into this new paradigm has been proceeding at a snail's pace, indeed, one death at a time.

Recently, biology and physics have been secretly collaborating on a new partnership that some now call "quantum biology."[3] Each field is basically disclosing the fact that matter is weird and wonderful. The fundamental basis of everything that exists is nothing like our everyday experience of the world. The word "mystery" may be relevant here, referring to that which is ineffable, hidden, beyond the conceptual grasp. Modern physics is, in a sense, a mystical science that stands in opposition to the notion that "science explains everything" or that "science gives us the truth." Physics is in fact a description, not an explanation. The laws of nature are concisely integrated descriptions of our observations and experiments, descriptions that use creative abstract concepts like "charge" or "spin" and the abstract language of mathematics. The goal is to provide a "model" or "representation" of the measurable objective aspects of our experience. Physics is an abstract description of nature, although there are no abstractions in nature. What you see is not necessarily what is there. The map is not the territory.

If our vision of nature deceives us, then what is nature? Science is discovering a vast and complex universe of life that defies reductionism. Albert Einstein's theory of relativity revolutionized

---

1. Peter Russell, *From Science to God: A Physicist's Journey into the Mystery of Consciousness* (Novato, CA: New World Library, 2010), 22.

2. Max Plank, *Scientific Autobiography and Other Papers,* trans. Frank Gaynor (New York: Philosophical Library, 1949), 33–34.

3. See Johnjo McFadden and Jim Al-Kalilli, *Life on the Edge: The Coming of Age of Quantum Biology* (New York: Crown, 2016).

our understanding of nature in ways that we still do not understand. The weirdness of nature is that nature is not merely the stuff of material things but also the elusiveness of energy. Quantum physics is a branch of science that focuses on quantum mechanics, where the term "mechanics" refers to the set of principles used to describe the behavior of matter and energy at the most fundamental levels. There are approximately eighteen different interpretations of quantum mechanics, and it is difficult to say which interpretation is correct, but there is a fundamental basis to quantum physics: energy is the stuff of the universe. Matter is energy moving slowly enough to be seen.

The first aspect of quantum reality we need to consider is the fact that the basis of material things is not material. This view opposes our experience of the world, but, according to Diogo Ponte and Lothar Schaeffer, it follows Erwin Schrödinger's view that "the electrons in atoms and molecules are not . . . little balls of matter, but standing waves or forms."[4] Ponte and Schaeffer write: "When an electron enters an atom, it ceases to be a material particle and becomes a wave . . . that is, the electrons in atoms are probability fields."[5] Probabilities are dimensionless numbers, ratios of numbers. Probability waves are empty and carry no mass or energy, just information on numerical relations. The interferences of atomic wave patterns, for example, determine what kind of molecules can form. Hence, the visible order of the world is determined by wave interference.[6] Surprisingly, the new insights of quantum physics bear a resemblance to early Greek science. In the sixth century BCE, Pythagoras was already teaching that "all things are numbers" and that "the entire cosmos is harmony and number." Plato thought that atoms are mathematical forms.[7] What

---

4. Diogo Valadas Ponte and Lothar Schafer, "Carl Gustav Jung, Quantum Physics and the Spiritual Mind: A Mystical Vision of the Twenty-First Century," *Behavioral Sciences* 3 (2013): 601–18.

5. Ponte and Schafer, "Carl Gustav Jung, Quantum Physics and the Spiritual Mind," 603.

6. Ponte and Schafer, "Carl Gustav Jung, Quantum Physics and the Spiritual Mind," 603.

7. Ponte and Schafer, "Carl Gustav Jung, Quantum Physics and the Spiritual Mind," 603.

the Greeks realized is what physicists now realize, that the language of mathematical relationship is perhaps the primal word of everything that exists. The basis of matter is thoroughly relational.

THE UNBROKEN WHOLE

As we travel into the world of quantum physics, we enter a misty sea of infinite potential. At this level, one wonders how anything exists at all. David Bohm recognized that features of quantum theory required that the entire universe be considered as an unbroken whole, with each element in that whole demonstrating properties that depend on the overall environment. He wrote: "Thus, if all actions are in the form of discrete quanta, the interactions between the different entities (e.g., electrons) constitute a single structure of indivisible links, so that the entire universe has to be thought of as an unbroken whole."[8] He called this unbroken wholeness the "implicate order," meaning that enfolding takes place in the movements of various universal fields, including electromagnetic fields, sound waves, and others.[9] The word "implicate" comes from the Latin *implicare*, which means "to enfold." The enfolded order is the basis of the explicit order that we perceive in the unfolded state. Bohm said there are two ways of seeing the universe. The first perspective is mechanistic. The universe is seen as a collection of entities existing independently in time and space and interacting through forces that do not cause any change in the essential nature of these entities. This is the Newtonian perspective, which follows fundamental laws of classical physics, in which each atom, molecule, cell, organism, or entity acts according to classical physical laws of motion.

The second perspective is based on quantum reality and cannot be accounted for by the mechanistic order. In quantum reality, movement is generally seen as discontinuous. An electron can move from one spot to another without going through any of the

---

8. David Bohm, *Wholeness and the Implicate Order* (London: Routledge and Kegan Paul, 1980), 175.

9. Bohm, *Wholeness and the Implicate Order*, 178.

space in between. Particles, like electrons, can have different properties depending on their environment: in some places they are particles, while in other places they are waves. Finally, two particles can have "non-local relationships," which means they can be separated by vast distances but react as if they are connected to each other.[10]

Thanks to the theory of relativity, we understand that what we usually think of as empty space is full of background energy. This immense background energy may be the basis of the implicate order and the undivided wholeness of the universe. Whereas classical physics is based on discreet parts making up discreet wholes, Bohm took relationships between parts as primary. At the quantum level each part is connected with every other part. Thus, the whole is the basic reality; primacy belongs to the whole. Systems are in movement, or what he calls "holomovement." Kevin Sharpe explains: "The holomovement model for reality comes from the properties of a holographic image of an object.... Any portion of the holographic plate (the hologram) contains information on the whole object."[11] Because reality is marked by relationality and movement, it has endless depth. Hence, Bohm directs us to think in terms of wholeness, relationality, and depth. What we know of reality does not exhaust it; properties and qualities will always be beyond us.

The notion of undivided wholeness emerged in the 1960s when scientists began to examine more carefully the notion of order in the universe. Bohm was shown a mechanical device that gave rise to his notion of enfoldments that occurs in implicate order. The device was made of two concentric glass cylinders, one placed within the other, with the space between filled with glycerin, a viscous fluid. When a droplet of ink was placed in the fluid and the outer cylinder was rotated, the ink drop was drawn out into the shape of a thread that finally disappeared. Bohm thought that the ink particles had become "enfolded" into the glycerin. However, when the cylinder was rotated in the opposite direction,

---

10. Bohm, *Wholeness and the Implicate Order*, 175.

11. Kevin J. Sharpe, "Relating the Physics and Metaphysics of David Bohm," *Zygon: Journal of Religion and Science* 25, no. 1 (March 1990): 105–22.

the threads of ink reappeared and finally turned once again into the droplet. Bohm concluded that when the ink spread through the glycerin by turning the cylinders, the ink was not in a state of disorder but was part of a hidden order, an enfolded order.

Another image Bohm used to explain his theory used pierced folded paper. If we take a piece of paper, fold it into a triangle, and pierce it to create a hole, when we unfold the sheet we see a pattern of holes that appear to be separate and unrelated. However, if we fold up the paper again, all the holes come together into the single spot through which it was pierced.[12] The implicate order means that everything is enfolded into everything, and the question of distinguishing what is hidden and what is apparent is a challenging one. Bohm thought that science was too fixated on explaining what was perceived or measured; what is hidden also exists and must be considered in any scheme that attempts to describe the whole, because that which is hidden has greater power than that which is seen.[13]

Bohm's ideas seem to touch on Plato's insights in his "Allegory of the Cave." What appears to be real in one dimension will look different in another dimension. For example, imagine that you have a clear glass fish talk filled with water. A fish is swimming back and forth in the tank. Then you aim two television cameras toward the tank. One camera focuses on the fish from the front of the tank, the other focuses from the side. Now, picture two television sets in the room, mounted high above the fish tank, one on each side of the tank. One television shows a fish swimming from a side view. The other television shows a fish swimming from a head-on or tail-end perspective. Which one is true? Well, both are. Every time one side of the fish moves, the other side has a corresponding movement. In reality, there is only one fish, but, from the perspective of the televisions, it looks like two fish; and if a viewer were to walk into the room where the actual fish tank sat, then the viewer could experience a three-dimensional view: the actual fish in the tank and the two television screen views of the swimming fish. According to Bohm, the

12. Bohm, *Wholeness and the Implicate Order*, 76.

13. Bohm, *Wholeness and the Implicate Order*, 71.

two fish-tank images are interacting actualities, but they do not represent two independently existent realities. Rather, they refer to a single actuality, which is the common ground of both. For Bohm, this single actuality is of higher dimensionality, because the television images are two-dimensional projections of a three-dimensional reality, which holds these two-dimensional projections within it. These projections are only abstractions, but the three-dimensional reality is neither of these; rather it is something else, something of a nature beyond both. Bohm also says that the implicate order has to be extended into a multidimensional reality. He explains:

> In principle this reality is one unbroken whole, including the entire universe with all its fields and particles. Thus, we have to say that the holomovement enfolds and unfolds in a multidimensional order, the dimensionality of which is effectively infinite. . . . Thus, the principle of relative autonomy of sub-totalities [what appears as individual entities]. . . is now seen to extend to the multi-dimensional order of reality.[14]

This holomovement image is the ground for both life and matter. Bohm provides a clear account of how a "particle" conception of matter causes harm not only to the sciences but also to the way we think and live:

> The notion that all these fragments is are separately existent is evidently an illusion, and this illusion cannot do other than lead to endless conflict and confusion. Indeed, the attempt to live according to the notion that the fragments are really separate is, in essence, what has led to the growing series of extremely urgent crises that is confronting us today and the creation of an overall environment that is neither physically nor mentally healthy for most of the people who live in it.[15]

---

14. Bohm, *Wholeness and the Implicate Order*, 240.

15. Bohm, *Wholeness and the Implicate Order*, 1–2.

Once we enter the world of matter and discover the strangeness of matter, we find ourselves in the midst of mystery. Our inability to say exactly what matter actually is lies in the nature of matter itself, in which consciousness and entanglement play fundamental roles.

In his book *Wholeness and the Implicate Order*, Bohm provides another example of the strangeness of reality: the phenomenon of quantum entanglement, an apparent paradox of quantum theory proposed by Einstein and two of his postdoctoral students, Boris Podolsky and Nathan Rosen in 1935.[16] Using a thought experiment based on quantum theory, they concluded that two particles that have interacted and split apart will continue to interact almost instantaneously, despite being separated by enormous distances. Their finding has come to be known as the Einstein-Podolsky-Rosen—or EPR—paradox. Einstein himself referred to it as "spooky action at a distance." Erwin Schrödinger coined the term "entanglement" to describe this weird connection between quantum systems.

Entanglement refers to the intrinsic relationality of matter. "To be entangled is not simply to be intertwined with another, as in the joining of separate entities, but to lack an independent, self-contained existence."[17] Bohm described a simplified description of the 1935 quantum entanglement experiment:

Consider a molecule of zero total spin, consisting of two atoms of spin [one plus, the other minus]. . . . Let this molecule be disintegrated by a method not influencing the spin of either atom. The total spin then remains zero, even while the atoms are flying apart and have ceased to interact appreciably. Now, if any component of the spin of one of the atoms (say A) is measured, then because the total spin is zero, we can immediately conclude that this com-

16. A. Einstein, B. Podolsky, and N. Rosen, "Can Quantum Mechanical Description of Reality Be Considered Complete?" *Physics Review* 47 (May 15, 1935): 777–80.

17. Karen Barad, *Meeting the Universe Halfway: Quantum Physics and the Entanglement of Matter and Meaning* (Durham, NC: Duke University Press, 2007), ix.

ponent of the spin of the other atom (B) is precisely oppo-site. Thus by measuring any component of the spin of atom A, we can obtain this component of the spin of atom B, *without interacting with atom B in any way.*[18]

Jim Marion further explains that "if atom A is now in Los An-geles and B is now in Paris and A and B are still moving farther away from each other," the measurement of molecule A will af-fect molecule B simultaneously. The effect is nonlocal (since A and B are effectively separated and only A was measured), and it is instantaneous, that is, faster than the speed of light. The effect on B happened exactly at the same time as the measurement of A. However, nothing physical can travel faster than the speed of light, so how are these results explained? Bohm answers this question by returning to the two fish on the television screens, which he likens to atoms A and B. Just as any movement of one television fish instantaneously affects the other television fish, so too do atoms A and B affect each other even though they are sep-arated by a vast distance. What accounts for the entangled activ-ity? Just as the fish are two when seen in two dimensions but only one when seen in three dimensions, so too, Bohm says, what appears as two distinct atoms is really one reality in a higher di-mension. Marion states: "The supposedly separate atoms are three-dimensional projections into the world of space-time of a six-dimensional reality. This six-dimensional reality is unseen and perhaps unseeable. It is the implicate order from which the 'being' of the atoms arises and from the vantage point of which the two atoms are seen as one."[19]

---

18. Barad, *Meeting the Universe Halfway*, 91–2. The 2022 Nobel Prize in Physics was recently given to Alain Aspect, Anton Zellinger, and John Clauser for their work in demonstrating the behavior of particles in entangled states, providing a foundation for a new era of quantum technology. See Daniel Garisto, "The Universe Is Not Locally Real and the Physics Nobel Prize Winners Proved It," *Scientific American* (October 6, 2022), https://www.scientificamerican.com/article/the-universe-is-not-locally-real-and-the-physics-nobel-prize-winners-proved-it/.

19. Jim Marion, *The Death of the Mythic God: The Rise of Evolutionary Spiri-tuality* (Charlottesville, VA: Hampton Roads Publishing Company), 82.

Bohm suggests that quantum theory infers a higher dimensional reality. "In this respect, the physical universe is not only not all there is but is only one of many possible 'explicate' orders that could theoretically arise out of the hidden 'implicate' order."[20] Something invisible, in other words, continually gives rise to the whole of space-time, and to everything that exists in space-time. The implicate order is not a material order because it exists outside the three dimensions of space and outside time. Everything that appears to our senses, including ourselves, is generated from, sustained by, and will eventually vanish into the vast sea of invisible energy. Bohm's model of implicate order flirts with metaphysics as a brilliant paradigm to explain the unity of reality.

COSMIC CONSCIOUSNESS

If physics is science, then quantum physics breaks all protocol because nothing is really what it seems to be. Causal explanations based on measurement and observation give way to poetic descriptions of approximate reality. Perhaps the most startling aspect of this strange science is the fundamental role of consciousness. In the early twentieth century, physicist Max Planck spoke of consciousness as fundamental to matter, indicating that we cannot consider matter apart from consciousness:

> All matter originates and exists only by virtue of a force which brings the particle of an atom to vibration and holds this most minute solar system of the atom together. We must assume behind this force the existence of a conscious and intelligent mind. This mind is the matrix of all matter.[21]

Like Planck, Schrödinger thought that consciousness is absolutely fundamental to matter and is always experienced in the

---

20. Marion, *The Death of the Mythic God*, 83.

21. Susan Borowski, "Quantum Mechanics and the Consciousness Connection," *AAAS* (July 16, 2012), https://www.aaas.org/quantum-mechanics-and-consciousness-connection.

singular; everything begins with consciousness, which itself is nonmaterial.[22] The philosopher Bertrand Russell said that "we know nothing about the intrinsic quality of physical events except when these are mental events that we directly experience."[23] Such insights have led to "the hard problem of matter," the realization that we cannot talk about matter apart from consciousness.[24]

In the 1950s, astrophysicist James Jean wrote: "The universe looks more like a great thought than a great machine. Mind no longer appears as an accident intruder into the realm of matter. . . . The quantum phenomena make it possible to propose that the background of the universe is mindlike."[25] No one really knows what consciousness is, but we do know that consciousness is fundamental to existence itself. Without mind, matter would not exist or, put it this way, how could we know if matter exists apart from the mind? According to philosopher Gaylen Strawson, "The hard problem is not what consciousness is, it's what matter is."[26] He goes on to say: "The ultimate intrinsic nature of the stuff of the universe is unknown to us—except insofar as it is consciousness."[27] Bohm said that consciousness itself is part of a higher dimension of reality of the implicate order, but it is difficult to say what this could mean, scientifically, apart from consciousness. In their book *The Conscious Universe*, Menas Kafatos and Robert Nadeau argue that, if the universe is an indivisible wholeness, everything comes out of this wholeness and everything belongs to it, including our own consciousness. Thus, consciousness is a cosmic property.[28]

---

22. Erwin Schrödinger, *What is Life?*, trans. Verena Schrodinger (Cambridge: Cambridge University Press, 2012, reprint edition), 93–95.

23. Bertrand Russell, "Mind and Matter," 1950, https://russell-j.com/19501110_Mind-Matter.HTML.

24. Gaylen Strawson, "Consciousness Isn't a Mystery. It's Matter," *New York Times* (May 16, 2016), https://www.nytimes.com/2016/05/16/opinion/ consciousness-isnt-a-mystery-its-matter.html.

25. James Jeans, *The Mysterious Universe* (New York: Macmillan, 1931), 158.

26. Strawson, "Consciousness Isn't a Mystery."

27. Strawson, "Consciousness Isn't a Mystery."

28. Menas Kafatos and Robert Nadeau, *The Conscious Universe: Parts and Wholes in Physical Reality* (New York: Springer, 1990).

Let us be frank. Consciousness is such a mysterious phenomenon, that has garnered much attention in the last few decades, that it is almost impossible to say with any degree of certainty what exactly consciousness is. Because consciousness is a fundamental starting point for everything else, it must somehow correspond to quantum reality. Ponte and Schaefer offer an interesting interpretation of consciousness that corresponds to other physical descriptions, such as that offered by Michio Kaku, among others. Beginning with the phenomenon of entanglement, they affirm that, in a holistic universe, decisions made by an observer in one part of the world can have an instantaneous effect on the outcome of processes somewhere else. In earlier paradigms, it was thought that no influence can travel at a speed faster than the speed of light; in the quantum paradigm, influences can act instantaneously over long distances, from one end of the universe to another. This aspect of relational wholeness can be described in connection with the wave properties of elementary particles. Electrons in atoms are waves until they are noticed. The act of observation collapses the wave into a particle, so when we see an electron, it appears as a material particle. In his book *Infinite Potential*, Schaefer writes:

> At the foundation of the visible world we find Entities, which always appear to us as Elementary Things, when we interact with them. However, when they are on their own, they become waves. As waves, they have lost all mass, and they have become pure forms, patterns of information, something mindlike or thoughtlike. Accordingly, we can call the units of existence at the foundation of the world "ETs," meaning Elementary Things, or Elementary Thoughts or simply Entities.[29]

Because the ET is without mass and exists in a wave state, it is also a state of potentiality. We can think of the visible world as an

---

29. Lothar Schafer, *Infinite Potential: What Quantum Physics Reveals About How We Should Live* (New York: Random House, 2003), 198; cited in Ponte and Schafer, "Carl Gustav Jung, Quantum Physics and the Spiritual Mind," 604–5.

ocean. The ETs in the ocean are hanging together, like water waves in an ocean do, so that the nature of reality is an indivisible wholeness. If the ETs in the realm of potentiality did not form a coherent whole, the empirical world emanating out of the cosmic potentiality would be chaotic. However, the visible is not chaotic but appears as a coherent system.[30]

Sir Arthur Eddington was perplexed by the immateriality of quantum physics and suggested that the background of atoms is mindlike. To Eddington, the "unity" of the universe made it necessary to conclude that, behind all empirical appearances of the world, "there is a background continuous with the background of the brain."[31] Unity, in this context, means coherence. That the universe is a coherent system can be suggested on the basis of the unity of our mind: "If the unity of a man's [sic] consciousness is not an illusion, there must be some corresponding unity in the relations of the mind-stuff, which is behind [the visible surface of things]."[32] Thus, from our inner sense of unity, we infer the unity of the world. If the universe were not a coherent system, but a random collection of disconnected piles of material debris, the unity of our thinking would be an illusion. On the other hand, if the universe is a coherent whole, the existence of our personal mind suggests that the background of the universe is mindlike. According to Eddington,

> the universe is of the nature of "a thought or sensation in a universal Mind." ... To put the conclusions crudely — the stuff of the world is mind-stuff. As is often the way with crude statements, I shall have to explain that by "mind" I do not here exactly mean mind and by "stuff" I do not at all mean stuff. Still, this is as near as we can get to the idea in a simple phrase.[33]

---

30. Ponte and Schafer, "Carl Gustav Jung, Quantum Physics and the Spiritual Mind," 605.

31. Sir Arthur Eddington, *The Nature of the Physical World* (New York: Macmillan, 1928), 312.

32. Eddington, *Nature of the Physical World*, 315.

33. Eddington, *Nature of the Physical World*, 259–60.

"Consciousness is not sharply defined," Eddington explained, "but fades into subconsciousness; and beyond that we must postulate something indefinite but yet continuous with our mental nature. This I take to be the world-stuff."[34] What Eddington and others realized is that, at the foundation of reality, *entities with mind-like properties are found.* "It is not unreasonable to imagine," physicist John Wheeler wrote, "that information sits at the core of physics, just as it sits at the computer."[35] In passing through a system of slits, as in in the double-slit experiment, electrons seem to *know* how many slits are open, and they adjust their behavior accordingly. In a vacuum, pairs of particles can appear out of nothing, provided they exist for such a short time that we cannot *know* for sure that they existed. A particle that forms a singlet state with another particle seems to *know* whether or not a measurement was made on its twin a long distance away. The physicist Henry Stapp offers a provocative thought:

> The central mystery of quantum theory is how does information get around so quick? How does the particle know that there are two slits? How does the information about what is happening everywhere else get collected to determine what is likely to happen here? How does the particle know that it was looked for in some far-away place and not found?[36]

From the mind-like aspects of elementary particles, Eddington generalized: "The universe is of the nature of a thought or sensation in a universal Mind ... the stuff of the world is mind-stuff."[37] Mind involves relationship, and matter is that which it

---

34. Eddington, *Nature of the Physical World*, 280.

35. John Wheeler and Kenneth Ford, *Geons, Black Holes, and Quantum Foam: A Life in Physics* (New York: W. W. Norton and Company, 1998), 340.

36. Henry Stapp, "Are Superluminal Connections Necessary?" *Nuovo Cimento*, 40B (1977): 191.

37. Sir Arthur Eddington, *The Philosophy of Physical Science* (New York: Macmillan, 1939), 151.

relates. Neither on its own could evolve or express anything; together they give us ourselves and our world.[38]

MIND-MATTER WHOLENESS

The relationship of mind and matter has been at the heart of philosophical reflection since the times of the ancient Greeks. We do not think about this relationship in our everyday activities, but it is a fundamental relationship. It may be good to stop and ask: "As I think about these ideas, what is the 'I' doing the thinking?" Is it my grey-mattered brain or glial-bounded neurons or some mysterious spirit within me? Is my matter thinking? What happens when the brain no longer works properly, as in Alzheimer's disease? How does thinking go haywire? These are difficult questions for scientists to explore, but they raise a fundamental point: matter and mind are related.

Wolfgang Pauli, who was one of early pioneers of quantum physics, said: "It would be most satisfactory if physis (matter) and psyche (mind) could be conceived of as complementary aspects of the same reality."[39] This view is known as "dual-aspect monism." By way of definition: "Two or more descriptions are complementary if they mutually exclude one another and yet are together necessary to describe the phenomenon exhaustively."[40] Dual-aspect monism excludes reductionism of either an idealist (the primacy of consciousness) or a materialist (the primacy of matter) nature while being necessarily incompatible with dogmatic physicalism and scientific materialism. Writing with Bohm's implicate order in mind, philosopher Paavo Pylkkänen summarized the shift from the atomism of classical, mechanistic physics to the holism characteristic of the quantum revolution. He noted:

---

38. Danah Zohar, *The Quantum Self: Human Nature and Consciousness Defined by the New Physics* (New York: Quill and William Morrow, 1990), 236.

39. Cited in Harald Atmanspacher, "Dual-Aspect Monism à la Pauli and Jung," *Journal of Consciousness Studies* 19, no. 10 (2012): 6.

40. Atmanspacher, "Dual-Aspect Monism à la Pauli and Jung," 6.

"With quantum physics . . . the whole scheme of philosophical atomism is challenged and one is forced to consider some radically holistic basic principles. . . . In the context of Bohm's implicate order, mind and matter are analogous to non-locally connected (entangled) quantum systems."[41]

The Jesuit scientist Pierre Teilhard de Chardin said that consciousness is the stuff of the universe and exists as the "inside" of matter. Life, he said, is "a specific effect of matter turned complex; a property that is present in the entire cosmic stuff."[42] He considered matter and consciousness not as "two substances" or "two different modes of existence, but as two aspects of the same cosmic stuff."[43] The complementarity of mind and matter, or dual-aspect monism, explains both the rise of biological complexity and the corresponding rise of consciousness. The universe orients itself toward intelligent, conscious, self-reflective life.

What scientists are realizing today (although this is still controversial) is that the whole of life, from the Big Bang onwards, is the emergence of mind or consciousness. The greater the exterior levels of physical complexity, the greater the interior levels of consciousness. A system is conscious if it can communicate or process information, which in turn serves as its organizational function. Anything capable of self-organizing possesses a level of consciousness insofar as there is information flow. Biophysicist Fritz Popp states that the difference between a living and non-living system is the radical increase in the occupation number of the electronic levels.[44] In living systems, photons are exponentially more bunched together or squashed into a coherent Bose-Einstein condensate; in non-living systems, they are less tightly packed. According to Popp, the difference of consciousness between living

---

41. Paavo Pylkkänen, "Can Quantum Analogies Help Us to Understand the Process of Thought?" *Mind and Matter* 12, no. 1 (2014): 86–87.

42. Pierre Teilhard de Chardin, *Man's Place in Nature,* trans. Noel Lindsay (New York: HarperCollins, 1966), 34.

43. Pierre Teilhard de Chardin, *The Phenomenon of Man*, trans. Bernard Wall (New York: Harper and Row, 1959), 56–64.

44. Fritz-Albert Popp, "On the Coherence of Ultraweak Photoemission from Living Tissues," *Disequilibrium and Self-Organization,* ed. C. W. Kilmister (Dordrecht: D. Reidel Publ., 1961); cited in Zohar, *Quantum Self*, 223.

and non-living systems is one of degree, not principle.[45] Ilya Prigogine, whose work on complex, dynamical systems won him a Nobel Prize, said that communication or consciousness exists even in chemical reactions where molecules know, in some way, what the other molecules will do even over macroscopic distances. There is a creative and integral relationship between matter and consciousness on every level of life, for consciousness seems to be the fundamental basis of life.

If we ask, what is matter?, we can say that matter is a thought. At the basis of what we call matter, there is no-thing that is "material substance"; there is the conscious experience of some-thing and nothing more. The images that arise in the mind are nothing like the thing-in-itself. For example, I like the color blue, but the color blue does not really exist except in my mind, which registers the photons of light at a particular frequency. The same is true of sound. My speaking moves air molecules back and forth, but there is no sound out there. The sound of my voice is something that appears in my conscious mind. The same with matter. The physical world appears to be made of solid matter, but what we observe to be a golf ball or basketball is just that: a conscious experience that language shapes into something we hold in common.

Scientists are baffled as to how a purely physical brain gives rise to a subjective experience, such as the color blue or the sound of a guitar. Philosopher David Chalmers called this "the hard problem of consciousness," that is, how something apparently material gives rise to a subjective immaterial experience of consciousness. This is the puzzle of physics, for consciousness is not a human phenomenon or a brain phenomenon, but a fundamental phenomenon of all cosmic life. Nothing can be said about anything that exists apart from consciousness. If consciousness is the "inside" of matter, then everything has consciousness—not just human beings or other animals, but all that exists, from rocks and spoons to dirt and trees. The capacity for awareness goes all the way down to the level of a simple bacterium. What has evolved are the forms that appear in consciousness or the contents of consciousness. As life grows more complex, so does experience. The

---

45. Zohar, *Quantum Self*, 223.

inner world evolves into richer and more diverse forms of experience. Once we have seen that the physics of human consciousness emerges from quantum processes and that, in consequence, human consciousness and the whole world of its creation shares a physics with everything else in this universe—with the human body, with all other living things and creatures, with the basic physics of matter and relationship, and with the coherent ground state of the quantum vacuum itself—it becomes impossible to imagine a single aspect of our lives that is not drawn into a coherent whole.[46]

THE WISDOM OF THE EAST

The Eastern sages have known that consciousness is our fundamental reality, but Western science (and religion) has never accepted consciousness as integral to matter. The relationship between mind and matter can be traced back to the ninth century BCE monistic Indian philosophers who taught that pure consciousness is the substratum of everything. In other words, there is one subtle order, namely, pure consciousness, which takes the form of an infinite number of sub-orders. Neuroscientist Marjorie Woollacott explains how, in studying Patanjali's *Yoga Sutras*, a classic yogic text, she realized the profound wisdom of the *sutras* or teachings. For example, Sutra 1 of the *Pratyabhijna-hrdayam* is a definition of supreme consciousness, *chitti*. The *sutra* is this:

Chitti svatantra vishva siddhi hetuhu

Woollacott explains the words, one at a time:

  chitti: consciousness, the power of ultimate consciousness,
      the Absolute
  vishva: all pervading, omnipresent
  svatantra: freedom, independence, self-rule
  siddhi: attainment, perfection, power
  hetuhu: cause, means

---

46. Zohar, *Quantum Self,* 236.

She then translates the above as: *consciousness freedom totality power attainment cause*. There is no verb. Hence, one must ask, what is the relationship between these words? Woollacott maintains that since *chitti* or consciousness is the first word, it is consciousness that is being defined. In neuroscience, "consciousness" is awareness. In Kashmir Shaivism, "consciousness" is synonymous with freedom, with everything in the universe, with all power and attainment, and it is also the cause of all that is. She states that, based on this *sutra*, "consciousness, out of its own freedom, is the source and power of everything. Consciousness takes form as an act of pure self-determination."[47] Based on another *sutra*, she writes: "Consciousness itself descends from the expanded state to become the mind, contracted by the objects of perception."[48]

The Indian sage views pure consciousness, the consciousness of the universe, as a united whole, with one exalted and essential nature. In our everyday existence, it is difficult to see how we can be part of a reality that is an indivisible wholeness, without parts and divisions; the only way we can understand this is to acknowledge the presence of Mind in the universe as an intrinsic aspect of all things in space and time. The Mind or consciousness that permeates nature is the same flow of activity that each of us inherits in a unique way. In the ordinary world of our sense experience, the only known entity that can react to the flow of information is a conscious mind. What is noteworthy in Woollacott's discussion is that consciousness is not identical to mind but integrally related to it. Pure consciousness has the capacity to contract into the separate awareness of the individual—defined here as the mind—taking the form of the individual's material reality. This "material reality" is whatever a person chooses to perceive and understand about that perception.[49] Joseph Bracken suggests that mind is the place where synthesizing activity occurs.[50] In a sense, the mind is

---

47. Marjorie Hines Woollacott, *Infinite Awareness: The Awakening of a Scientific Mind* (New York: Rowman and Littlefield, 2018), 84–85.

48. Woollacott, *Infinite Awareness*, 85.

49. Woollacott, *Infinite Awareness*, 84–85.

50. Joseph Bracken, *Does God Play Dice?* (Collegeville, MN: Liturgical Press, 2012), 26.

the whole realm of inner experience, including our perceptions, sensations, intuitions, feelings, emotions, memory, imagination. Mind is itself an instance of an activity that is going on everywhere in the universe at the same time. To reflect upon the mind as an instance of pure activity is to gain an insight into the nature or deeper reality of the universe as a whole.

EVOLUTION AND QUANTUM WHOLENESS

Bohm held that mind and matter are different aspects of one whole and unbroken movement and saw a parallel between the activity of consciousness and the implicate order in general. The physical world can no longer be explained by positing only a material universe. There is an implicate order that underlies the physical world. This order is nonmaterial; it is invisible but real. Not only does it underlie the physical universe, but it also in some way actually gives rise to the material universe. Bohm suggests that the implicate order may be a realm of many dimensions, a world of vast complexity that science has hardly begun to investigate. Consciousness is integral to the implicate order, and he conceives of consciousness as more than information and the brain because it involves "awareness, attention, perception, acts of understanding, and perhaps yet more."[51] As the implicate order evolves, one moment gives rise to the next, in which each context that was previously implicate is now explicate, while the previous explicate context has become implicate. Consciousness is an interchange, a feedback process that results in a growing accumulation of understanding.

The complexity of consciousness and matter impelled Bohm to consider the human individual to be an intrinsic feature of the universe. The universe would be incomplete in some fundamental sense if the person did not exist. He believed that individuals participate in the whole and consequently give it meaning. Because of human participation, the "implicate Order is getting to

---

51. Bohm, *Wholeness and the Implicate Order*, 251–52.

know itself better."[52] Bohm developed a philosophy of participation based on the implicate order that has merit for our time. The individual is part of the whole of humankind, and yet each person is the "focus for something beyond humankind."[53] Using the analogy of the transformation of the atom ultimately into a power and chain reaction, Bohm believed that the individual who uses inner energy and intelligence can transform humankind. The collectivity of individuals has reached the "principle of the consciousness of mankind," but does not have quite the "energy to reach the whole, to put it all on fire."[54] Bohm suggested that an intense heightening of individuals who have shaken off the "pollution of the ages" (worldviews that propagate ignorance), who come into close and trusting relationship with one another, can begin to generate the immense power needed to ignite the whole consciousness of the world. In the depths of the implicate order, there is a *"consciousness, deep down—of the whole of humankind."*[55] and remains so for our time.

Each human person is responsible for contributing toward the building of this consciousness of humankind. "There's nothing else to do, there is no other way out. That is absolutely what has to be done and nothing else can work."[56] Bohm noted that, as a human being taking part in the process of this *totality,* one is fundamentally changed in the very activity in which one's aim is to change that reality, namely, consciousness.[57] As the Buddha claimed, the mind is everything. What you think, you become.

---

52. Lee Nichol, ed., *The Essential David Bohm* (London: Routledge, 2003), 200.

53. Nichol, *Essential David Bohm,* 207.

54. Nichol, *Essential David Bohm,* 199.

55. Nichol, *Essential David Bohm,* 200.

56. Nichol, *Essential David Bohm,* 290.

57. Bohm, *Wholeness and the Implicate Order,* 266.

2
Teilhard de Chardin and the Human Convergent

Anselm of Canterbury clearly argued that the core of Christian faith is based on the fall of Adam and Eve, for, if Adam had not sinned, then Christ would not have come. Pope Pius XII affirmed the doctrine of original sin and the concept of inherited guilt due to a single couple in his 1950 encyclical, *Humani Generis*.[1] Science is telling us something very different about matter and person-hood, however, something that ultimately makes a difference as to how we conceive of the human person and thus how we conceive of religion. Quantum physics discloses a startling insight: matter is not what we think it is. If this is so, what about the human person? Are we not what we think we are, as well? This is a pivotal question, both for science and religion. The relational holism of mind and matter is like a spiral complexifying with the dynamic unfolding of spacetime, so that the human person is the thinking portion of the universe aware of infinite numbers and ultimate meaning.

---

1. See Pope Pius XII, *Humani Generis* (August 12, 1950), ## 36–37.

David Bohm considered what his theory would mean in terms of the evolution of life. He said that the word "evolution" is too mechanistic to describe what is really going on in the successive "unfolding" of living forms. Later living forms, such as humans, are not "caused" by what went on before, except in minor ways, because each species continuously arises more or less independently from the multidimensional implicate order and is a projection of a reality in that order. While Bohm's idea of implicate order in evolution is worth further reflection, one would have to consider how implicate order and emergence work together in evolution. Philip Clayton defines emergence as "the theory that cosmic evolution repeatedly includes unpredictable, irreducible, and novel appearances."[2] He writes: "Emergent properties are those that arise out of some subsystem but are not reducible to that system. Emergence is about *more than but not altogether other than*.... The world exhibits a recurrent pattern of novelty and irreducibility."[3] With emergence, something is constituted from components in such a way that it has new properties which are not reducible to the properties of the components.[4] The mark of emergence is *irreducible novelty* which pertains not only to the properties of the new emerging entity but to the entity itself as new.[5] The big question concerns how quantum physics and biology work together to explain evolution and the emergence of life.

Teilhard de Chardin was an evolutionary biologist who saw the implications of the new physics for understanding the human person and the spiritual depths of nature. He claimed that we are linked organically and psychically with all that surrounds us. "We realize," he wrote, "that which is emerging in us is the great

---

2. Philip Clayton, *Mind and Emergence: From Quantum to Consciousness* (New York: Oxford University Press, 2006), 39. Although evolution is marked by novelty in nature, it does not mean naïve optimism, which I find frequently articulated by those unfamiliar with science. A more thorough explanation of evolution would include aspects of devolution, mutations, and punctuated equilibrium over long periods of developmental processes.

3. Clayton, *Mind and Emergence*, 39.

4. Clayton, *Mind and Emergence*, 39.

5. Clayton, *Mind and Emergence*, 39.

cosmos."[6] Just as Max Planck spoke of consciousness as fundamental to matter, so, too, Teilhard thought that awareness or
what he called "seeing" brings matter into existence. Teilhard's
paradigm is like a hologram in movement and requires a capacity
to see the whole. Vision is everything, as he writes: "To see is to
develop a homogenous and coherent perspective of our general
experience as it extends to the human being; that is, to see a
whole that unfolds."[7] To see is to know and unite: "One can say
that the whole of life lies in seeing—if not ultimately, at least essentially... unity grows... only if it is supported by an increase of
consciousness, of vision."[8] Those who see "have the sense of the
world as a unified whole in movement. Those who do not see, do
not see beyond the multiplicity of things. They perceive the
world as fragmented and ultimately absurd."[9] Teilhard goes on to
say, "if we lack these qualities of sight, no matter what anyone
does to show us, the human being will indefinitely remain for
us... an erratic object in a disconnected world."[10]

Teilhard's thought bends in the direction of mysticism: matter
is like a mirror. Matter has no being in itself. The great paradox of
matter is not that it is "being" but that it is "non-being." Like a
mirror, empty in itself, matter reflects back only what is presented to it. When we look into the depths of matter, we find that
our vision plunges us into "the infinite that lies beyond us."[11] Of
course, this idea belies our everyday experience of matter, since
we can look at a tree and say "that is a tree and nothing more
than a tree and all that a tree can be." But what if the tree is me
looking at itself? This is the mystery of matter. Matter is not stuff

---

6. Pierre Teilhard de Chardin, *Science and Christ*, trans. René Hague (New
York: Harper and Row, 1968), 27.

7. Pierre Teilhard de Chardin, *The Human Phenomenon*, trans. Sarah Appleton-Weber (Brighton: Sussex Academic Press, 1999), 6.

8. Teilhard de Chardin, *The Human Phenomenon*, 3.

9. Appleton-Weber, Introduction to *The Human Phenomenon*, xix.

10. Teilhard de Chardin, *The Human Phenomenon*, 5.

11. Pierre Teilhard de Chardin, *The Heart of Matter*, trans. René Hague
(New York: Harcourt Brace Jovanovich, 1979), 225; cited in Thomas M. King,
Teilhard's Mysticism of Knowing (New York: Seabury Press, 1981), 30.

but energy. As one sees, matter ceases to be noticed as matter and instead one is drawn into the ineffable depths of the being seen.

Although Teilhard does not explicitly present a philosophy of matter, his ideas suggest that the being *in* matter is the being *of* matter. That which makes matter a mirror is something of the mind reflected in the mirror. The mirror image of matter and the mirrored image of the one who sees are the same. The mirror of matter gives itself to the one who looks at it and whom it mirrors. The mirror image not only receives its being from the "other," it also directs itself to its "other" and is what it is *for* its other. Without the "other" whom it mirrors, matter would virtually cease to exist. It is only by working our way through matter that our minds can expand to the God-dimensions of the universe.

As an evolutionary biologist whose work brought him into intimate contact with the earth, Teilhard recognized the power of matter: "In the beginning was *Power,* intelligent, loving, emerging ... there was the *Fire.*"[12] This power of matter was the ultimate real for him, an indestructible presence not subject to the forces of entropy. He experienced this power in rocks and minerals, as well as within himself. He wrote: "We must say of every man that he contains in himself, besides a body and a soul, a certain physical entity that relates him in his entirety to the universe (the final universe) in which he reaches his fulfillment."[13] Because of this power of matter within all things, "each human ego is co-extensive with the entire universe."[14] Teilhard blesses matter, not for what it tells us about itself, but because we would remain ignorant both of ourselves and of God without it.[15] In his "Hymn to Matter," he writes:

I bless you, matter ... in your totality and your true nature.
You I acclaim as the inexhaustible potentiality for existence

---

12. Teilhard de Chardin, *The Heart of Matter*, 121–22.

13. Pierre Teilhard de Chardin, *Writings in Time of War*, trans. René Hague (New York: Harper and Row, 1968), 296.

14. Pierre Teilhard de Chardin, *Activation of Energy*, trans. René Hague (New York: Harcourt Brace Jovanovich, 1963), 218.

15. Pierre Teilhard de Chardin, *Hymn of the Universe*, trans. Gerald Vann, OP (New York: Harper and Row, 1965), 69.

and transformation. . . . I acclaim you as the universal power which brings together and unites. . . . I acclaim you as the divine milieu, charged with creative power. . . . Raise me up then, matter . . . until, at long last, it becomes possible for me in perfect chastity to embrace the universe.[16]

Matter is neither fallen nor profane. Rather, through matter we enter the world, and the world enters us. The observer is part of what is observed. Teilhard said that the more we try to break down matter into isolated entities, the more we can see its fundamental unity. He writes: "[T]here are no isolated things in the world. There are only elements of a whole in process."[17] We live in a participatory universe of inseparability; everything is connected to everything else.

Teilhard sees matter as essential to God. Matter is not only good; it is holy. Matter gives birth to God, as he poetically expressed: "A Being was taking form in the totality of space . . . The rising Sun was being born in the heart of the world. God was shining forth from the summit of that world of matter whose waves were carrying up to him the world of spirit."[18] Matter is God-bearing. There is an inextricable relationship between God and matter, as Teilhard realized: "I see in the world a mysterious product of completion and fulfillment for the Absolute Being himself."[19] We do not go to God directly; we go to God in and through matter. "Matter puts us in touch with the energies of earth and together with the earth we find ourselves looking to the 'Unknown God' who is to come."[20] Without matter, God could not be experienced because God would have no form. Matter matters to God.

---

16. Teilhard de Chardin, *Hymn of the Universe*, 69–70.

17. Appleton-Weber, Introduction to *The Human Phenomenon*, xix.

18. Teilhard de Chardin, *Hymn of the Universe*, 68.

19. Teilhard de Chardin, *Heart of Matter*, 54.

20. Celia Deane-Drummond, ed., *Pierre Teilhard de Chardin on People and Planet* (London: Routledge, 2006), 185.

THE HUMAN PHENOMENON

The magnitude of the human story for Teilhard begins on the level of matter's first forming of the planet earth, encompassing the human future within its globe and motion. Tracing the composite human back to its source in the stuff of the universe, he identifies the three major pillars of life as matter, energy, and plurality, and he positions the human phenomenon within the unfolding of space-time. He begins the work with the "stuff" of the universe:

> Moving an object back into the past is equivalent to reducing it to its simplest elements; followed as far as possible in the direction of their origins, the last fibers of the human composite are going to merge in our sight with the very stuff of the universe.[21]

By tracing the human back to its origin in the universe, Teilhard finds a collective, the *totum* or whole, which influences activity from the bottom-up. In a 1942 essay, he wrote:

> We have gradually come to understand that no elemental thread in the Universe is wholly independent in its growth of its neighboring threads. Each forms part of a sheaf; and the sheaf in turn represents a higher order of thread in a still larger sheaf—and so on indefinitely.... This is the organic whole of which today we find ourselves to be a part, without being able to escape from it ... in countless subtle ways, the concept of Evolution has been weaving its web around us. We believed that we did not change; but now ... we are becoming aware of the world in which neo-Time, organizing and conferring a dynamic upon Space, is endowing the totality of our knowledge and beliefs with a new structure and a new direction.[22]

---

21. Teilhard de Chardin, *The Human Phenomenon*, 11.

22. See his essay "The New Spirit" (1942) in Pierre Teilhard de Chardin, *The Future of Man*, trans. Norman Denny (New York: Image Books, 2004), 74–89.

Teilhard looks for structural patterns throughout the development of life by which he can understand the construction of the universe and the properties of thought that distinguish the human. He tells us at the end of the prologue of *The Human Phenomenon* that he particularly chose the expression "human phenomenon" to affirm that "the human" is authentically a fact in nature, falling (at least partly) within the province of the requirements and methods of science.

Teilhard's subject is the ever-evolving human phenomenon as it is developing in and around us at this very moment, a unique biological, collective, and global phenomenon, whose past, present, and future are intimately bound up with the formation, life, and ultimate transformation of the earth. "The human is not the static center of the world . . . but the axis and arrow of evolution," which then, Teilhard adds, "is much more beautiful" than being a mere center.[23] The human person is "evolution become conscious of itself." He continues: "[T]he consciousness of each of us is evolution looking at itself and reflecting upon itself."[24] Thus, the human person emerges from the evolutionary process and is integral to evolution. Each human is "the point of emergence in nature, at which this deep cosmic evolution culminates and declares itself."[25] The human phenomenon is the cosmic phenomenon on the level of thought: "We discover we are not an element lost in the cosmic solitudes but that within us a universal will to live converges and is hominized."[26]

He posits a fundamental principle of evolution, the law of complexity-consciousness. This principle works as the background for human emergence, as well as the future of human evolution, so that the "option for the evolving future of the earth and her thinking layer (ourselves) lies in our own hands."[27] Teilhard identifies evolution with the advance of thought and claims that

23. Teilhard de Chardin, *The Human Phenomenon*, 7.

24. Pierre Teilhard de Chardin, *The Phenomenon of Man*, trans. Bernard Wall (New York: Harper and Row, 1959), 221.

25. Pierre Teilhard de Chardin, *Human Energy*, trans. J. M. Cohen (New York: Harcourt Brace Jovanovich, 1969), 23.

26. Teilhard de Chardin, *The Phenomenon of Man*, 36.

27. Appleton-Weber, Introduction to *The Human Phenomenon*, xxvii.

the very end of thought is to have no end. With the emergence of the self-reflective mind, humankind enters a new age where a new spirit of the earth is born. Evolution is, fundamentally, the rise of consciousness.

In 1940, Teilhard completed his most important work, *The Human Phenomenon*, in which he described the fourfold sequence of the evolution of galaxies, Earth, life, and consciousness. The human person is not a ready-made fact but the outflow of billions of years of evolution, beginning with cosmogenesis and the billions of years that led to biogenesis. The realization that humans are part of a larger process involving long spans of developmental time brings about a massive change in all of our knowledge and beliefs. Teilhard described evolution as a "biological ascent," a movement toward more complexified life forms in which, at critical points in the evolutionary process, qualitative differences emerge. At some point, evolution reaches a reflexive state that generates the idea of evolution: "There is only one real evolution, the evolution of convergence, because it alone is positive and creative."[28] We are earthlings to the core.

Teilhard recognized that, at all known levels of the universe, there are units or "grains" that include stars, atoms, molecules, cells, people, and so forth. Sometimes the particles are found together in aggregations (for example, a pile of sand or a galaxy of stars); sometimes they link together to form a crystal. While a crystal builds up through indefinitely repeating the same molecular pattern, life builds up by uniting into ever more complex and intricate structures of relatedness. This "center-to-center" bonding of complexity, which is characteristic of all living things, captured Teilhard's attention.[29] His paradigm for the build-up of life can be described in three stages of evolution: increasing organization, convergence, and the radiation of consciousness throughout the whole.

The first stage is one of of increasing organization. Billions of years after the creation of the universe there came a point at which

---

28. Pierre Teilhard de Chardin, *Christianity and Evolution: Reflections on Science and Religion*, trans. René Hague (New York: Harcourt Brace Jovanovich, 1971), 87.

29. Teilhard de Chardin, *Activation of Energy*, 120; Teilhard de Chardin, *Christianity and Evolution*, 87.

inert elements merged and formed the first living cell. All the separate elements had been there before the cell appeared, but the union of these elements caused a new entity to emerge that was more than the sum of its parts. "True unity does not fuse the elements it brings together," Teilhard wrote. "Rather, by mutual fertilization" it "renews them; union differentiates."[30] The movement toward complex unions means that each individual cell continues to reach beyond itself to find new elements and incorporate them into its unity. Evolution is the game of "plus one," the many become one and are increased by one.[31] Unfolding life is an incredible confluence of processes working together, testing new relationships, picking up and moving when the right time comes. In Teilhard's view "life has constructed organisms of ever greater complexity, and with this increased complexity the organism has also shown an increase in consciousness, that is, an increase of intention, of acting with a goal."[32]

The second stage is one of convergence toward a projected point of maximum human organization and consciousness. In the course of evolution, the human person emerges from a general searching of the world; thought is born. Teilhard sees consciousness as intrinsic to the process of evolution and states that evolution is fundamentally the rise of consciousness. He does not see the human person lost or insignificant in view of evolution; rather, he sees the human person as truly unique—not a chance arrival but an integral element of the physical world.

The third stage is the maximization of thought whereby consciousness radiates throughout the whole, in every aspect of the cosmos, as the cosmos is recapitulated on the level of the human person. In light of evolution, Teilhard described the human as distinct in three ways: (1) the extreme physic-complexity of the human brain indicates that the human person is the most highly synthesized form of matter known in the universe; (2) the human is the most perfectly and deeply centered of all cosmic particles

---

30. King, *Mysticism of Knowing*, 32.

31. Alfred North Whitehead, *Process and Reality*, ed. David Ray Griffin and Donald W. Sherburne (New York: Free Press, 1979), 21.

32. King, *Mysticism of Knowing*, 33.

within the field of our experience; and (3) the high degree of mental development (capacity for reflection, thought) places the human person above all other conscious beings known to us, not in an ontological sense but as the recapitulation of all cosmic life.[33] The human person is integrally part of evolution in that we rise from the process, but in reflecting on the process, we stand apart from it. We can strive to know the very processes that make knowing possible in the first place. Teilhard defines reflection as "the power acquired by a consciousness to turn in upon itself, to take possession of itself *as an object* . . . no longer merely to know, but to know that one knows."[34] The human person therefore is essential to the continuation of evolution because we are evolution on the level of self-reflective thought. How we think is how we act and how we act shapes what we become.

MATTER, THE MATRIX OF CONSCIOUSNESS

Teilhard was aware of the problem of consciousness as a fundamental problem of matter. In the seventeenth century, René Descartes had split reality into two separate realms. On the one hand, there was the *res extensa*, the world of solid bodies extending in space and independent of human mental processes; on the other hand, there was the *res cogitans*, the inner realm of the perceiving mind. Only the former was capable of consistent mathematical description and was gradually developed into the intricate mechanistic concept of reality. The realm of the mind involved strict mathematical treatment. Consequently, it was removed from the areas of both science and religion. In the early eighteenth century, amid general exultation with the triumphs of modern science, Bishop Berkeley accused the scientific materialists (that is, those who saw materialism as inert stuff and self-explanatory) of drawing unwarranted conclusions about reality. Reality, he said, is no more than a

---

33. Teilhard de Chardin, *The Future of Man*, 90. For Teilhard, the human person is everything the universe is, but the human is distinguished by the capacity for self-consciousness.

34. Teilhard de Chardin, *The Phenomenon of Man*, 165.

complex of sensations, actual or remembered, in the perceiving mind. Berkeley anticipated the rise of quantum physics.

Teilhard, as a disciple of the new physics in the twentieth century, held to a dual-aspect monist position to explain evolution. As noted in chapter 1, dual-aspect monism means that the mental and the material are different aspects or attributes of a unitary reality, which itself is neither mental nor material, a theory that aligns with Bohm's implicate order. Dual-aspect monism gives greater emphasis to matter, in contrast to panpsychism, which states that all matter has some degree of consciousness.[35] Teilhard's views on mind and matter fall between dual-aspect monism and panpsychism, and one can detect a development in his thought toward panpsychism. Life, he wrote, is "a specific effect of matter turned complex; a property that is present in the entire cosmic stuff."[36] He considered matter and consciousness not as "two substances" or "two different modes of existence," but as "two aspects of the same cosmic stuff."[37] Matter is united in ever greater patterns of physical complexity, supporting greater consciousness and ultimately self-consciousness.

In his essay on "The Heart of Matter," Teilhard describes matter as the matrix of consciousness: "For me, matter was the matrix of consciousness; and wherever we looked, consciousness, born of matter, was always advancing towards some ultra-human."[38] Matter is unitive and transcendent. Teilhard spoke of matter as having a "withinness" and "withoutness," or what he called radial energy and tangential energy.[39] The power to enhance organic unity relates to radial energy, while the power of matter to complexify is tangential energy. Matter is always in the process of greater physical organization as consciousness increases; and the increase in

---

35. See Philip Goff, *Consciousness and Fundamental Reality* (New York: Oxford University Press, 2017).

36. Pierre Teilhard de Chardin, *Man's Place in Nature*, trans. René Hague (New York: Harper and Row, 1966), 34.

37. Teilhard de Chardin, *The Phenomenon of Man*, 56–64.

38. Teilhard de Chardin, *The Phenomenon of Man*, 45.

39. Teilhard de Chardin, *The Phenomenon of Man*, 45.

conscious matter entails a higher level of energized relationship or spirit. Spirit is the energy portion of matter.[40] He writes: "Matter is the matrix of Spirit. Spirit is the higher state of matter."[41]

The human person is complexified matter, a self-conscious agent of convergence, one who can bring matter together through higher levels of consciousness and increase the energy of matter toward spirit. Teilhard saw each human—and humanity itself—as the basis of evolution, converging toward a community of greater spirit, a universal human organism that works by the same power that undergirds the physical complexity of the human brain. He wrote: "How can we fail to see that the process of convergence from which we emerged, body and soul, is continuing to envelop us more closely than ever, to grip us, in the form of—under the folds of, we might say—a gigantic planetary contraction?"[42]

In Teilhard's view, there is no dualism between matter and spirit. As individuals come into contact with the unifying power moving through evolution, they progress from being individual and move toward personhood, toward becoming relational beings whose individuality is intensified by their relation to the whole. The key to wholeness lies in consciousness. As we come into contact with one another, consciousness shifts and relationships change. And the relationships change us, so that we are further shaped as individuals rather than being dissolved in a featureless collectivity. To the extent that the individual relates to the universal power operative in the universe, union in relationships differentiates the individual beyond itself. Ultimately, Teilhard sees that each ego is destined to complexify beyond itself into some mysterious super-ego.[43] We are in evolution and will continue to increase in complexified consciousness (realized today with computer technology). As consciousness grows through shared information, we humans will converge by coming together, as persons, communities, and nation-states. Evolution is

---

40. Teilhard de Chardin, *Heart of Matter*, 26–30.

41. Teilhard de Chardin, *Heart of Matter*, 35.

42. Teilhard de Chardin, *Heart of Matter*, 36.

43. Teilhard de Chardin, *Heart of Matter*, 38.

the movement toward the maximization of consciousness or thought, and this invisible process of evolution is our current reality.[44] The more we can be in touch with the reality of evolution, the greater we can align ourselves with its fundamental forces so that we can flow peacefully into the new dynamic wholeness that is taking shape.

OMEGA

The basis of Teilhard's paradigm is a unifying power in evolution, which he calls "Omega." Omega is a centrating principle, similar to Bohm's idea of a quantum potential undergirding the implicate order. It is within the cosmic order and yet not subject to the laws of physics; in nature yet not subject to the forces of nature; distinct yet intrinsic; autonomous and independent. Omega, as Teilhard's concept of the dynamic impulse in cosmic life, is part of nature yet other than nature.

In a sense, Omega is not a new idea. The early Greek philosophers, beginning in the sixth century BCE (around the time of axial consciousness), began to speculate on a divine spark within the soul that animated life toward transcendence. The Greek philosopher Heraclitus (ca. 500 BCE), for example, used the term *ethos anthropo* to indicate that there was some higher, spiritual nature within humanity. The Greek word *ethos* signifies "home," "hearth," or "the innermost part of the house." The term can be understood in the sense that "the god(ly) is home to man," which means that in the center of the person or central to one's innermost personality, there is something godly.[45] We also find the idea of some inner God or godlike inner voice in the famous Platonic dialogue "The Apology of Socrates." Socrates, who in the end is sentenced to death for "introducing new gods," confirms that he experiences an inner voice that sometimes warns him against

44. Teilhard de Chardin, *Heart of Matter*, 28.

45. Harald Walach, "Higher Self—Spark of the Mind—Summit of the Soul: Early History of an Important Concept of Transpersonal Psychology in the West," *The International Journal of Transpersonal Studies* 24 (2005): 18.

doing things, but never advises him in the positive to do something.[46] Endre von Ivánka, who traced the history of the concept of the One in Platonic and neo-Platonic traditions, noted that the Stoics also had a concept of the "spark of the soul," a universal fire as the source of everything as well as the trace of this fire in everything as a fiery, cosmic seed.

For Teilhard, Omega deeply influences nature's propensity toward greater complexity and consciousness.[47] It is the principle of cosmic wholeness and is irreducible to isolated elements. Omega accounts for the "*more* in the cell than in the molecule, *more* in society than in the individual, and *more* in mathematical construction than in calculations or theorems."[48] Omega is the most intensely personal center that makes beings personal and centered because it is the attractive center of love that empowers every center to love.[49]

But what is Omega? Is it the collective unconscious? The standing waves of quantum physics? Teilhard never identifies Omega explicitly, but he describes Omega as the prime mover of evolution. It is operative from the beginning of evolution, acting on pre-living cosmic elements, even though they are without individualized centers, by setting them in motion as a single impulse of energy.[50] Omega moves into the field of consciousness as it emerges from the organic totality of evolution, and it is the goal toward which evolution tends.[51] Omega is the absolute whole that makes wholeness in nature not only possible but also intensely personal. Teilhard identifies Omega with God: "Only a God who is functionally and totally 'Omega' can satisfy us."[52]

46. See E. V. Ivánka, *Plato Christianus: Übernahme ud Umgestaltung des Platonisumus durch die Väter* (Einsiedeln: Johannes Verlag, 1964).

47. Teilhard de Chardin, *The Phenomenon of Man*, 257–260.

48. Teilhard de Chardin, *The Phenomenon of Man*, 268.

49. Teilhard de Chardin, *Activation of Energy*, 112.

50. Teilhard de Chardin, *Activation of Energy*, 121.

51. Teilhard de Chardin, *Activation of Energy*, 114.

52. Teilhard de Chardin, *Christianity and Evolution*, 240; *The Phenomenon of Man*, 268–72.

MONIST HIGH TENSION

Teilhard's knowledge of science and his experience of matter as the whole—the stuff of rocks, metals, and dirt—put him in opposition to Greek metaphysics with its philosophical influences on Christian doctrine. For Teilhard, the soul is not other than the body, spirit is not other than matter, and the human person belongs to the animal kingdom. What gave rise to everything before the human is enfolded in the human. Nor did evolution stop at the level of thinking humans or *homo sapiens*. We continue to evolve through higher levels of consciousness and complexity, especially in our global internet age. For Teilhard, God is at the heart of matter itself. He espoused a "Christian pantheism," a term he used reverentially, although it has been severely misinterpreted. As he declared, he found himself in "monist high tension," because of his ideas on matter, life, and energy.[53]

Teilhard's insights are consonant with Bohm's ideas on implicate order, but he cloaked his ideas in poetic language to blur the radicality of his thought from the authority of the Church. A careful reading of his essay on "The Heart of Matter," however, clearly shows him struggling to convey the deep insights that Bohm and others more freely expressed, namely, that the physical cosmos emerges out of and is integral to a cosmic plenum or wholeness. Here was a Jesuit priest writing on the power of rocks and metal to convey the deepest truths of existence—a faith in matter itself. He tells us how he was first attracted to the world of rocks which, he claimed, helped him broaden "*the foundations of my interior life.*"[54] When he discovered minerals, he was set "on the road towards the 'planetary.'"[55] He woke up to "the stuff of things." This stuff began to emerge in the direction of a fundamental basis of everything, so that matter ultimately became for Teilhard the place of the Absolute.[56] "The truth is," he wrote, "that even at the peak

---

53. Teilhard de Chardin, *Heart of Matter*, 25.

54. Teilhard de Chardin, *Heart of Matter*, 20.

55. Teilhard de Chardin, *Heart of Matter*, 20.

56. Teilhard de Chardin, *Heart of Matter*, 20.

of my spiritual trajectory I was never to feel at home unless immersed in an Ocean of Matter."[57] He felt himself to be in contact "with the Cosmic 'in the solid state.'"[58] When he discovered physics, he realized that on either side of matter stood life and energy: "There gradually grew in me, as a *presence* much more than an abstract notion, the consciousness of a deep-running, ontological, total current which embraced the whole universe in which I moved; and this consciousness continued to grow until it filled the whole horizon of my inner being."[59] In short, Teilhard discovered a new and vital God, not a God dominating the world with power, but a God integral to the world's becoming. The world had taken on new meaning, no longer the fragmented state of a static cosmos, but the organic state and vitality of a cosmogenesis, with the human as the vanguard.[60]

There is a deep interrelatedness among consciousness, space, unity, and love in Teilhard's thought, which could be summed up in the word "creativity." Alfred North Whitehead believed that creativity is the fundamental principle of everything, including God. In his masterful work *Process and Reality*, Whitehead identified creativity as the "category of the ultimate." In his view, creativity is "that ultimate principle by which the many, which are the universe disjunctively, become the one actual occasion, which is the universe conjunctively."[61] He then adds by way of explanation: "The novel entity is at once the togetherness of the 'many"; hence his maxim, "the many become one, and are increased by one."[62] He notes: "This category of the ultimate replaces Aristotle's category of 'primary substance.'"[63] Since primary substance for Aristotle represents that which in the first place is, what Whitehead appears to be saying here is that creativity, as an ongoing passage from the many to the one and back to the many, is even

---

57. Teilhard de Chardin, *Heart of Matter*, 20.

58. Teilhard de Chardin, *Heart of Matter*, 22.

59. Teilhard de Chardin, *Heart of Matter*, 25.

60. Teilhard de Chardin, *Heart of Matter*, 25.

61. Whitehead, *Process and Reality*, 21.

62. Whitehead, *Process and Reality*, 20.

63. Whitehead, *Process and Reality*, 20.

more ultimate than the individual actual occasions that are constituted in virtue of that activity.

While the reductionistic principles of evolution such as natural selection, adaptation, and self-organization may undergird evolution, creativity provides a metaphysical basis as to why anything changes at all. Thus "creativity is at work in atoms and molecules unconsciously, even as it is at work both consciously and unconsciously in the workings of the human mind," Joseph Bracken writes.[64] Creativity is a fascinating way to describe the energy of newness. It includes the power of the mind to imagine, the power of matter to shape and be shaped, and the freedom to explore ideas or potentials never before envisioned. Creativity is the heart of cosmic life.

To reflect upon the mind as an instance of pure creative activity is to gain an insight into the nature or deeper reality of the universe as a whole. Modern philosophy has interpreted the mind as a distinct center of intellectual power, disconnected from the outer universe. Quantum physics tells us otherwise: there is no outer universe without the inner universe, because there is no matter without mind. We have mastered the outer universe sufficiently to know that it is much larger than we could have ever imagined. Our attention now needs to shift to the inner universe if we are to understand the whole of reality. The inner universe is not secondary to the outer universe; rather, it *is* the outer universe on the level of consciousness. If religion is a function of consciousness, then religion and spirituality may have as much authority as science to tell us how the universe works. Religion is fundamental to evolution.

RELIGION AS COSMIC PHENOMENON

In his essay "The Position of Man in Nature and the Significance of Human Socialization," Teilhard indicated that intelligent life cannot be considered in the universe any longer as a superficial

---

64. Joseph Bracken, *Does God Play Dice? Divine Providence for a World in the Making* (Collegeville, MN: Liturgical Press, 2012), 26.

accident;[65] rather, the universe orients itself toward intelligent, conscious, self-reflective life. He declared: "[M]an discovers that he is nothing else than evolution become conscious of itself. . . . The consciousness of each of us is evolution looking at itself and reflecting upon itself."[66] The human person rises from evolution and, in turn, can reflect on evolution. Teilhard went on to ask, "How indeed could we incorporate thought into the organic flux of space-time without being forced to grant it the first place in the process? How could we imagine a cosmogenesis reaching right up to mind without being thereby confronted with a noogenesis?"[67] Human knowledge redounds on the very processes that make knowledge possible because knowledge is a function of evolutionary emergence. The mind creates by perceiving the phenomena of reality and, in doing so, continues the fundamental work of evolution. "To discover and know is to actually extend the universe ahead and to complete it," Teilhard wrote.[68] The knower is a unifier: "each time the mind comprehends something it unites the world in a new way."[69]

By including consciousness as part of the material world, Teilhard opened up a place for religion in nature, transcending the abstraction of supernaturalism and reframing religion as the depth and breadth of evolution. Religion is an emergent dimension of matter itself and hence of evolution. He wrote: "To my mind, the religious phenomenon, taken as a whole, is the simple reaction of the universe as such, of collective consciousness and human action in process of development."[70] Religion begins with the genesis of the universe: "Religion, born of the earth's need for the disclosing of a god, is related and coextensive with not the individual man but the whole of humankind."[71] Teilhard's notion of god (lower

65. Teilhard de Chardin, "The Position of Man in Mature and the Significance of Human Socialization," *Future of Man*, 211–17.

66. Teilhard de Chardin, *The Phenomenon of Man*, 221.

67. Teilhard de Chardin, *The Phenomenon of Man*, 221.

68. King, *Mysticism of Knowing*, 35.

69. King, *Mysticism of Knowing*, 36.

70. Teilhard de Chardin, *Christianity and Evolution*, 118–19.

71. Teilhard de Chardin, *Christianity and Evolution*, 119.

case) as a principle of wholeness is not to the exclusion of a personal God but a conceptual principle of the whole that makes every wholeness, including the wholeness of God, possible. This principle of the whole is, in my view, Omega. Ursula King states: "Teilhard is one of the few modern thinkers on religion for whom evolution provided the dominant note of his entire work."[72] The basic structure of an evolutionary perspective underlies all his thought on religion. In 1916, he claimed:

> Religion and evolution should neither be confused nor divorced. They are destined to form one single continuous organism, in which their respective lives prolong, are dependent on, and complete one another, without being identified or lost.... Since it is in our age that the duality has become so markedly apparent, it is for us to effect this synthesis.[73]

Religion, therefore, is not strictly a personal matter of personal belief but is integral to nature. In his essay "The Spirit of the Earth" (1931), Teilhard wrote that the true function of religion, not always clearly perceived in the past, is to sustain and spur on the progress of life. Thus, the religious function increases in the same direction and to the same extent as the development and growth of the human in evolution. As nature changes, religion changes. The sacred ordering of nature is an ongoing process. Religious meanings do not disappear; they change, and new forms of treating nature as sacred are generated. The function of religion is to create stories of mythic depth, stories of meaning and purpose that animate human life toward wholeness and goodness. Spirituality proposes what reality can become.

Teilhard understood that our idea of nature has changed along with our ideas of the sacred largely because science and technology have redefined our world. The scientific and technological transformation of nature belongs to the new story of reli-

---

72. Ursula King, *Teilhard de Chardin and Eastern Religions: Spirituality and Mysticism in an Evolutionary World* (Mahwah, NJ: Paulist Press, 2011), 179.

73. King, *Teilhard de Chardin and Eastern Religions*, 179–80.

gion. Teilhard sought a new story of the whole, Omega in evolution. To articulate this story, he emphasized that religion grows continuously with the human being by taking on a new form with each new phase of humankind.[74] Unless religion changes and adapts to the evolving world, it cannot do what it has the capacity to do: enkindle a zest for life.

Western religion is about a personal, Absolute something or Someone at the heart of the universe, drawing the world into the fullness of unity. Eastern religion is about attaining pure consciousness of the whole. On the human level, religion is expressed on the levels of thought and action; however, no one religion can satisfy the religious spirit of the earth, Teilhard thought. Religion is directly concerned with the universe and its evolution toward Omega. As he wrote, "[T]he comparative value of religious creeds may be measured by their respective power of evolutive activation."[75] Religion is to energize the human toward greater wholeness and unity. Faith in Omega is faith in the power within to increase life in the face of resistance; the power to create, change, to become something new. Carl Jung came to a similar conclusion. Both Teilhard and Jung contribute to a new religious myth of relational holism that will cause your heart to stop or to beat faster. Either way, we are in the midst of a God revolution.

---

74. King, *Teilhard de Chardin and Eastern Religions*, 186.

75. Pierre Teilhard de Chardin, "The Christic," section D, available at http://www.users.globalnet.co.uk/~alfar2/Christic.htm.

3

Carl Jung and the Cosmic Psyche

Teilhard de Chardin offers insights into the implicate order of mind and matter, in which consciousness is the fundamental basis of cosmic life; however, he never explored the depths of conscious life, perhaps because the Western world has, historically, displayed a certain degree of antagonism toward the relationship between psychology and theology. For the most part, theologians have been suspicious that psychologists harbor an unacknowledged antipathy toward religion. As early as 1891, Pere Maisonneuve, of the Catholic Scientific Congress in Paris, declared that "psychology is an enemy of Christian philosophy."[1] The tendency toward suspicion of psychology and its methods was strengthened by the publication of Sigmund Freud's works on religion. Freud claimed that religion was no more than a defense against the superior forces of nature and a meager consolation for the shortcomings of civilization. As such, he felt it was

---

1. Karen A. Palmer, "Paul Tillich and Carl Jung: A Dialogue Between Theology and Psychology" (master's thesis, McMaster University, 1996), 1.

"the universal obsessional neurosis of humanity."[2] Freud's analysis of religion helped to usher in a long period of virtual silence between psychology and theology. Even in the late 1970s, the relationship between these disciplines was cautious and tentative.

Carl Jung was a student of Freud who rejected his teacher's diagnosis of religion. John Dourley, whose brilliant work on Jung and Teilhard is influential here, notes that Jung's psychology was a sustained effort to re-connect the individual and through the individual, society, with the depths of the soul and the fuller life such reconnection offered. A master at putting complex epistemology into succinct psychological terms, Jung wrote: "It is therefore psychologically quite unthinkable for God to be 'wholly Other,' for a 'wholly Other' could never be one of the soul's deepest and closest intimacies, which is precisely what God is."[3] He, like Teilhard, lamented the ecclesial suppression of pantheism. In Jung's view, the dissociation of body and spirit was problematic, for the contemporary spirit had now been reduced to intellectual and technological superficiality.

Teilhard was apparently influenced by Jung's ideas, and Jung knew Teilhard's work as well. It is said that Jung was reading Teilhard's *Human Phenomenon* shortly before he died; a copy was found on his night table. Although Jung's psychology is *not* exclusively positive in its evaluation of religion (and Christianity in particular), he attempted to articulate a theology that would be more open to religious phenomena and their doctrinal expressions. His criticisms made possible a deeper appreciation of Christian symbols and doctrines by revealing their source in the depths of the psyche. His corpus is vast, and the amount of Jungian scholarship is enormous. I make no pretense of being a Jungian expert, nor do I know much about psychology. However,

2. Sigmund Freud, *The Future of an Illusion*, trans. and ed. James Strachey (New York: W. W. Norton and Company, 1961), 43; cited in Palmer, "Paul Tillich and Carl Jung," 2.

3. Carl Jung, "Introduction to the Religious and Psychological Problem of Alchemy," *Collected Works* 12 (Princeton: Princeton University Press, 1944), para. 11n6; cited in John Dourley, "Jung's Equation of the Ground of Being with the Ground of the Psyche," *Journal of Analytical Psychology* (2011) 56: 517.

the more I read Jung and Teilhard together, the more I am convinced that the paradigm shift needed to rekindle the religious spirit and, in a particular way, the Christian spirit, requires the integration of psychology, theology, cosmology, and quantum physics as we understand these sciences within the processes of evolution.

John Dourley describes Jung's spirituality as being directed to the recovery of the lost depths of the human psyche in the interests of a greater fullness of individual and societal life. Diogo Valadas Ponte and Lothar Schaefer expand this idea by explicitly linking Jung's ideas to quantum reality and, in an implicit way, to Bohm's implicate order:

> Jung's teaching is more than psychology: it is a form of spirituality. By "spirituality" we mean a view of the world that accepts the numinous at the foundation of the cosmic order. In the same way, Quantum Physics is more than physics: it is a new form of mysticism, which suggests the interconnectedness of all things and beings and the connection of our minds with a cosmic mind.[4]

Jung's abiding sense of a radical immanence led him to see divinity as approaching consciousness from no other source than one's own inner being. In recovering a wider sense of the holy, humanity gives birth to a new myth, the co-redemption of the divine and human in one single and historically prolonged process. To state this in brief: we are God-makers. This shocking idea startles us. But Jung makes a bold move that corresponds to the insights of quantum physics: the mind must connect to its deepest self if we are to be made whole.

---

4. Diogo Valadas Ponte and Lothar Schafer, "Carl Gustav Jung, Quantum Physics and the Spiritual Mind: A Mystical Vision of the Twenty-First Century," *Behavioral Sciences* 3 (2013): 602.

The Psyche as Central

In *Memories, Dreams, Reflections,* Jung tells us that his life's work was dedicated "to service of the psyche."[5] The psyche is the *numinosum,* the realm of the holy or divinity, to which he religiously devoted his career. In his 1937 Terry Lectures, he stated:

> Religion, as the Latin word denotes, is a careful and scrupulous observation of what Rudolf Otto aptly termed the *numinosum,* that is, a dynamic agency or effect not caused by an arbitrary act of will. On the contrary, it seizes and controls the human subject, who is always rather its victim than its creator. The *numinosum*—whatever its cause may be—is an experience of the subject independent of his will.[6]

Jung describes how, in the years after his break from Freud and up to the end of World War I, he was seized by material from the unconscious, which he also refers to as the psyche itself. His experience is similar to the fire within that Teilhard describes in *The Heart of Matter.* Jung writes:

> But then, I hit upon this stream of lava, and the heat of its fires reshaped my life. That was the primal stuff which compelled me to work upon it, and my works are a more or less successful endeavor to incorporate this incandescent matter into the contemporary picture of the world.... The years when I was pursuing my inner images were the most important in my life—in them everything essential was decided. It all began then; the later details are only supplements and clarifications of the material that burst forth

---

5. Carl Jung, *Memories, Dreams, Reflections,* ed. Aniela Jaffe (New York: Vintage Books, 1961), 192.

6. Carl Jung, "Psychology and Religion" (The Terry Lectures), *Collected Works* 11 (Princeton: Princeton University Press, 1938/1940), para. 6.

from the unconscious, and at first swamped me. It was the *prima materia* for a lifetime's work.[7]

Teilhard also had a deep, inner experience of the ineffable whole that inspired him to return to matter as the place of the Absolute. Writing in the midst of World War I, Teilhard recounts his inner journey into the All:

> I allowed my consciousness to sweep back to the farthest limit of my body, to ascertain whether I might not extend outside myself. I stepped down into the most hidden depths of my being, lamp in hand and ears alert, to discover whether in the deepest recesses of the blackness within me, I might not see the glint of the waters of the current that flows on, whether I might not hear the murmur of their mysterious waters that rise from the uttermost depths and will burst forth no man knows where. With terror and intoxicating emotion, I realized that my own poor trifling existence was one with the immensity of all that is and all that is still in the process of becoming.[8]

It is Jung, however, who probes the mind as the field of the Absolute. What does Jung mean by "psyche"? It is not a question easily answered. His conception of "psyche" is the immensity of consciousness and unconsciousness, the realm of the Self: "The psyche, as a reflection of the world and man, is a thing of such infinite complexity that it can be observed and studied from a great many sides."[9] Jung's philosophy rests on the teleology of the unconscious becoming progressively conscious, as the core meaning of personal and collective history.[10]

---

7. Jung, *Memories, Dreams, Reflections*, 199.

8. Pierre Teilhard de Chardin, *Writings in Time of War*, trans. René Hague (New York: Harper and Row, 1968), 25.

9. Carl Jung, "The Structure and Dynamics of the Psyche," *Collected Works* 8 (Princeton: Princeton: University Press, 1969), para. 283.

10. John Dourley, *Paul Tillich, Carl Jung and the Recovery of Religion* (London: Routledge, 2008), 111-26.

For Jung, the recovery of his own soul enabled him to perceive soul in the reality of his immediate surroundings: "in things and men."[11] This recovery of soul grew into the meaning of the *unus mundus*, the one world, a symbol that strongly undergirds the recovery of soul as the conscious recovery of the unconscious through a progressive incarnation of self, leading to an intensified sense of one's affinity with all that is. Jung's description of the *unus mundus* sounds very much like Bohm's implicate order. He wrote:

> Undoubtedly the idea of the *Unus Mundus* is founded on the assumption that the multiplicity of the empirical world rests on an underlying unity, and that not two or more fundamentally different worlds exist side by side or are mingled with one another. Rather, everything divided and different belongs to one and the same world, which is not the world of sense.[12]

Jung's relentless pursuit of the inner universe emerged from a felt need to reconcile body and soul. He felt that Christianity had become a "dead system," imprisoned in isolated dogmatic certitudes; religion had become a matter of the head and not of the total person.[13] Teilhard similarly lamented: "Christianity no longer stimulates the need to worship for the modern mind, but rather paralyzes it."[14] For Jung and Teilhard, the need to critique early twentieth-century Western religion may have been provoked by the problem of a specifically Christian need to recover its own lost soul and with it the symbolic life. In time, this critique became much more extensive and deeper.

As Jung's work on the issue of religion progressed, it took on three broader features. First, his psychology became an apology

---

11. Carl Jung, *Modern Man in Search of a Soul*, trans. W. S. Dell and Cary F. Baynes (Eastford, CT: Martino Fine Books, 2017), 232.

12. Carl Jung, "Mysterium Coniunctionis," *Collected Works* 14 (Princeton: Princeton University Press, 1970), para. 767.

13. Jung, *Modern Man in Search of a Soul*, 226–54.

14. Pierre Teilhard de Chardin, *The Heart of Matter*, trans. René Hague (New York: Harcourt Brace Jovanovich, 1979), 54.

for no religion in particular, but for religion itself as an ineradicable function of the human psyche. Second, his psychology slowly brought him to the realization that Western confessional religion had little to offer in terms of reconnecting the modern person with the depths of the soul. Third, in his later psychology, he concluded that, in the West, a new individual and societal myth was emerging from the one matrix of the many religions.[15]

THE COLLECTIVE UNCONSCIOUS

Jung's *collective unconscious* is a non-personal part of the human psyche. It is a realm of forms—*the archetypes*—which can appear spontaneously in our consciousness and act in it, influencing "our imagination, perception, and thinking."[16] The archetypes are "typical modes of apprehension,"[17] which shape, regulate, and motivate the conscious forms in our mind in the same way in which the virtual states of atoms and molecules shape and control empirical phenomena. Peter Todd states that "the archetypes transcend the finiteness of both individual and collective humanity while providing intimations of something infinite. And the eternal present in a perennial now [is] that of the boundless unconscious psyche."[18] Jung describes archetypes as collective material, motifs that repeat themselves in almost identical form all over the earth as constituents of myths as well as individual products of unconscious origin.[19] The archetypes exist as timeless, cosmic ordering and regulating principles and are the realm

---

15. Carl Jung, "Psychology and Alchemy," *Collected Works* 12, paras. 202–25.

16. Carl Jung, "The Archetypes and the Collective Unconscious," *Collected Works* 9 (Princeton: Princeton University Press, 1969), para. 44.

17. Jung, "The Structure and Dynamics of the Psyche," *Collected Works* 8, para. 137.

18. Peter Todd, "The Numinous and the Archetypes as Timeless, Cosmic Ordering and Regulating Principles in Evolution," *C. G. Jung Society of Sydney Presentations* (2011): 11.

19. Jung, "Psychology and Religion," *Collected Works* 11, para. 88.

of the numinous. They are discernable through their verifiable influence in both the phenomenal and internal worlds.[20] Among the archetypes is the Self, which "is not only the center but also the whole circumference which embraces both consciousness and unconsciousness; [the Self] is the center of this totality, just as the ego is the center of the conscious mind."[21] We must constantly reach into the realm of the archetypes and actualize their virtual forms in order to live and to give meaning to life.

Ponte and Schaefer make an interesting comment on Jung's archetypes by comparing them to the wave forms of quantum states. Like the wave function of quantum systems, archetypes of the collective unconscious are pure, non-material forms. Just as molecules are guided in their actions by the wave forms of their quantum states, like inner images, so too, we are guided by thoughts or ideas which are archetypes, that is, potential realities or forms which must be actualized to exist. The power of human imagination can plumb the cosmic arena of archetypes, both conscious and unconscious, to draw out new realities that form the world. "We can understand the world, because the forms within our mind and the structures of the world outside both derive from the same cosmic source."[22] Beyond the narrow confines of our personal psyche, Jung pointed out, the collective unconscious is

> a boundless expanse full of unprecedented uncertainty, with apparently no inside and no outside, no above and no below, no here and no there, no mine and no thine, no good and no bad…where I am indivisibly this and that; where I experience the other in myself and the

---

20. Kalervo Vihtori Laurikainen, *Beyond the Atom: The Philosophical Thought of Wolfgang Pauli* (New York: Springer-Verlag, 1988); cited in Todd, "The Numinous and the Archetypes," 10.

21. Jung, "Psychology and Alchemy," *Collected Works* 12, para. 44.

22. Ponte and Schaefer, "Carl Gustav Jung, Quantum Physics and the Spiritual Mind," 610. See Stephen Asma, "Imagination: A New Foundation for the Science of Mind," *Biological Theory* (July 16, 2022). He claims that our "understanding of imagination is still in a pre-Linnean phase."

other-than-myself experiences me.... There I am utterly one with the world, so much a part of it that I forget all too easily who I really am.[23]

This reconciliation of our personal psyche with the collective consciousness is what many of the mystics—East and West—attained. One of the best examples comes from the thirteenth-century Franciscan mystic Angela of Foligno. In her spiritual memoir *Memorial,* she describes a mystical experience in which prayer brought her into the conscious awareness of the All within and without:

> Afterward [God] added: "I want to show you something of my power." And immediately the eyes of my soul were opened, and in a vision I beheld the fullness of God in which I beheld and comprehended the whole of creation, that is, what is on this side and what is beyond the sea, the abyss, the sea itself, and everything else. *And in everything that I saw, I could perceive nothing except the presence of the power of God, and in a manner totally indescribable. And my soul in an excess of wonder cried out: "The world is pregnant with God!"* Wherefore I understood how small is the whole of creation—that is, what is on this side and what is beyond the sea, the abyss, the sea itself, and everything else—but the power of God fills it to overflowing.[24]

When the outer world and the inner world form one seamless world, the *unus mundus,* then we are fully alive in the All. As Teilhard wrote: "If I am to be All, I must be fused with All."[25]

---

23. Jung, "The Archetypes and the Collective Unconscious," *Collected Works* 9, para. 21.

24. Paul Lachance, *Angela of Foligno: Complete Works* (Mahwah, NJ: Paulist Press, 1993), 169–70.

25. Teilhard de Chardin, *Heart of Matter,* 21.

THE PROBLEM OF THE SKY GOD

Jung's exploration of the human psyche was based on the premise that religion is a natural part of the process of individuation, of becoming a person, a fully integrated and relational being. This process of personal formation challenged the traditional notion of God as a transcendent wholly other being who sustains and governs all life. The notion of finding oneself in God rather than in oneself is not an invitation to leave oneself behind by focusing attention on a transcendent being; rather, it is to enter into the unreconciled self, the field of the mind, to see what we are being called to as well as to face our fears, doubts, and anxieties. At the center of the human heart is a burning desire to reach for wholeness in love, for God is already there. A theology of transcendence that diverts attention away from embodied life toward supernatural life can turn into abandoning earth life for an imaginary God.

Jim Marion distills supernatural theology into plain talk by describing a "sky God." The sky God is the "supernatural" God, dwelling outside this world and invading the world periodically to accomplish the divine will. In Marion's view, many Christians have become stuck on the level of mythic consciousness—a level of adolescent consciousness that functions within the narrow limits of law and order. It is the level of what we might call binary thinking. At the mythic level, the child [or adult] thinks concretely, which is why mythic thinking is concrete operational thinking.[26] God is seen as a being who lives in the sky (heaven), a (male) being separate from humans and all creation, a being who, in response to prayer, supernaturally intervenes in the human condition.[27] At the level of mythic consciousness, one has not made the conceptual leap from a lawful God to true universality. Personal talk of God is universalized; in other words, the only

---

26. Jim Marion, *The Death of the Mythic God: The Rise of Evolutionary Spirituality* (Charlottesville, VA: Hampton Roads Publishing Company, 2004), 14.

27. Marion, *Death of the Mythic God*, 28.

real God is *my* God. The mythic conception of God has almost completely colored Christianity's understanding of Jesus and his teachings. Jesus has been primarily understood not as a human being who realized his own divinity but as a god or divine being who was sent down from the sky. This god died on the cross to appease his Father, the sky God, for the sins of humanity (supposedly incurred by the first humans, Adam and Eve, in the Garden of Eden). Marion notes that "Christians go to church on Sunday as if entering a time warp, putting the modern scientific worldview aside for an hour or two to submit to the old mythic worldview. Then they emerge to take up once again the scientific worldview that guides their lives and professions during the week."[28]

Marion's caricature of the "sky God" reflects a fundamental concern for theology that both Jung and Teilhard shared. If religion is a cosmic and personal phenomenon and God symbolizes the interior depth of consciousness, then how do we still preach and teach a sky God? The explosion of consciousness studies in the late twentieth and early twenty-first centuries reveals the urgent need to explore the relationship of the mind and the psyche to the powerful word "God." Many psychologists have mapped out stages of consciousness that can help us understand the development, including the religious development, of the human person. Marion sums it up this way:

> As our consciousness evolves up the ladder of consciousness, we become less and less egocentric and more and more universally compassionate. An infant (archaic consciousness) has what Freud called "primary narcissism." It is not that the infant is selfish in the moral sense, it is just that the infant can recognize only itself, at first not even distinguishing itself from its mother. At the magical level, one identifies with one's family and blood relatives, one's tribe. At the mythic level, one identifies with one's ethnic group, race, nationality, or religious sect. Thus, the mythic level is ethnocentric or sociocentric.

---

28. Marion, *Death of the Mythic God*, 32.

Each level of consciousness broadens one's concern, compassion, and identification until finally, at the causal or Christ Consciousness level, one no longer identifies with the human personality at all but with Spirit in whom resides the entirety of creation...the highest levels of human consciousness—the causal (or Christ) consciousness and nondual consciousness.[29]

The question we have to face, theologically, is this: If divinity is transcendent, personal Being, what does this mean in terms of consciousness and the psyche? Is God a shorthand term for the infinite wholeness of potential life, the collective unconsciousness, or is God the transcendence of consciousness itself?

PANTHEISM OR ENTANGLEMENT?

Jung wrestled with the problem of the supernatural as an extrinsic source of divine perfection. He approached the question of God not from the point of philosophical religion but from the perspective of the mind seeking wholeness. God is the name of the Whole of the whole, the transcendence of the psyche. God is within, as archetype, yet more than the collective unconsciousness. Jung spoke of the soul as image of God, indicating that the soul has divine life but that God is beyond the soul. He recognized the importance of transcendence but saw transcendence as the openness and depth of nature, not another existence beyond nature. He was criticized for reducing Christianity to a pantheistic, natural religion, a claim that was made of Teilhard, as well. But is this claim justified?

Pantheism, as we saw in the introduction, identifies God with the universe or considers the universe to be a manifestation of God. Monism views God as identical with the cosmos and sees nothing as existing outside of God. Neither Jung nor Teilhard support monism. A distinction may be drawn between *distributive pantheism*, the view that each thing in the cosmos is divine; and

---

29. Marion, *Death of the Mythic God*, 72–73.

collective pantheism, the view that the cosmos as a whole is divine.[30] Richard Dawkins in *The God Delusion* complains that "pantheism is sexed-up atheism."[31] Einstein was a pantheist but rejected any notion of a personal God.[32] William Mander describes different versions of pantheism, one of which is the Absolute Idealist scheme, where history culminates in the complete realization of God or Absolute spirit in the world.

One can find hints of pantheism among Christian writers throughout history, such as the ninth-century philosopher John Scotus Eriugena, who taught an emanation-theory of creation that had pantheistic tendencies. Baruch Spinoza in the seventeenth century said that God is the same as the cosmos. What is referred to as "God" is one and the same as the complex unit referred to as "nature" or "the cosmos." As the nineteenth-century philosopher G. F. Schelling put it, in the last days, "God will indeed be *all in all,* and pantheism will be true."[33] Samuel Alexander posited that the universe evolves in a steadily progressive manner and will finally "attain deity," where deity is thought of as an unknown but superior quality that will "emerge" from the complex whole in rather the same way as, at a lower level, consciousness "emerges" from complex organizations of organic matter. Teilhard's ideas are along these lines as well, but not as Alexander wrote: "God as actually possessing deity does not exist but is an ideal always becoming; but God as the whole universe tending towards deity does exist."[34] Alexander suggests that the universe *becomes* God, whereas Teilhard indicates that the universe *completes* God. That is, God does not depend on the universe to be God; rather, the universe depends on God to be itself, and to

---

30. Graham Oppy, "Pantheism, Quantification and Mereology," *The Monist* 80, no. 2 (1994): 325.

31. Richard Dawkins, *The God Delusion* (Boston: Houghton Mifflin Company, 2007), 40.

32. Walter Isaacson, *Einstein: His Life and Universe* (New York: Simon and Schuster, 2007), 384–93.

33. See William Mander, "Pantheism," *Stanford Encyclopedia of Philosophy* (October 1, 2012), https://plato.stanford.edu/entries/pantheism/.

34. Samuel Alexander, "Some Explanations," *Mind* 120 (October 1921), 428.

be itself is to fulfill its God potential. In fulfilling this potential, God is completed in God's own relational life. In *The Divine Milieu* Teilhard wrote:

> Pantheism seduces us by its vistas of perfect universal union. But ultimately, if it were true, it would give us only fusion and unconsciousness; for, at the end of the evolution it claims to reveal, the elements of the world vanish into the God they create or by which they are absorbed. Our God, on the contrary, pushes to its furthest possible limit the differentiation among the creatures he concentrates within himself. At the peak of their adherence to him, the elect also discover in him the consummation of their individual fulfillment. Christianity alone therefore saves...the essential aspiration of all mysticism: *to be united* (that is, to become the other) *while remaining oneself.* More attractive than any world-Gods, whose eternal seduction it embraces, transcends and purifies...our divine milieu is at the antipodes of false pantheism. The Christian can plunge himself into it whole-heartedly without the risk of finding himself one day a monist.[35]

For many pantheists, identification of the whole cosmos as divine involves rejection of a personal God.[36] Although Jung and Teilhard use the language of pantheism, their intention is to overcome the dualistic language and thinking that have crept into Western religion. However, the concept of pantheism involves a substantive understanding of being that diminishes their insights, which are better expressed in terms of divine complexity and entanglement. Pantheism assumes a philosophical position that makes ontology the basis of theology. One could see how pantheism arises if God is regarded as *being itself,* so that there is an identification of divine being with created being, resulting in a

---

35. Pierre Teilhard de Chardin, *The Divine Milieu*, trans. Bernard Wall (New York: Harper & Row, 1960), 116.

36. See Michael P. Levine, *Pantheism: A Non-Theistic Concept of Deity* (London: Routledge, 1994).

conflation or loss of distinction between God, human, and cosmos. To avoid this, some type of ontological transcendence was thought to be necessary. Hence, God must be a supernatural Being (read: "sky God").

Panentheism, on the other hand, means God (theos) is *in* (en) all (pan) and all is *in* God, without collapsing God into world. It finds its source in the Acts of the Apostles (17:28), where Saint Paul writes of God "in whom we live and move and have our being." Panentheism is what Thomas Aquinas had in mind when he described his metaphysics: God is *in* the world and the world is *in* God. We live in God, as God lives in us. However, if God is first and foremost, the experience of ultimate meaning or concern, then the descriptive language must be experiential as well. The panentheistic view is that everything that exists is alive; there is no such thing as dead matter. The world lives in God and God lives in the world, and the mutual influence between God and the world is similar to the way the cells of our body influence us. This position is close to Jung's ideas. Victoria LePage writes:

> The heart of the panentheistic exposition lies in the twin concepts of divine holism and divine love, which imply a voluntary self-limiting on God's part, a voluntary self-transformation. So does a mother interact with the child in her womb in such a way that both are undergoing a growth and an evolution together, in mutual love, while remaining distinct entities. On this interpretation, the best of the biblical tradition is the God of love.... For proponents of panentheism, God is a meaningless abstraction unless he is the Whole, the one universal Life acting in all particularities yet transcending them, the One who is also Many, the Being who is also Becoming. Such a God is nameless, genderless, formless, a universal and all-merciful divinity beyond race or creed: not the Lord Jehovah, but the unknown and incomprehensible God of the Gnostics, the Ain Soph of the Kabbalists, the Brahma of the Vedantists.[37]

---

37. Victoria LePage, "The God Debate: Monotheism vs. Pantheism in Postmodern Society," *The Theosophic Society in America* 87, no. 6 (December

While panentheism is a helpful concept, the language of pantheism and panentheism is based on concepts of "being" and "nature" that can lead to misguided images of distinct beings in relation to one another. A more useful concept to describe the inextricable relationship of God and matter is "divine entanglement," because it points to a mutual, reciprocal, and interactive relationship. God and the world form a complementary whole. Another useful concept is Raimon Panikkar's notion of cosmotheandric holism: divinity, humanity, and cosmos as three interlocking realities united in a single reality or a "cosmotheandric reality."[38]

Jung's views incorporated the notion of entanglement although he never explicitly used this term. In his psychology, the ego is never wholly without the experience of its origin in the deeper psyche itself, never wholly at one with that origin, yet ever driven to a closer conscious unity with it, just as the origin is ever driven to become increasingly conscious in the ego. To put such psychology in religious terms, God's desire for an ever-deeper union with human consciousness intersects with a consciousness that can neither wholly resist nor exhaustively satisfy the constant address of divinity to become ever more incarnate, that is, divinity conscious of itself in human self-consciousness. "The experience of such ultimacy is inextricably psychological and religious and points to an experientially God-haunted humanity," Dourly writes.[39] Jung maintained that an authentic religious function in the unconscious imbues humanity with a natural sense of the divine as the basis of religion universally.[40] Religion is a natural process of individuation. This natural process

---

1999), https://www.theosophical.org/publications/quest-magazine/1572-sp-514974763.

38. For a discussion on Christ as the Cosmotheandric Mystery, see Raimon Panikkar, *Christophany: The Fullness of Man* (Maryknoll, NY: Orbis Books, 2004), 180–88; Cheriyan Menacherry, *Christ: The Mystery in History A Critical Study on the Christology of Raymond Panikkar* (Frankfurt am Main: Peter Lang, 1996), 117–20.

39. Dourley, "Jung's Equation of the Ground of Being with the Ground of the Psyche," 518.

40. Jung, "Psychology and Religion," *Collected Works* 11, para. 3.

is evident in humanity's collective affirmation that God is real because God is really experienced.[41] Here, Jung joins Paul Tillich in grounding the ontological argument that God is a necessary experience in the universal sense of the divine as humanity's ultimate concern.[42]

Jung and Teilhard sought to clarify the elusiveness of the term "pantheism" and to reaffirm nature as the place of the holy. Pantheism is a pre-quantum idea and reflects an atomistic understanding of matter. Jung and Teilhard were writing in view of the new science in which quantum physics changes everything. Once the role of mind becomes inseparable from matter, we are in an entirely new field of God and matter. Clearly, Jung evokes new ideas of divinity not conceived by the early Church Fathers who wrote theology in a pre-scientific age. His conception of the God-matter relationship, like that of Teilhard, is much more consonant with quantum physics than with pre-Newtonian physics. Applying the charge of pantheism as a type of reductionism to them is simply misguided. The term "relational holism" is more suitable to their system of thought. The operative conceptual model for both Jung and Teilhard is religious holism or "theohology," that is, God (*theos*) is the divine Whole (*holos*) of every whole. Theology is talk of the whole God-matter-mind complex.

JUNG AND THE NOTION OF TRANSCENDENCE

Jung regarded the Self as the archetype of wholeness experienced by the human, comprised of both consciousness and unconsciousness. What the Christian myth sees as the intervention of the divine into one human being—the Messiah or Jesus Christ—Jung sees as an intervention from the collective unconscious of the archetypal self which, he hypothesizes, all humanity shares.

---

41. Jung, "Psychology and Religion," *Collected Works* 11, para. 4.

42. Carl Jung, "The Relativity of the God-Concept in Meister Eckhart," *Collected Works* 6 (Princeton: Princeton University Press, 1921), paras. 61–62; See also Paul Tillich, *Systematic Theology: Reason and Revelation, Being and God*, vol. 1 (Chicago: University of Chicago Press, 1973), 205–7.

For him, Christ is the archetype of the human who is awakened to one's own unconsciousness. This is not unlike Raimon Panikkar's insights on "Christophany," in which every person is an icon of Christ.

Writing from an intercultural perspective, Panikkar's view was that Christianity is essentially a non-dual religion. What has distorted this awareness has been the attempt to process Jesus's experience through a rigid Western interpretation of Abrahamic monotheism that sees creator and creature as separated by an unbridgeable abyss. But Jesus himself neither taught nor experienced this. Like Jung, Panikkar writes that knowing Christ from the inside involves a spiritual subject-to-subject or "I-I" *interabiding* rooted in our own deepest experience of spiritual seeking and finding. I discover myself as the "thou of an I" ("God is the I, and I am God's Thou"). This is the genuine experience of Christian *advaita* or non-dualism ("not one, not two, but both one and two"), preserving both the interpenetration of identity and the reality of personhood. As we awaken to the God-depth of our life, we become more than human; we become "ultrahuman" or "Christic," which impels us to move beyond the "ego" toward the "super-ego," the "hyperpersonal," which is the completion of the self as the God-self. Panikkar writes: "Man . . . is more than 'Man.' . . . [One is] a spark of the Divine."[43] He continues:

> Our destiny is to become God, to reach the other shore where divinity dwells by means of the transformation that requires a new birth in order to enter the kingdom of heaven . . . Without pleroma there would be no place for God, and human existence would make no sense. "Man" is more than "Man"; when one wants to be merely "Man" one degenerates into a beast. He is destined for higher things.[44]

---

43. Raimon Panikkar, *Cultures and Religions in Dialogue,* Opera Omnia vol. VI, *Part 2: Intercultural and Interreligious Dialogue* (Maryknoll, NY: Orbis Books, 2006), 77.

44. Panikkar, *Intercultural and Interreligious Dialogue,* 77.

Panikkar seems to be echoing Jung: the human person is divine by nature. It is a dialectical mystery because the root reality of all existence, God, cannot be reduced to mere materiality, yet materiality cannot exist without its divine root. In his later psychology, Jung engaged the theological question of God as the transcendent source of life. He reflected on divine transcendence within humanity's experience of divinity, described as immanent, because it is experienced within the human and creation. In other words, just as we cannot speak of transcendence apart from immanence, we cannot speak of God apart from consciousness and the matrix of consciousness, which is matter.

Jung reverses the priority of transcendence over immanence. He does not eliminate these terms but radically revises the premises of their distinction. He does this by denying that divinity can be understood as a transcendent object or entity. Effectively, divinity becomes the *experience of divinity*, and this experience is wholly generated by intra-psychic forces, or more precisely, by the impact of numinous archetypal powers, especially of the (unconscious) self, seeking concrete expression in consciousness. The basis of transcendence for Jung lies in the importance of dreams and memories. These powers are numinous "types"—unconscious contents, processes, and dynamisms—and such types are immanent-transcendent. They are immanent because they exist within the human psyche. They are transcendent because they transcend the ego with which they are organically connected in the total psyche and in which they seek to become conscious. Archetypes are transcendent precisely because their creative potential is inexhaustible. The infinite potential of archetypes falls within the purview of nature, but nature itself falls within the purview of the mystical.

Jung's position could be interpreted as panentheist, but there is an operative holism in his work that better describes his thought as the entangled wholeness of God and person. Quantum physics suggests that matter is transcendent by nature because matter reflects mind and mind has no limits. If mind is the matrix of consciousness, as Teilhard claimed, and consciousness is unlimited, then God is the name of transcendent wholeness of mind or consciousness, as Eastern religions affirm. Jung would contend that

God is transcendent to consciousness itself. God is the Whole beyond whole, the fountain fullness of Wholeness, that Whole of which no greater can be conceived. God is the ground of cosmic life.

Transcendence, then, has to do not with God's transcendence but with matter's transcendence; divine transcendence is the transcendence of matter. Matter is never at rest; rather, it is restless and always yearning for something more, because matter is open to divinity. We are so conditioned by Western dualism that it is difficult for us to think that matter itself is open to divine life; however, the quantum world invites us to consider anew both God and matter. The transcendence of God *is* the transcendence of matter, and the transcendence of matter is the transcendence of God. Maurice Merleau-Ponty described the divinity of the new materialism this way:

> God is not simply a principle of which we are the consequence, a will whose instruments we are. . . . There is sort of an impotence of God without us, and Christ attests that God would not be fully God without becoming fully man. . . . God is not above but beneath us—meaning that we do not find him as a suprasensible idea, but as another ourself which dwells in and authenticates our darkness. Transcendence no longer hangs over man; he becomes, strangely, its privileged bearer.[45]

The transcendence of matter invites a new model of the God-world relationship that allows Jung's insights to be situated within the paradigm of relational holism, with its underlying fundamental concept of entanglement. Entanglement is the inextricable and insuperable relationality of all that is, including God. If pantheism conjures up the collapse of God into matter, then entanglement holds everything together in a relational whole. There is no transcendence without immanence and no immanence

---

45. Maurice Merleau-Ponty, *Signs* (Evanston, IL: Northwestern University Press, 1964), 106; cited in Richard Kearney, *Anatheism* (New York: Columbia University Press, 2010), 9.

without transcendence; there is no God without matter and no matter without God. God and matter form a complementary whole.

A NOTE ON ENTANGLEMENT

I have been using the language of entanglement to describe the God-matter or God-world relationship because it is the most modern symbol for conveying the mystery of matter in its divine potential. It is time now to look more closely at the concept of entanglement. As noted in chapter 1, according to the Einsten-Podolsky-Rosen paradox, the result of a measurement on one particle of an entangled quantum system can have an instantaneous effect on another particle, regardless of the distance between them.

Einstein, Podolsky, and Rosen were dealing with scientific aspects of entanglement. It was the physicist Niels Bohr who approached the science of entanglement from a philosophical perspective. Bohr rejected atomistic metaphysics, which takes "things" as ontologically basic entities, holding instead to the view that things do not have inherently determinate boundaries or properties, and words do not have inherently determinate meanings.

To be clear about what Bohr was rejecting, we need to go back to the early modern period, when René Descartes's search for true and certain knowledge impelled him to separate mind and matter, giving rise to distinct "internal" and "external" domains. In a sense, the internal realm of the knowing subject replaced the cosmos as the place of knowledge. The turn to the subject became a new metaphysics in the work of Immanuel Kant, who proposed that the mind imposes its mental structures of representations by constructing meanings of the world. In the twentieth century, Ludwig Wittgenstein described the power of language to construct meaning according to game rules, turning Cartesian representationalism into the power of linguistic construction.

Bohr called into question the Cartesian belief in the inherent distinction between subject and object, knower and known, since nothing can be said apart from an act of *conscious* knowing. He rejected the notion of language and measurement as performing *mediating* functions. There is no mediator between mind and matter. Language has functioned as a mediator, but, in doing so it has artificially carved up the world. In Bohr's view, the conceptual and physical are intertwined. Language does not represent the truest state of affairs, and measurements do not represent measurement-independent states of being.[46]

Karen Barad, a student of Bohr's philosophy, explicitly dismisses language as a source of meaning, wondering aloud, "When did language become so important?" She declares that "language has been granted too much power" and should no longer be the order of the day.[47] Barad writes that representationalism separates the world into the ontologically disjointed domains of words and things.[48] Essentially, words carve up the world into separate things which we analyze and judge. If words are untethered from the material world, how do representations gain a foothold? She coins a term—"thingification"—to indicate that we humans turn relations into "things," "entities," or "relata"; that is, words form things and things have relationships. The construction of a "thing-world" infects much of the way we understand the world and our relationship to it, including God. Instead, the focus should be on "matter," in all its "mattering." Hence, Barad rejects the traditional notion of representationalism, with its dependence on "reflection," that is, the turning of relationships into "things" and subsequent reflection on "things" as objects. Existence is not an individual affair. Barad offers new concepts such as diffraction and intra-action to recontextualize the role of the human in the whole. Intra-action means everything affects everything else, since relationships form things, rather than things forming relationships. An intra-action is an action of mutual and reciprocal relationality. The agential cut is a choice

---

46. Karen Barad, "Posthuman Performativity: Toward an Understanding of How Matter Comes to Matter," *Signs: Journal of Women and Culture in Society* 28, no. 3 (2003): 813.

47. Barad, "Posthuman Performativity," 801.

48. Barad, "Posthuman Performativity," 804.

made from the relationship, actualizing an event by effecting a separation between "subject" and "object." In Barad's view, agency is not a center of action but a center of relationship; agency is not something one has but what one "is."[49] All matter is agential matter. Life is a complexity of intra-acting processes, whereby matter interacts reciprocally. Shared information or shared life becomes an ontological performance of the world in its ongoing articulation and differential becoming.

THE ENTANGLED JUNG

Jung wrote with a view of modern science in mind and, although he was not familiar with entanglement, his way of thinking leads in this direction. He was aware that new concepts of time, space, matter, and motion were characterized by a closer interdependence than their classical equivalents. Time and space were shown to be inextricably bound to form a four-dimensional continuum, while matter and motion were reduced to a quantitative transformation of the spatio-temporal medium. These revised physical concepts implied the existence of an intrinsic unity in nature extending beyond the relationships admitted and analyzed by classical science. The universe is not an agglomeration of particles but rather is an organism whose inter-connectedness is so intricate that no part of it, including God, can be clearly delineated from the whole.

For Jung, the experience of the immanent archetypal dimension of the psyche is the experience that brings God into focus. Archetypes are potentials, the realm of the ineffable and unknowable, the mystical realm. In this view, the psychogenesis of divinity is entirely from within, emerging from the entangled infinite potential of matter. Jung does concede that divinity is not and cannot be divested of a transcendent element because the fontal wealth of the archetypal, the collective unconscious, will never cease the drive to fuller realization. In this respect, it will always transcend the degree of its incarnation in the individual. Jung de-

---

49. Barad, "Posthuman Performativity," 815.

scribes the surpassing plenitude of the creative energy of the un-conscious as "of indefinite extent with no assignable limits."[50] By saying this, he means that there is an ongoing infinite seeking ever-fuller realization in what must remain finite. And yet, the re-lationship between ego and unconscious is the foundation of in-dividuation, a process which can no more be evaded, because it is as natural as the psyche. While the unconscious always tran-scends consciousness, nothing transcends their interaction within the extended psyche whose creative potential is open to the infi-nite. In this way, he eliminates the reality and imagining of an on-tologically distinct, divine transcendent agency impinging on the psyche from a position wholly beyond it and foreign to it.

Jung makes us aware of the unity in nature that extends from objects to perceiving minds. Thus, our individual conscious-nesses also have the capacity to merge beyond time and space into "a single continuous stream of life," something which Teil-hard also realized.[51] Transcendence is no longer above or onto-logically beyond us; transcendence is the openness of incomplete matter or matter in evolution toward wholeness. Transcendence is the stretching of matter into the future, the orientation of mat-ter toward the absolute wholeness of life, toward God Omega.

---

50. Carl Jung, "Transformation Symbolism in the Mass," *Collected Works* 11, para. 390; cited in John Dourley, "Conspiracies of Immanence: Paul Tillich, Pierre Teilhard de Chardin and C. G. Jung," *Journal of Analytical Psychology* 60, no. 1 (2015): 78.

51. Dourley, "Conspiracies of Immanence," 83.

4
The Question of God

Quantum physics revolutionized nature by turning measurable entities into descriptive processes. Atomic particles are now seen to be a constellation of quarks, bosons, gluons, and leptons dancing around each other in fields of endless energy. Matter is nothing like it seems. Quantum physics disrupted nature in its naïve appearance, without ever intending to do so. Talk about "nature" as a thing in itself has been left to poets, artists, and theologians. Scientists instead talk about spin, motion, charge, entanglement, and the essential but elusive role of the mind. Instead of the conceptual categories of matter and form, nature is seen to be open, chaotic, and emergent. Given enough time and the right environment, nature will do new things. Hence, talk about nature must begin with humility, reverence, openness, and wonder. Any nature-talk of finality is likely not to be talking about nature at all. If talk about nature has become carefully orchestrated, how can we talk about God? Better yet, if nature is a constellation of relationships, what is God?

As a psychiatrist and a psychotherapist, Jung lamented that Christianity had induced a type of "religious schizophrenia" because it separates God from the rest of nature and insists on talk-

ing about God and world as two separate entities. The stubborn-
ness of Christian language in the face of modern science may be a
reason why Christianity is thinning out. In 2011, a new translation
of the Catholic Mass reinserted the Latin term "consubstantial"
into the Nicene Creed to denote the belief that Jesus Christ is one
in substance with the Father. People were confused by this archaic
term, and even those who knew what it meant (or checked it out
on Google) found it abstract and irrelevant. Religious language,
like religious myth, is meant to animate and inspire us to see
meaning and purpose in the whole cosmic order. Adhering to religious language and principles based on old philosophical ideas
and terms confuses people and enervates their desire for wholeness because it separates the mind from the reality of nature. This
can result only in planetary failure. If we seek religion only to govern and save ourselves, we will lose everything.

How the Sky God Was Born

Jung and Teilhard, among others in the twentieth century, recognized the problem of Greek philosophy as the basis of theology.
On June 12, 1946, Teilhard jotted down in a diary a short sentence
that read: "The death of God (Nietzsche) and the rebirth of God
(Omega)." He had just returned to Paris after a long stay in China
and was impacted by the prevalence of existentialist thought in a
postwar milieu. The struggle for life was surrounded by anxiety
and despair. Modernity had collapsed, and there seemed to be no
way out of the mess humans had made. He was aware of a certain pessimism bordering on and leading to atheism. Teilhard
asked if the real problem might be a sense of unsatisfied theism, a
shrinking of God into nice, neat formulas, a God who no longer
"nourishes in us the interest to go on living and living on a
higher plane."[1] When the growth of science and technology out-
strips our spiritual growth, the human person is reduced to data
and eventually obliterated as a subject of infinite proportions.

---

1. Pierre Teilhard de Chardin, *Activation of Energy*, trans. René Hague
(New York: Harcourt Brace Jovanovich, 1963), 239.

Teilhard thought that the God of Jesus Christ had to be reborn as the God of Evolution. "The human world of today," he wrote, "has not grown cold but it is ardently searching for a God proportionate to the new dimensions of a universe whose appearance has completely revolutionized the scale of our faculty of worship."[2] The two terms, the death of God and the rebirth of God, were meant to underscore several ideas:

1. Religion is too individualistic and needs to be reframed within the scope of the cosmos; religion is a cosmic phenomenon not an individual one.
2. Christianity, with its emphasis on transcendence and other-worldliness, has become irrelevant.
3. The rebirth of God requires a rebirth of religion as the whole, since all religions have a role in the future of humankind.
4. The new physics invites a new emphasis on the birth of God in matter.

Teilhard thought we go to God in and through matter. The more conscious we become of God in our own embodied lives, the more conscious we become of God in every aspect of life. "Matter puts us in touch with the energies of earth, where we find ourselves looking to the 'Unknown God' who is to come."[3] Teilhard's ideas were consonant with those of Bohm, Jung, and other mystics informed by science. By awakening to matter's infinitely entangled divine life, we help complete God by realizing the potential of our own creaturely existence.[4] We cannot understand divine completion, however, using Greek philosophy or metaphysics. Quantum physics and evolution turn ontological transcendence into nostalgia. The only way to conceive of God in a new way is to begin with our cosmic reality of relational wholeness. Hence, we

---

2. Teilhard de Chardin, *Activation of Energy,* 281.

3. Thomas M. King, *Teilhard's Mysticism of Knowing* (New York: Seabury Press, 1981), 94.

4. Pierre Teilhard de Chardin, *The Heart of Matter,* trans. René Hague (New York: Harcourt Brace Jovanovich, 1979), 53.

need a new theology of the whole, or theohology, and we need to understand why theohology rejects the notion of the supernatural.

The word "supernatural" is not found in scripture but is a theological term of later origin. The concept of the supernatural appears for the first time in the Latin translations of the fifth-century mystic the Pseudo-Dionysius, and later in the writings of Hilduin and John Scotus Erigena in the ninth century. Peter Lombard does not use the term. Only with Thomas Aquinas does its usage become general. The term "supernatural" appeared for the first time in decrees of the Council of Trent and the propositions of the Bull of Pius V.

The term arises out of Greek philosophy, particularly Aristotle's ideas on substance and form. Aristotle relocated the Platonic forms as essences of things in nature. Plato held that the ideal forms exist in a realm outside the world. Aristotle opposed this while seeking to preserve pure forms. For him, the prime category of the real was essence, and the unreal was the phenomenal, the accidental. Essence was called "substance" insofar as it was the basis for accidents. The medieval adoption of Aristotle's philosophy was based on the categories of substance and accidents. Substance pertained to essence and nature, while accidents pertained to things related to nature. Substance was to center as accident was to periphery.

In 1879, Pope Leo XIII made the theology of Thomas Aquinas the official theology of the Catholic Church.[5] Thomas drew heavily upon the Muslim philosopher Avicenna, who carefully distinguished between the ways in which metaphysicians and natural philosophers discuss agent (or efficient) cause.[6] Avicenna wrote: "The metaphysicians do not intend by the agent the principle of movement only, as do the natural philosophers, but also the principle of existence and that which bestows existence, such as the creator of the world."[7] Avicenna distinguished between two kinds

---

5. See Pope Leo XIII, *Aeterni Patris* (August 4, 1879).

6. Jitse M. van der Meer and Scott Mandelbrote, eds., *Nature and Scripture in the Abrahamic Religions: 1700–Present*, vol. 1 (Leiden: Brill Publishers, 2008), 236.

7. Cited in van de Meer and Mandelbrote, *Nature and Scripture in the Abrahamic Religions*, 236.

of agent causes: one that acts through motion, and one that is "a giver of being."[8] It is the latter type of agency that undergirds the oneness of God, independent of any other existence. Such an agent needs only the power to create and nothing else. All beings other than God, he said, require a cause in order to exist. God is both essence and existence, while creatures exist by the power of God.

Joseph Kenny states that Thomas's most important borrowing from the Arab philosophers is the explicit recognition of a real distinction between essence and existence outside of God, so that everything depends on an exterior cause for the continuation of its existence.[9] Thomas's notion of God finds its philosophical roots in Aristotle's notion of being. Being (*esse*) is the act of existing; "to be" means *that* a thing is. It is distinguished from essence, which explains *what* a thing is. God is being itself (*ipsum esse subsistens*) and, thus, the immediate source of existence in all things.[10] God, therefore, is absolute Being who freely gives Being to being and as such is Creator, cause, and goal of all that exists. The act of creation, therefore, is God himself: "Creation signified actively means the divine action, which is God's essence."[11] Creation is not something in between God and creatures by which God brings creatures into existence, nor is creation the passive of something already somehow "there" to receive the new actuality. The creation of creatures, instead, implies "a certain relation to the Creator as to the principle of its being," an indispensable relationship since, without it, the creature would cease to exist.[12] God is immediately and most intimately present to the creature as the

---

8. Cited in van de Meer and Mandelbrote, *Nature and Scripture in the Abrahamic Religions*, 236.

9. See Joseph Kenny, O.P., "Thomas Aquinas, Islam, and the Arab Philosophers," http://www.catholicapologetics.info/apologetics/islam/thomas.htm.

10. Aquinas's works are cited from Thomas Aquinas, *Opera omnia ut sunt in Indice Thomistico cum hyper- textibus in CD-ROM [ITOO]*, cur. Robert Busa, SJ, (Trend, 1996). For a complete list of references to *The Book of Causes* in Aquinas's other works, see C. Vansteenkiste, OP, "Il *Liber de Causis* negli scritti di San Tommaso," *Angelicum*, 35 (1958): 325–74. The list is reprinted in *Commentary*, 169–78.

11. Thomas Aquinas, *Summa Theologica*, I, 45, 3, co.

12. Aquinas, *Summa Theologica*, I, 45, 3, co.

source of its being.[13] Any relationship somehow "added on" to God's existence would only diminish God's immanence in the creature, since it would make God a being of the same order as the created thing and so unable to be the source of its being and most intimately present to it. God is simply the beginning and end of all things.

Medieval theology placed theological or revealed truths at the core and called them the substance of faith to show their central, eternal, and unchanging character. Within this worldview and from its philosophical categories, the notion of the supernatural was understood and formulated. The supernatural pertained to that which was not constitutive of nature but over and above it. Hence, Thomas's statement, "grace builds on nature," means that grace is a supernatural divine gift that perfects nature. For Thomas, God is the supernatural Truth, the supernatural cause, the supernatural principle, because God's essence is existence itself. The divine call to union becomes a supernatural perfection of human nature. In other words, union with God is above nature and beyond the powers of nature to attain and thus is only possible with God's grace.

In the classic dispute regarding nature and grace, the question was whether or not the natural desire for the Beatific vision is innate. Thomas wavered and said sometimes the desire for the Beatific vision was innate and at other times there was no natural desire for it. Eventually, however, Thomas claimed that the human desire to see God is not innate. It is divinely elicited, conditional, and of itself inefficacious. While we have a desire to see God as the author of nature, that desire is simply a disposition toward this vision; we do not have the power to attain it without supernatural grace. Twentieth-century theologians, such as Maurice Blondel and Karl Rahner, began to question this theology because the supernatural seemed to be something accidental and extrinsic to nature, an add-on to the natural order rather than an intrinsic part of nature. Elevation to the divine nature seemed like a divine afterthought rather than an innate desire. This extrinsic notion of grace which found its way into modern theology in some ways aided the rise of scientism and naturalistic humanism. It seemed

---

13. Aquinas, *Summa Theologica*, I, 45, 3, co.

to justify the autonomy and self-sufficiency of nature by stating that there are two orders extrinsic to one another, nature and grace, and that the natural order is the primary order that can be perfected by a divine gift outside the natural realm. In this paradigm, nature is created by God to serve as a substratum for and organ of the supernatural life.

THE QUESTION OF GOD AND WORLD

The various interpretations of Thomism following the High Middle Ages complicated the God-world relationship by forging it into a structure of asymmetrical relationships. Franciscan theology differed from that of Thomas Aquinas by placing an emphasis on divine love and relationality; however, the Catholic Church turned its back on the Franciscan theologians following the rise of nominalism and modern science. By officially mandating the theology of Aquinas as the official theology of the Church in 1879, the Church closed itself off from supporting a living God-world relationship in a world of change. In the Middle Ages, "cosmology was a part of theology as long as the cosmos was believed to be God's creation."[14] However, cosmology has shifted over time, from the Ptolemaic cosmos to the Copernican cosmos to the Big Bang cosmos, so that the hierarchically structured Aristotelian-Thomistic synthesis, which held sway in the medieval to modern periods, has become theologically stifling. Raimon Panikkar wrote: "[T]heology, like philosophy, rests on a particular worldview that is our ultimate myth."[15] He continues:

> God is always God for a World, and if the conception of the World has changed so radically in our times, there is little wonder that the ancient notions of God do not appear convincing. To believe that one might retain a traditional idea of God while changing the underlying cosmology implies giving up the traditional notion of God and substitut-

---

14. Raimon Panikkar, *The Rhythm of Being: The Gifford Lectures* (Maryknoll, NY: Orbis Books, 2010), 186.

15. Panikkar, *The Rhythm of Being*, 207.

ing an abstraction for it, a *Deus otiosus*. One cannot go on simply repeating "God creator of the world," if the word "world" has changed its meaning since that phrase was first uttered—and the word "creator," as well.[16]

With the rise of modern science, notions such as final and formal causes have gradually dropped out of consideration, since they cannot be represented mathematically.[17] Mario Bunge writes:

> When science was born, formal and final causes were left aside as standing beyond the reach of experiment; and material causes were taken for granted in connection with all natural happenings.... Hence, of the four Aristotelian causes only the efficient cause was regarded as worthy of scientific research.[18]

The rise of modern science, with its corresponding shift in cosmology, did not usher in a new understanding of God or the God-world relationship; however, God became less a prime mover than a prime mechanic. Christian theology remained bound to the Ptolemaic cosmos and the Thomistic-Aristotelian synthesis, which ultimately gave rise to two distinct worldviews and, in a sense, two metaphysical orders: science and religion. The response of the Marquis de la Place to the emperor Napoleon when asked about the role of God in his system was symptomatic of the age: "Sir, I no longer have need for such a hypothesis."[19] The separation of empirical science from divine causality or divine relationality yielded a "decosmologization" of nature, a reduction of cosmos to world.[20]

16. Panikkar, *The Rhythm of Being*, 207.

17. See William A. Wallace, OP, *Causality and Scientific Explanation,Volume 2: Classical and Contemporary Science* (Ann Arbor: University of Michigan Press, 1972), 246.

18. Mario Bunge, *Causality and Modern Science* (New York: Dover, 1979), 32.

19. Pierre Simon Marquis de Laplace, *A Philosophical Essay on Probabilities*, trans. F. W. Truscott and F. K. Emory (New York: Dover, 1961), 4.

20. Rémi Brague, *The Wisdom of the World: The Human Experience of the Universe in Western Thought*, trans. Teresa Lavendar Fagan (Chicago: University of Chicago Press, 2003), 98. By using the term "cosmologization," Brague

If causality, including divine causality or God intervening in nature, was now thought of only as physical force, then divine causality had to be explained in those terms. Einstein sensed this when he argued that there was simply no "room" in the universe for divine causality: "The more man is imbued with the ordered regularity of all events the firmer becomes his conviction that there is no room left by the side of this ordered regularity for causes of a different nature. For him neither the rule of human nor the rule of divine will exists as an independent cause of natural events."[21]

The artificial separation between science and religion lies at the heart of our contemporary theological confusion. Yet, underlying this separation is a philosophical intransigency, a refusal to relinquish a Neoplatonic conceptual ordering of creation as a logical understanding of existence in relation to God. Can we speak of a distinct conceptual order of creation at all, if science now contends that nature is dynamically energized and entangled; more so, that mind itself emerges from nature?[22] Without the mind, nature is a passionless idea to be accepted or rejected. Panikkar laments that the rise of the philosophical concept dispels the content of love as transformative knowledge:

> The destiny of western theology has been greatly influenced by a genial philosophical discovery: the concept, which is due mainly to the no less genial figure of Socrates. ... Since concepts have proved themselves to be so rich and useful, the *Sophia* intended by philosophy and theology has

---

suggests that, for the Greeks, the celestial bodies influenced the earth and their circular movement governed the linear temporality of human history. Christian polemics against astrology, he claims, reversed this relationship and spoke of a historization of cosmology. The same could be said for the rise of modern science and the alienation of religion from science.

21. Albert Einstein, *Out of My Later Years* (New York: Wisdom Library, 1950), 32.

22. On the emergence of mind, see David Chalmers, *The Conscious Mind: In Search of a Fundamental Theory* (New York: Oxford University Press, 1996); James Jeans, *The Mysterious Universe* (New York: Macmillan, 1931); Lothar Schäfer, "Quantum Reality, the Emergence of Complex Order from Virtual States, and the Importance of Consciousness in the Universe," *Zygon* 41 no. 3 (2006): 505–32.

been overshadowed by the *epistēmē* of concepts, specifically, of general concepts. Theology then slowly becomes a conceptual system, and once the concept has emancipated itself from all its emotional constituents, theology can dispense with love as a constitutive ingredient. The concept does not need love to be a clear and distinct concept. Love becomes relegated to piety or devotion and no longer to theology, which increasingly grows into a conceptual science.[23]

The distinction between a conceptual order and one of real relationship undergirds the difference between classical theology and the new relational holism of theohology. In exploring this new relational holism, Alfred North Whitehead realized that God cannot be the great exception to creation; rather, God must be its chief exemplar.[24] Whitehead and the school of process philosophy sought to understand a new metaphysics of the whole. Process reality is a philosophical paradigm that tries to see reality as an open system in which every entity is interrelated and connected through a dynamic process whereby events influence each other. Even the smallest beings (such as atoms) are organic, which means they "grow, mature, and perish."[25] The essence of reality, however, is *not* being but becoming. Reality is a dynamic process of "ongoing transformation."[26] Taking his cue from quantum physics, Whitehead developed a God-world relationship of mutuality and reciprocity: God affects the world, and the world affects God. He coined a term for this process of becoming: "philosophy of organism,"[27] and he situated both God and creaturely life within the model of organic wholeness. If God is the highest reality, then God must be the ultimate form of

---

23. Panikkar, *Rhythm of Being*, 195.

24. Alfred North Whitehead, *Process and Reality*, ed. David Ray Griffin and Donald W. Sherburne (New York: The Free Press, 1979), 343.

25. Alfred North Whitehead, *A Key to Whitehead's Process and Reality*, ed. Donald W. Sherburne (Chicago: University of Chicago Press, 1981), 6.

26. Bruce Gordon Epperly, *Process Theology: A Guide for the Perplexed* (London: T & T Clark International, 2011), 11.

27. Whitehead, *Process and Reality*, 18.

the dynamic process of transformation. God and world are inter-connected and interdependent.

Process thinkers affirm that God is really related to us and that we are really related to God. The philosopher Charles Hartshorne argued persuasively that God's actuality is real, if not more real, than God's essential nature: "[I]t is the actuality of accidents not existence of substance that is prior."[28] While Hartshorne's position seems to contradict divine immutability, it actually enhances the God-ness of God. An analogy can be made to the human person who grows and changes without losing anything of one's distinct personhood. On the contrary, it is growth and change, integrated with a mature consciousness, that comes to define a person in a distinct way. So too with God. God is neither statically perfect nor immutable; neither omniscient nor omnipotent because none of these attributes really define God. God is simply the absolute and ultimate whole who is becoming more whole in and through the entangled emergence of evolving life. Hartshorne wrote: "God is the wholeness of the world, correlative to the wholeness of every sound individual dealing with the world."[29] An individual (other than God) is only a fragment or fractal of reality, not the whole. Cosmic wholeness, not infinity, is the essential concept of divinity. God is the whole of the whole of spacetime, and the whole itself is a dynamic and infinite relatedness. God is integral to the world's becoming.

Whitehead believed that God is the very source of the world's freedom: "Apart from God, there could be no relevant novelty."[30] God shares in the relational (creative) process as the one who lures the entire evolutionary enterprise to possibilities that enable the achievement of rich and complex values—values that ultimately reflect and enhance its very source. Divine love is the energetic lure; it is both alluring and affected by that which is lured. Authentic love preserves the freedom and integrity of the other by offering possibilities to the other without forcing the choice to

---

28. Charles Hartshorne, *Reality as Social Process: Studies in Metaphysics and Religion* (Boston: Beacon Press, 1953), 72.

29. Charles Hartshorne, *A Natural Theology for Our Time* (La Salle, IL: Open Court, 1967), 6.

30. Whitehead, *Process and Reality*, 164.

act. Love is always persuasive and never coercive: God's power is God's love.[31]

As the ground of freedom and novelty, God's power enables, sustains, and nurtures possibilities, but God's lure depends on creaturely freedom to respond. From God's side, the divine lure is to ever-increasing freedom, novelty, and relationship; to make available opportunities to envision a world beyond the world presently actualized.[32] Creation is not a solitary act but a social act between God and world. The incarnation is entangled divinity and humanity co-creating and co-actualizing potential new life in every creature open to the fullness of life. The main principles of Whiteheadian metaphysics are woven into the new narrative of the relational whole—the theohological narrative—described by Jung and Teilhard de Chardin.

COMPLEXITY AND CONSCIOUSNESS

Patristic and medieval theology are beautiful reminders of God's glorious history, but history cannot hold a candle to understanding the newness of matter open to a future that beckons us onward. We are living in a world never imagined by ancient scholars. We need to find a new way of thinking about God and humanity in evolution. To begin to do so, I will borrow a term from the sciences, "complexity," and suggest that complexity is a helpful concept in understanding the new God-world entangled whole in evolution. Complexity refers to the fact that most biological, cognitive, and social systems typically exhibit behavior that is nonlinear and involve multiple interacting elements or

---

31. John Cobb explains the distinction between coercive power and persuasive power. He describes coercive power as the measure to limit freedom by reducing one's possibilities. He describes persuasive power, in contrast, as the measure to enable the flourishing of freedom by presenting a wide range of possibilities for the greatest degree of novelty and union. Furthermore, many process theists will argue that God's radical relationality, by its very definition, necessitates a respect for the freedom of the other. For more detail, see John Cobb, Jr., *God and the World* (Eugene, OR: Wipf and Stock Publishers, 1998), 83.

32. Lewis S. Ford, *Two Process Philosophers: Hartshorne's Encounter with Whitehead* (Tallahassee, FL: American Academy of Religion, 1973), 87.

components. God and world form a system, and the most distinguishing feature of the system is the appearance of new being. In the new theohological narrative, complexity means that each term must be considered in relation to the other.

While the phrase "complex dynamical system" lacks a concise definition, many researchers agree that complex dynamical systems exhibit three key characteristics. First, they consist of multiple interacting components or agents. Second, these systems exhibit emergence: their collective behavior can be difficult to anticipate from knowledge of the individual components that make up the system, although they exhibit some coherent pattern and, in some cases, apparent purposiveness. Third, complexified emergent behavior is self-organized and does not result from either a central or an external controlling component process or agent. Rather, it is precisely the interaction of entities that undergirds emergent new life. Whereas classical theology, following the Neoplatonic scheme, posited the One giving rise to the many, the new theohology of evolution posits the One arising from the many. God is no longer the essence of simplicity. God is complexifying oneness in evolution.

Thomas Aquinas would agree that God and creation cannot be separated. The question is, how are they related? Thomas distinguished essence from existence, divine Being from created being; however, quantum physics overturns this. Without mind there is no matter, and without matter, which is the condition for divine emergence, there is no God. Jung said that the ground of experience from which all deities are born requires a sense of radical immanence. God approaches consciousness from no other source than "one's own being." In this way, God and humanity are functions of each other.[33] Failure to acknowledge this radical interiority is a failure of religion itself. To recover a sense of the holy requires birthing a new myth of the co-redemption of the divine and human in one single, prolonged process of personal and cosmic evolution. Both Teilhard and Jung agree on the principle of theogenesis or "God-birthing." The so-called "supernatural

---

33. John Dourley, "Jung's Equation of the Ground of Being with the Ground of the Psyche," *Journal of Analytical Psychology* 56 (2011): 521.

transcendent" begins on the level of the collective unconsciousness, the infinite psyche of the human person. Teilhard wrote:
"We must say of every man that he contains in himself, besides a
body and a soul, a certain physical entity that relates him in his
entirety to the universe (the final universe) in which he reaches
his fulfillment."[34] In this respect, Teilhard saw that "each human
ego is co-extensive with the entire universe."[35] We are cosmic,
earthly beings to the core. He wrote: "Bathe yourself in the ocean
of matter; plunge into it where it is deepest and most violent;
struggle in its currents and drink of its waters. For it cradled you
long ago in your preconscious existence; and it is that ocean that
will raise you up to God."[36]

Teilhard reframed the God-world relationship as a complementary pair of mutually affirming opposites. The key to this relationship is creative union. He did not hold to a separate doctrine
of creation but saw creative union as the integral core of creation,
which includes the mysteries of incarnation and redemption. The
creative process involves a unification of multiplicity and a struggle against the forces of dispersion. Creation, incarnation, and redemption are coextensive with the total space-time continuum. In
one of his journals he wrote:

> Christianity, influenced by the conquests of modern thought,
> will finally become aware of the fact that the three funda-
> mental personalistic mysteries upon which it rests are in
> reality simply three aspects of one and the same process
> (christogenesis), depending on whether one looks at it
> from the point of view of its principal moving power (cre-
> ation), or its unifying mechanism (incarnation), or its ele-
> vating effort (redemption).[37]

---

34. Ursula King, *Pierre Teilhard de Chardin* (Maryknoll, NY: Orbis Books,
1999), 87.

35. Teilhard de Chardin, *Activation of Energy*, 218.

36. King, *Teilhard de Chardin*, 42.

37. Donald Gray, *The One and the Many: Teilhard de Chardin's Vision of
Unity* (London: Burns and Oates, 1969), 67.

The God-world relationship can be likened to a complex dynamical system in that God and world cannot be considered sepa-
rately but must considered in relation to each other. If creativity is
the ultimate principle for divine and creaturely life, then dynamic
being and relationality are one and the same. To be is to be related.
Novelty is intrinsic to God's identity or, as Gordon Kaufman
points out, God *is* creativity.[38] Since love is the most intense relationship that unifies and forms absolute wholeness, love is the
most characteristic of being itself. Being is the dynamism of love,
and love is always the movement from potentiality to actuality, a
movement of creativity. We might consider this creative movement of love as the ever-dynamic movement of divinity itself, the
unoriginated source (Father), expression (Son), and breath (Spirit)
of love's infinite potential life. Divine being moves itself from potency to actuality in virtue of its own intrinsic dynamism. God is
always active as the subject of the ongoing act of existence, or the
ongoing subject of relationality, because God is the name of persons or personal relationships in a dynamism of love and so is
continuously coming into being as God.[39] As Meister Eckhart
wrote: "God is the newest thing there is, the youngest thing there
is. God is the beginning, and if we are united to God, we become
new again. It is in the coming to be that God is."[40] God is the
newest thing there is, and all who seek God live in the newness of
life. Love is what God is; and God is always seeking to be more in
love. The world is restlessly yearning for the fullness of life because the heart of yearning is the heart of love. Evolution is an
ever-newness of life born out of the ever-newness of divine love.[41]

Teilhard's insights impel us to reconsider the doctrine of creation. Creation is not the appearance of something out of nothing;
rather, it is an act of immanent unification by which the world is

---

38. See Gordon Kaufman, *In the Beginning ... Creativity* (Minneapolis,
MN: Fortress Press, 2004).

39. Bracken, *Divine Matrix*, 30.

40. Matthew Fox, *Meditations with Meister Eckhart* (Santa Fe, NM: Bear
and Company, 1983), 32.

41. Pierre Teilhard de Chardin, *Christianity and Evolution: Reflections on
Science and Religion*, trans. René Hague (New York: Harcourt Brace Jovanovich), 171–72.

in the process of being created. Teilhard states that God and world can be thought of as the complementary union of the uncreated and created, infinite and finite, distinct, yet each having a need both to exist in themselves and to be combined with each other. In this way, the absolute maximum of possible union is effected *in natura rerum* (in the things of nature).[42] Elsewhere, he states: "We are inevitably making our way to a completely new concept of being: in this the hitherto contradictory attributes of the world and God would be combined in a general synthetic function: 'God completely other than the world and yet unable to dispense with it.'"[43] God does not create in time, as if God is a supernatural being outside time reaching in; rather, time, as a function of matter organizing spatially, is the emergence of God.

Time is the appearance of new forms of matter or the movement of matter to higher forms of complexity and new levels of consciousness. What happens in time is what happens with God. John Haught writes: "It is because God *is not-yet* that there is room for time and the coming of a new future."[44] He continues: "It is because God *is not-yet* that there is room for hope. It is because God *is not-yet* that the passage of time is not a threat but the carrying out of a promise."[45] The not-yet God is the God of the future, the God who is coming to be. The drama of cosmic awakening, therefore, contributes to the very identity of God.[46] God and world cannot be separated because matter, and the potential of matter to become something more, undergird existence, and the heart of existence is the infinite wellspring of love, which is the energy of life itself. Hence, transcendence does not belong to

---

42. Teilhard de Chardin, *Christianity and Evolution*, 227.

43. Pierre Teilhard de Chardin, *Science and Christ*, trans. René Hague (New York: Harper and Row, 1969), 182. Teilhard writes: "What I have in mind here is a synthetic re-definition of being, which, taken in its most general form, would include, *both simultaneously*, an absolute term and a participated term. What makes the God-world antinomy insoluble is that we first split up a natural pair and then persist in considering the two terms *in succession*" (note 3).

44. John Haught, *God after Einstein* (New Haven: Yale University Press, 2022), 14.

45. Haught, *God after Einstein*, 12.

46. Haught, *God after Einstein*, 200.

God alone but to the *God-world unity* in its infinite potential to become something more *together*.

If the universe is unfinished, then God is unfinished as well. God is not yet completely realized in this unfolding spacetime universe, which means the "Garden of Eden" (Gen 2:8) is not behind us but before us. The Garden of Eden symbolizes the hope of the world's becoming. Teilhard's ideas are developmental. Every state of the world is the necessary result of the previous state of biological existence. Development is more than a combinatorial unfolding of the world, traceable back to the past chain of causes and effects; rather, development involves emergence and complexity. Clayton defines emergence as "genuinely new properties which are not reducible to what came before, although they are continuous with it."[47] Emergence pertains not only to the properties of the new entity but to the entity itself as fundamentally new. God emerges in evolution as a New Being, the New Person, a union of divinity and materiality, signified by the Christ.

GOD IN EVOLUTION

Traditional theology postulates God as *the cause* of all things (cf. Gen 1:1); Teilhard descrobes God as *the goal* of all things. God is the whole that comes into clearer vision with each new stage of consciousness. Evolution brings God into focus. God is the *goal* toward which all things are moving. Traditional theology begins with the Godhead, while emergence points to the God-ahead. God's creative activity cannot be thought of simply as enabling things to exist. Rather, such activity must be seen as enabling things to evolve and to become what is new. God is creative, and so too are we. Consciousness is a creative act because the mind acts on potentials and brings them into actual existence. Each person who acts consciously co-creates the universe. God and world co-create the universe as a whole because they are becoming something more together in evolution. It is not just creatures who are becoming new in evolution;

---

47. Philip Clayton, *Mind and Emergence: From Quantum to Consciousness* (New York: Oxford, 2004), 39.

God also is becoming new.[48] Teilhard rejects creation *ex nihilo* (creation "out of nothing") as being out of touch with modern biology. It is too asymmetrical, he claimed, since it posits a one-way relationship between God and world. Rather, he posits a mutual and interactive relationship between God and world because God and world share a real, mutual relationship. This idea is in contrast to traditional theology in which God has a real relation to creatures, but creatures do not have a real relationship with God, only a rational relationship. A real relationship is mutual in that entities affect one another; that is, the relationship makes a difference to that which is related. A rational relationship is one in which the mind can know the other without being affected by the other. Both Jung and Teilhard opt for a real relationship between divinity and humanity.

The model of relational holism based on implicate order and divine entanglement means that God affects the world and the world affects God. God can change and grow because matter changes and grows. Only what is alive can change, and only what can change can grow. Thus, entangled relational holism or theohology rejects omnipotence and immutability. Teilhard was critical of speaking about divine power as an abstraction, something that affects but is unaffected by development processes. He spoke, instead, of a bilateral and complementary relationship between God and world and maintained that what gives life to Christianity is not so much the contingency of the world but the sense of the mutual completion of God and world. Whitehead put it this way: "It is as true to say that God creates the World, as that the World creates God."[49] If the universe is unfinished, it is because the entangled whole—including God—is not yet finished. The universe is evolving. Whitehead said: "[T]he creativity of the world is the throbbing emotion of the past hurling itself into a new transcendent fact."[50] Without the physical universe, it is not possible to conceive of God, and without God, the universe

---

48. See Donald Viney, *Charles Hartshorne and the Existence of God* (Albany: State University of New York Press, 1985).

49. Whitehead, *Process and Reality*, 348.

50. Alfred North Whitehead, *Adventures of Ideas* (New York: Macmillan, 1993), 177.

does not exist. God and world are a complementary pair and, together, they form a unified whole.[51] In Whitehead's words: "The world lives by its incarnation of God in itself."[52]

RELATIONAL HOLISM

In our everyday existence, it is difficult to see how we can be part of a reality that is an indivisible whole, without parts and divisions. We must become attentive to the experience of the whole in order to experience the whole. The German philosopher Immanuel Kant described the whole as an integrative relational structure in which there is a constant interplay of parts. The whole is constantly unified while the parts are reconfigured and change: whole and parts are codependent and coevolve. Bohm and others, like Karl Pribam, elaborate on wholeness, explaining wholeness as an integral relationship of mind and matter. Physicist and philosopher Carl Friedrich von Weizsäcker said that taking quantum mechanics seriously predicts a unique, single quantum reality underlying the multiverse. To become aware of and understand the whole is to acknowledge the presence of consciousness in the universe as an intrinsic aspect of all things in space and time. The consciousness that permeates nature is the same flow of activity that each of us inherits in a unique way. In and through our minds, we are part of an undivided whole that is our home, the cosmos.

Cosmic holism refers to nature's "seamless garment" of life in which mind, matter, and nature's ability to change are integrally related. Nature is an interlocking network of systems, an "unbearable wholeness of beings" as Steven Talbott writes. Nature is more flow than fixed. "The body," Talbott states, "is a *formed* stream."[53] Structures once stably formed do not necessarily stay

---

51. Teilhard de Chardin, *Christianity and Evolution*, 227.

52. Alfred North Whithead, *Religion in the Making* (New York: Macmillan, 1926), 149.

53. Steven L. Talbott, "The Unbearable Wholeness of Beings," (Fall, 2010), https://www.thenewatlantis.com/publications/the-unbearable-wholeness-of-beings.

that way. Many of the body's structures are more like standing waves than once-and-for-all constructed objects. Organisms show a meaningful coordination of activities whereby a functioning and self-sustaining unity engages in flexible responses to the myriad stimuli of the environment. Nature is a choreographed ballet, a symphony in which every organism is dynamically engaged in its own self-organization, pursuing its own ends amid an ever-shifting context of relationships. Self-organization is maintained by openness to the environment, spontaneity, and new patterns of order. We humans are part of a cosmic relational whole, nature's interlocking wholeness of intricate systems.

In his 1923 essay on "Pantheism and Christianity," Teilhard devoted his attention to the Whole. Building on the mind-matter relationship, wholeness was, for him, a matter of "seeing" and thus a matter of consciousness. He indicated that each personal consciousness is a "particular actualizing on the whole."[54] In seeking a new understanding of reality, he was amazed by the coincidence of consciousness and wholeness:

> The really amazing thing is that the countless points of view represented by our individual thoughts should have a point of coincidence; that, intellectually, we should all appreciate one and the same pattern in the universe; that we should understand one another. The reason for the existence of this mutual understanding, of this intellectual concurrence in our collective penetration of the real, can be found only in the existence of a principle which controls and unifies individual perceptions.... We must go further and admit that all consciousnesses, taken as one whole, are dominated, influenced and guided by a sort of higher consciousness; and that it is this which animates, governs and synthesizes all the different apprehensions of the universe effected by each monad in isolation. There is a center which is the center of all centers, and without which the entire edifice of thought would disintegrate into dust.... Thus, from the patient, prosaic, but cumulative work of

54. Teilhard de Chardin, *Christianity and Evolution*, 61.

scientists of all types, there has spontaneously emerged the most impressive revelation of the Whole that could possibly be conceived. . . . The vital question for Christianity today is to decide what attitude believers will adopt towards this recognition of the value of the Whole, this "preoccupation with the Whole." Will they open their hearts to it, or will they reject it as an evil spirit?[55]

We humans have the ability to know the "Whole" in such a way that we can reflect on it and act toward it. We act on behalf of the "Whole" when we have a consciousness of belonging to a whole. We stifle or crush the whole when we are unconscious of it or refuse to acknowledge our own reality of wholeness. Einstein had a profound insight into the inclusive nature of the whole:

A human being is a part of the whole called by us universe, a part limited in time and space. He experiences himself, his thoughts and feeling as something separated from the rest, a kind of optical delusion of his consciousness. This delusion is a kind of prison for us, restricting us to our personal desires and affection for a few persons nearest to us. Our task must be to free ourselves from this prison by widening our circle of compassion to embrace all living creatures and the whole of nature in its beauty.[56]

A conscious awareness of the whole is more evident today than in ages past due to the way computer technology has complexified consciousness. Bohm saw the implications of the implicate order and discussed the need to be aligned with the whole; he thought that any other position was an illusion of reality. We may seem separate, he said, but each person is part of the cosmic whole and shares in the same cosmic process. The rise of the "holonomic" person, or one who lives with a consciousness of the whole, is characteristic of younger generations who are invested

---

55. Teilhard de Chardin, *Christianity and Evolution*, 61, 63-64.

56. Albert Einstein, "Letter of 1950," *New York Times* (March 29, 1972).

in the community of planetary life, concerned about such issues as shared economic resources, global warming, racial and gender equality. The world is converging through a rise in consciousness into a new complexified whole, emerging through computer technology and the global brain.

Bohm pointed to the problem of the ruptured whole brought about by dualistic thinking and monotheistic religion: God and world, heaven and earth, body and spirit. To live with a sense of separate existences, as if God is a supernatural existence and heaven is an other-worldly place, is to split the earth into fragments. In 1967, the historian Lynn White published a controversial essay entitled "The Historic Roots of our Ecological Crisis," in which he claimed that Christianity is the primary source of the environmental problem. Christianity, with its emphasis on human salvation and dominion over nature, he said, "made it possible to exploit nature in a mood of indifference to the feelings of natural objects."[57] White listed several factors important to Christian belief that have contributed to our environmental problems: (1) an ambivalent attitude toward creation; (2) a stance of dominion that has led to exploitation; (3) an other-worldly focus; (4) a preoccupation with sin and guilt that has led to intense preoccupation with self; and (5) an emphasis on personal salvation. He insists that Christians are responsible for the ecological crisis because they have taken God's command to have dominion over creation as a command to dominate and subdue it (Gen 1:27–28). He argues that no religion has been more focused on humans than Christianity and none has been more rigid in excluding all but humans from divine grace and in denying any moral obligation to lower species.[58] White claims that we will continue to have an ecological crisis until we reject the Christian axiom that nature has no reason for existence except to serve us.[59] Since "the roots of our environmental problems are religious," he wrote, "then the remedy must

57. Lynn White, "The Historical Roots of Our Ecological Crisis," *Science* 155 (March 10, 1967): 1205.

58. White, "Historical Roots of Our Ecological Crisis," 1205.

59. White, "Historical Roots of Our Ecological Crisis," 1207.

be religious as well. We must rethink and re-feel our nature and our destiny."[60]

To rethink and re-feel our nature is the invitation awaiting the response of the new person and the new religious mind. The whole is our deepest reality. The more we can connect to the root of this reality, the more we will live in wholeness and unity. This is an inner and outer reality that requires our complete attention and commitment. We have become so conditioned by partials and fragments that wholeness seems unnatural. We fear deep relationships because we fear losing our individuality. But that fear is baseless. The one who lives deeply in awareness of the whole lives freely by the life of the whole. The wholeness one experiences within is the same wholeness that holds the universe together. The Whole of every whole is the ineffable love of God. To live freely in the whole is to live as a holonomic person, a person conscious of the whole. One does not lose oneself at the highest level of conscious wholeness; rather, one who lives by the life of the whole lives in the fullness of personhood. To be part of the whole is to be uniquely person, for it is the distinct personality of each person radiating divine light in a particular way that makes wholeness possible. A thousand million lights shining around the globe—with the divine light of love—can turn the darkness of the earth into the brilliance of heaven.

---

60. White, "Historical Roots of Our Ecological Crisis," 1205.

5

God, Ground, and Mystics

In his book *Eclipse of God*, the renowned Jewish scholar Martin Buber argued that Jung's psychology of religion is a religion of pure psychic immanence that reduces God to a mere psychic experience. Buber's complaint rests on the notion that Jung makes religion a function of the psyche. "If religion is a relation to psychic events, which cannot mean anything other than to events of one's own soul, then it is implied by this that it is not a relation to a Being or Reality which, no matter how fully it may from time to time descend to the human soul, always remains transcendent to it."[1] In Buber's view, Jung shows a professed agnosticism. In his attempt to relate to God in the depths of the human soul, he eliminates the possibility that God exists independently as well as in relation to the human subject.[2] Jung himself rejected the simplistic reduction of religion to psychology, while adopting the position

---

1. Martin Buber, *Eclipse of God: Studies in the Relation Between Religion and Philosophy* (Princeton: Princeton University Press, 1952), 67.

2. Buber, *Eclipse of God*, 81.

described by Jungian analyst Michael Fordham, namely, that the study of humanity must "reveal the nature of God as far as it can be understood by human beings."[3]

Clifford A. Brown sought to defend Jung from the kind of criticism being expressed by Buber and other theological critics of Jung's thought. They needed, he said, to take a closer look at Jung's psychological method before accusing him of reductionism. Brown suggests that Jung transposes doctrine from its exclusively theological and metaphysical context to a psychological context, opening up the religious mind to the psychic roots of language and life. This methodological strategy makes Christian doctrine relevant to the modern person's self-understanding and experience and reveals the symbolic dimensions of religious life. In Brown's view, Jung does not *reduce* the religious realm (and therefore God) to the psychological, but rather *translates* it into psychological terms. By translating religious doctrine and the concept of God into psychological terms, there is an opening and a need to retranslate the doctrine of God into new theological terms.

Paul Tillich, a prominent theologian of the twentieth century, saw the importance of depth psychology for the task of contemporary theology. According to Tillich, depth psychology provides new insight into the nature of the self and stands as an ally with theology in the fight against the dehumanizing effects of modern society. Depth psychology offers a heightened sense of sin as the universal estrangement of human beings from their essential nature. Tillich "did not think it is possible today to elaborate a Christian doctrine of the human without using the immense material brought forth by depth psychology."[4] Thus, he sought to correlate psychological accounts (as well as other nontheological, "existential" accounts) of the human condition with the Christian message. This is the essence of his theological

---

3. Michael Fordham, *Explorations into the Self* (London: Routledge, 1985), 184.

4. Charles W. Kegley and Robert W. Bretall, eds., *The Theology of Paul Tillich* (New York: The Macmillian Company, 1964), 19.

method of correlation in his *Systematic Theology*. Through this method, the theologian makes an analysis of the human situation out of which the existential questions arise and demonstrates that the symbols used in the Christian message are answers to these questions.

Like Jung, Tillich adopted a position that was at odds with the dominant trends within his discipline. His theology attempted to mediate between the demands of contemporary culture and the eternal message of Christianity, although not without conflict. He pursued his theological goal during what has been called "the Barthian captivity of modern Christian thought," in which Karl Barth claimed that "any attempt to reconcile the Christian revelation with philosophy or science was fundamentally erroneous and doomed to failure."[5] Barth's view dominated theological reflection in the twentieth century.

GOD AS GROUND

Jung, Teilhard, and Tillich all experienced the divine immanence as a universal power underlying all that is. This immanence of divine power is the basis of humanity's experience of the divine as transcendent. The notion of the ground is found in Jung's writings, although it is not widely used in his corpus. At one point, he refers to the Buddha and the Buddhist's repose on "the eternal ground of his inner nature, whose oneness with Deity, or universal being, is confirmed in other Indian testimonies."[6] He was intrigued by the Eastern fascination with the ground and its recovery. Essentially, the ground refers to the "deep root of all being, the many images of wholeness common to all religions . . . the universal

---

5. F. X. Charet, "A Dialogue Between Psychology and Theology: The Correspondence of C. G. Jung and Victor White," *Journal of Analytical Psychology* 35, no. 4 (October 1990): 437.

6. Carl Jung, "The Psychology of Eastern Meditation," *Collected Works* 11 (Princeton: Princeton University Press, 1943), para. 949; cited in John Dourley, "Jung's Equation of the Ground of Being with the Ground of the Psyche," *Journal of Analytical Psychology* 56 (2011): 515.

Ground, the deity itself."[7] Here, Jung unequivocally identifies the reality of the ground with the reality of God. Experience of the
ground is the experience of God. What is called "mystical union
with God" can be translated as the ground of the individual ego in
union with the ground of all that is and thus with the divine. It is
the highest level of consciousness of the individual before the One
who dwells within, that is, the One whose form has no knowable
boundaries, who encompasses the whole person on all sides, fath-
omless as the infinite potential of light and as vast as the heavens
themselves. The person who dwells in the ground of the One lives
from this center and dwells in all surroundings, within and without, the heavens above and in the depths of the earth below.

Mystical theology is a theology of the ground. Saint Augustine
was the first depth psychologist in the West who spoke of God as
the Ground of being: "Yet all the time you were *more inward than
my inmost self.*"[8] Francis of Assisi described his experience of God
in a simple phrase: "My God and my All" (*Deus meus et omnia*).[9]
Even more striking is the saying of Catherine of Genoa: "*My Me is
God*, nor do I recognize any other Me except my God Himself."[10]
The ninth-century Sufi mystic Mansur Al-Hallaj described mysticism in terms that prefigured the essence of Jung's insights:

> I saw my Lord with the eye of my heart
> I said: "Who are you?" He said: "You!"
> But for You, "where" cannot have a place
> And there is no "where" when it concerns You.
> The mind has no image of your existence in time
> Which would permit the mind to know where you are.

---

7. Carl Jung, "Introduction to the Religious and Psychological Problems
of Alchemy," *Collected Works* 12 (Princeton: Princeton University Press, 1944),
para. 8; cited in Dourley, "Jung's Equation of the Ground of Being with the
Ground of the Psyche," 515.

8. Saint Augustine, *Confessions*, trans. Henry Chadwick (Oxford: Oxford
University Press, 1991), Book 3, para. 11.

9. See Elizabeth Goudge, *My God and My All: The Life of Saint Francis of
Assisi* (New York: Plough Publishing House, 1959).

10. Dennis Hart, *Visions: The Remembering* (New York: Writer's Showcase,
2001), 163.

You are the one who encompasses every "where"
Up to the point of no-where
So where are you?[11]

Augustine had a similar question: Where are You, O God? He goes on to say, "I was looking without but You were within."[12] The universality of the mystical quest across religious traditions undergirds the depth of the psyche in its search for wholeness and meaning. Both Jung and Tillich were influenced by the German medieval mystic, Meister Eckhart, whose use of the term "ground" functioned as a power word. Eckhart wrote that no one was ever lost, except by leaving one's ground and settling abroad. Bernard McGinn states that the ground gave to Eckhart's mysticism its unique novelty and force and differentiated it from previous forms of Western mysticism.[13]

Etymologically, the meaning of ground ranges from simply the earth on which we stand to that which is most individual, one's essence. The term "essence," used philosophically and religiously in association with "ground," refers to that point where the divine and human coincide in human nature and eternity.[14] In quantum physics, however, distinguishing essence and existence does not make much sense.

Eckhart's notion of the ground prefigured the mysticism of relational holism. In his writings, he describes a "breakthrough," *Durchbruch,* in which he experienced an absolute identity of himself with the divine in the Godhead. "The eye with which I see God is the same eye with which God sees me; my eye and God's eye are one eye, one seeing, one knowing and one love."[15] The

---

11. William Stoddart, *Sufism: The Mystical Doctrines and Methods of Islam* (St. Paul, MN: Paragon House, 1976), 83.

12. Augustine, *Confessions*, Book 10, para. 38.

13. Bernard McGinn, *The Harvest of Mysticism in Medieval Germany* (New York: Crossroad Publishing Company, 2005), 86–90.

14. Dourley, "Jung's Equation of the Ground of Being with the Ground of the Psyche," 516.

15. Meister Eckhart, *Qui Audit Me*, Sermon on Sirach 24:30, *The Complete Mystical Works of Meister Eckhart*, trans. and ed., Maurice O'C. Walshe (New York: Crossroad, 2009), 298.

experience he describes is one of unitive consciousness, whereby both self and God are dissolved in an abyss wholly stripped of all form and activity, yet one from which all form and activity flow. He writes: "Here God's ground is my ground, and my ground is God's ground."[16] In his famous sermon on poverty, Eckhart boldly described a God-ness of the self that was close to what Jung intuited: "For in this breakthrough it is bestowed upon me that I and God are one."[17] Dourley notes that, in reading Eckhart, Jung identifies Eckhart's breakthrough as a moment when ego and unconscious, the human and divine, attain an identity beyond distinction. Jung writes: "God disappears as an object and dwindles into a subject which is no longer distinguishable from the ego."[18] Such total regression constitutes for Jung the experience of an identity with the reality of God. He explains: "As a result of this retrograde process, the original state of identity with God is re-established."[19] Return from this moment of identity then becomes the moment of intensified creativity and renewal of life for the ego. In Beatrice Bruteau's words: "The 'I' is God's creative activity, God's creative action."[20] Eckhart's spirituality is what Jung called, "individuation," the full flowering of the human person which is made possible by the actualization of divinity or incarnation through the reconciliation of opposites. The cycle of the ego's birth from the divine, a recovered identity with the divine, and a return from this moment, becomes the cycle of individuation itself. Jung sees the religious dimension of human personality as essential to self-actualization and human fulfillment. To para-

---

16. Meister Eckhart, "In This Was Manifested the Love of God" (Sermon XIII), *Meister Eckhart*, ed. F. Pfeiffer, trans. C. de B. Evans, Volume I (London: John M. Watkins, 1857), 49.

17. Meister Eckhart, "Blessed Are the Poor," *Meister Eckhart, Mystic and Philosopher*, trans. Reiner Schurmann (Bloomington: Indiana University Press, 1978), 219.

18. Carl Jung, "The Relativity of the God-Concept in Meister Eckhart," *Collected Works* 6, para. 430; cited in Dourley, "Jung's Equation of the Ground of Being with the Ground of the Psyche," 520.

19. Jung, "The Relativity of the God-Concept in Meister Eckhart," 431.

20. Beatrice Bruteau, *The Grand Option: Personal Transformation and a New Creation* (Notre Dame, IN: University of Notre Dame Press, 2007), 75.

phrase Irenaeus of Lyons: The vitality of God is the human person consciously alive.

MONISTIC PANTHEISM

Paul Tillich explored the notion of ground as the origin or cause of what flows from it, yet is never separable from its effect or influence. One participates in the ground and does so consciously at the human level.[21] The term "ground" affirms that the relationship of the human to its origin could never be one of total discontinuity in either being or consciousness. Creation and fall come to coincide in the individual, with a universal awareness that one is estranged from the ground of one's being (the fall), but driven to recover it by the lingering memory and allure of a prior identity or entanglement with it (creation).[22] Tillich deepens the intimacy between the ground and human awareness of it when he further contends that the ground remains the substance of what stands out from it, but never in the sense that what stands out can be unqualifiedly identified with the ground.[23] The human in existence continues to participate in the substance of its origin but never in the sense of wholly and exhaustively appropriating it. These characteristics of ground give to it the notes of a creative power which is never wholly severed in being from what flows from it, nor is what flows from it ever divorced from the immediate awareness of that from which it flows or separated from substantial participation in it.

The dialectic that the term ground describes—between the religious and philosophical—is well suited to describe the basic dynamic of individuation, the rhythm of the ego's birth from its origin, return to its origin, and the redemption of both origin and ego in the latter's subsequent return to consciousness. The term

---

21. Paul Tillich, *Systematic Theology*, vol. 1 (Chicago: University of Chicago Press, 1951), 156, 237, 238.

22. Paul Tillich, *Systematic Theology*, vol. 3 (Chicago: Chicago University Press, 1957), 33–36, 39–44.

23. Tillich, *Systematic Theology*, vol. 1, 238.

"ground" thus suggests a differentiated monism or a type of pantheism integral to the foundational movement of the psyche. As
soon as the ego is born, it is aware of its distance from its psychic
origin and, at the same time, its connectedness to it. In religious
language, divinity and humanity have, from the birth of consciousness, been in an ongoing process of mutual redemption,
within an all-inclusive cosmic organism or monad. This is the
basis of incarnation, as Jung will describe.

GOD AS DEPTH

In his theories of the unconscious, Sigmund Freud brought to
light a dimension of depth in human consciousness, which the
narrow rationalism of the nineteenth century had not allowed. In
scientific terms, Freud achieved what Tillich described as the
emancipation of psychology from domination by physiology.
Freud's great achievement was to defeat the notion that consciousness could be reduced to its physical underpinnings and
then explained as a biological or chemical process. Tillich states:

> This discovery was important ethically and religiously
> particularly because it recognized—with questionable over-
> emphasis, to be sure—the fundamental importance of the
> erotic sphere for all aspects of the psychical life. It was an
> insight of which religion has never been aware and which
> only the conventions of bourgeois society have relegated
> to the limbo of forgotten truth.... Speaking in the lan-
> guage of religion, psycho-analysis and the literature allied
> with it cast light upon the demonic background of life.
> But wherever the demonic appears, there the question as
> to its correlate, the divine, will also be raised.[24]

While Freud insisted that his theories had discredited the
truth claims of religion, Tillich saw that psychoanalysis actually
confirmed many elements of religious tradition. Freud insisted

---

24. Paul Tillich, *The Religious Situation* (New York: Meridian, 1956), 62.

that belief in God represented nothing more than the projection of images from the erotic experience of the infant into a supernatural realm, but Tillich drew parallels between Freud's psychic projects and the biblical notion of idol worship and idolatry. He also turned Freud upside down when he suggested that, even when one sees that every idea and image of God is a projection, one must then follow the metaphor one step further and notice that "projection always is a projection *on to* something—a wall, a screen, another being, another realm.... The realm against which the divine images are projected is not itself a projection. It is the experienced ultimacy of being and meaning. It is the realm of ultimate concern."[25]

In the years prior to World War II, Tillich laid the theoretical foundations for what he called "belief-ful realism." He continually asserted that the existence of God is not open to argumentation. The existence of God is not something that can be proved or disproved because God is not an object. In the first volume of his *Systematic Theology,* he wrote:

> It would be a great victory for Christian apologetics if the words "God" and "existence" were very definitely separated except in the paradox of God becoming manifest under the conditions of existence.... God does not exist. He is being-itself beyond essence and existence. Therefore, to argue that God exists is to deny him.... If we derive God from the world, he cannot be that which transcends the world infinitely.[26]

In one short sentence, Tillich states: "God does not exist," as if God is not a particular something, like a tree (or the "big guy in the sky"). Tillich is trying to state in the sharpest and clearest way possible that God is "beyond essence and existence." He tries to make the point that God is the depth of existence itself: "God does not exist ... *except* in the paradox of God becoming manifest

---

25. Tillich, *Systematic Theology*, vol. 1, 212.

26. Tillich, *Systematic Theology*, vol. 1, 212.

under conditions of existence."[27] Tillich, like Jung and Teilhard, sought to overcome Greek metaphysics by building on insights from the new physics of quantum reality. The name "God" does not signify an ontologically distinct being but the Whole of everything, the ground and depth of existence itself.

A NEW GOD FOR SCIENCE AND RELIGION

Religion concerns relationship with ultimate reality—divine being —but it is precisely this point that stifles the dialogue between science and religion. Science describes the impersonal laws of nature while religion speaks of a personal and transcendent God. What could science and religion possibly have in common? It is precisely this impasse that Tillich addresses in his theology:

> It is just this idea of religion which makes any understanding of religion impossible. If you start with the question whether God does or does not exist, you can never reach Him; and if you assert that He does exist, you can reach Him even less than if you assert that he does not exist. A God whose existence or nonexistence you can argue is a thing beside others within the universe of existing things. . . . It is regrettable that scientists believe that they have refuted religion when they rightly have shown that there is no evidence whatsoever for the assumption that such a being exists. Actually, they have not only not refuted religion, but they have done it a considerable service. They have forced it to reconsider and to restate the meaning of the tremendous word God. Unfortunately, many theologians make the same mistake. They begin their message with the assertion that there is a highest being called God, whose authoritative revelations they have received. They are more dangerous for religion than the so-called atheistic scientists. They take the first step on the road which inescapably leads to what is called atheism.

27. Tillich, *Systematic Theology*, vol. 1, 212.

Theologians who make of God a highest being who has given some people information about Himself provoke inescapably the resistance of those who are told they must subject themselves to the authority of this information.[28]

Tillich sought to reclaim the power of the word *God*. He used his "method of correlation" to make the connections between questions that arise out of the life situation of a particular people and the vast resources of the Christian tradition. Following Freud, who spoke of religion as "the dimension of depth," Tillich focused on the human passion for meaning, namely, what gives fire to our lives. Rising up from human awareness of finitude is an awareness of the infinite. The background of everything that exists is another existence. Openness is the law of existence. God symbolizes the openness of life to more life. God is the ungraspable openness of life. Divinity is not a super Being (that is, a "sky God") but the excess of life itself, experienced as a personal invitation to the fullness of life. We constantly dwell in this depth without focusing on it. It is the milieu rather than the object of our experience. Everything exists in God and God exists in all things. While Tillich refrained from identifying God or the depth existence of God as pantheistic, his ideas lean in this direction. God is not equal to matter but neither is God separate from matter. Rather, matter is non-being apart from mind, and mind extends infinitely beyond the individual existence of matter; hence, God is that depth and breadth of matter of which no greater can be imagined or experienced.

Is God Personal?

Tillich and Jung realized that interiority, which includes the levels of reason and the levels of the psyche, undergirds the realm of the ultimate. The human person experiences the numinous as rising from one's own depths. Without these depths, they suggested,

---

28. Paul Tillich, *Theology of Culture* (New York: Oxford University, 1959), 4–5.

there is loss not only of religious sensitivity but, more so, of a symbolic sense. Both losses are but two aspects of the same impoverishment. As the human person loses conscious touch with the sacred, the capacity to appreciate and respond to the way the sacred is expressed through symbol is inevitably lost. Religiously and theologically, the loss of the symbolic leads to the pathology of literalism. When the religious story is read literally, its true power and meaning are lost. As a consequence, access to the depths from which the story arises is also lost. Tillich and Jung were deeply concerned about literalism that conveys a type of revelation that is dropped from heaven. An other-worldly religion drives science to the brink of atheism. Tillich sought to bridge the gap between science and religion by renewing the powerful symbol of God.

A symbol allows the mind to access realms that are otherwise inaccessible or closed off to consciousness. Whereas a sign points to something other than itself, a symbol participates in that to which it points.[29] For Jung, the symbol is the product of the activation of an archetype in the unconscious. The unconscious works continuously to compensate for conscious imbalances and inadequacies, and so will produce symbols addressed to consciousness from a position beyond it and somewhat superior to it. Jung states that a symbol "has a life of its own . . . it cannot be invented or fabricated."[30] For Tillich, too, the symbol rises to consciousness from an area over which mind has no direct manipulative power.

In 1940, Tillich and Einstein participated in a conference in New York City on "Science, Philosophy, and Religion." Einstein identified God with the orderly laws of nature, and emphatically rejected the idea of a personal God. He asserted that the notion of a personal God is not essential for religion, that it is a mere superstition, that it is self-contradictory, and, most importantly, that it is incompatible with science. Einstein spoke of "the grandeur of reason incarnate in existence, which, in its profoundest depths, is

---

29. John Dourley, *The Psyche as Sacrament: A Comparative Study of C. G. Jung and Paul Tillich* (Scarborough, ON: Inner City Books, 1981).

30. Carl Jung, *Memories, Dream, Reflections*, ed. Aniela Jaffe (New York: Vintage Books, 1961), 335–36.

inaccessible to man."[31] This reference to a reality provoking in humanity a sense of the holy while remaining beyond human understanding was music to Tillich's ears, because Einstein was simultaneously speaking of God while denying the existence of a personal God! It is a common mistake made by many scientists. Steven Hawking, for example, wrote that when the unified theory of everything is discovered, then "[W]e shall know the mind of God."[32] The title of Richard Dawkins's popular book, *The God Delusion*, also reflects an erroneous idea of God and probably should be retitled, *The Human Delusion*, for the real delusion is being cut off from the numinous depth of existence and living with a constricted ego in the field of awareness.

Tillich accepted Einstein's view on religion as an invitation to offer a vital understanding of God: "Religion lives and tries to maintain the presence of, and community with, this divine depth of our existence. But since it is 'inaccessible' to any objectifying concept it must be expressed in symbols. One of these symbols is the Personal God."[33] Tillich admits that the symbolic character of the word "God" is not always realized and that the symbol is confused with some supernatural being existing "out there" in an imaginary world of pure spirit. Thus, he insists, the adjective "personal" can be applied to God only in a symbolic sense, as it is both affirmed and negated at the same time. He concludes his answer to Einstein:

> But why must the symbol of the personal be used at all? The answer can be given through a term used by Einstein himself: the supra-personal. The depth of being cannot be symbolized by objects taken from a realm which is lower than the personal, from the realm of things or sub-personal living beings. The supra-personal is not an "It," or more exactly, it is a "He" as much as it is an "It," and it is above both of them. But if the "He" element is left out,

31. Tillich, *Theology of Culture*, 130.

32. Stephen Hawking, *A Brief History of Time* (New York: Random House Publishing Group, 2011), 191.

33. Tillich, *Theology of Culture*, 130–31.

the "It" element transforms the alleged supra-personal into a sub-personal, as usually happens in monism and pantheism. And such a neutral sub-personal cannot grasp the center of our personality; it can satisfy our aesthetic feeling or our intellectual needs, but it cannot convert our will, it cannot overcome our loneliness, anxiety, and despair. For as the philosopher Shelling says: "Only a person can heal a person." This is the reason that the symbol of the Personal God is indispensable for living religion.[34]

For Tillich, God is the personal ground and depth of existence itself, the *supra-natural*. God's holy "otherness" is God's holy "withinness," a depth of the numinous open to levels of consciousness but never exhausted by even the highest level of consciousness. God is always the more, the overflow, the future of life's inexhaustible creative potential. Because we can unconsciously dwell in this divine milieu as we search for ultimate meaning and purpose, it is the personal experience of God that makes the living reality of the numinous alive and vital for the world.

TEILHARD'S GOD

The twentieth-century discoveries of the new science and depth psychology cannot be ignored or dismissed. Without them, theology will stumble into the future. Like Jung and Tillich, Teilhard realized that we need a renewed sense of the depth of matter, a vital pantheism; otherwise, the earth will continue to be plundered and the human species will be torn apart by war and violence. He noted that the God of scholasticism, forged out of Greek philosophy, no longer speaks to the world of modern science. God has become too small to nourish in us the interest to live on a higher plane. The pace of scientific knowledge has outstripped our spiritual growth. Teilhard felt that the world is searching for a God proportionate to the dimensions of the new universe. He combined

---

34. Tillich, *Theology of Culture*, 131–32.

insights from science with faith in the God of Jesus Christ, a God as wide as the universe and as warm as the human heart; a God who no longer "drapes" the world but a God who is the vitalizing center of a universe in movement. Thomas King described Teilhard's God as a God of matter: "God is not found through opposition to matter (anti-matter) or independent of matter (extra-matter) but through matter (trans-matter)."[35] We take hold of God in the finite; God is sensed as "rising" or "emerging" from the depths of physical evolution, born not in the heart of matter but *as* the heart of matter.[36] For Teilhard, God is dynamically engaged in matter: God is rising up in and through evolution. Christopher Mooney wrote: "[I]f God did not fully engage in evolution something would be absolutely lacking to God, considered in the fullness not of his being but of his act of union."[37] In his essay on the "Cosmic Life," Teilhard expresses his ideas on the ground as the Absolute of matter. He speaks of the divine ground as the infinite capacity for life:

> If man is to come up to his full measure, he must become conscious of his infinite capacity for carrying himself still further; he must realize the duties it involves, and he must feel its intoxicating wonder. He must abandon all the illusions of narrow individualism and extend himself, intellectually and emotionally, to the dimensions of the universe: and this even though, his mind reeling at the prospect of his new greatness, he should think that he is already in possession of the divine, is God himself, or is himself the artisan of Godhead.[38]

His essay recounts a divine entanglement and relational holism that is both monist and pantheist. For example, he writes:

---

35. Thomas King, *Teilhard's Mysticism of Knowing* (New York: Seabury Press, 1981), 66–67.

36. King, *Mysticism of Knowing*, 103.

37. Christopher Mooney, *Teilhard de Chardin and the Mystery of Christ* (New York: Harper and Row, 1966), 174.

38. Pierre Teilhard de Chardin, *Writings in Time of War*, trans. René Hague (New York: Harper and Row, 1968), 15.

When a man has emerged into consciousness of the cosmos, and has deliberately flung himself into it, his first impulse is to allow himself to be rocked like a child by the
great mother in whose arms he has just woken. For some
this attitude of surrender is a mere aesthetic emotion, for
others it is a rule of practical life, a system of thought, or
even a religion; but in it lies the common root of all non-
Christian pantheisms. The essential revelation of paganism
is that everything in the universe is uniformly true and
valuable: so much so that the fusion of the individual must
be effected with all, without distinction and without quali-
fication. Everything that is active, that moves or breathes,
every physical, astral, or animate energy, every fragment of
force, every spark of life, is equally sacred; for, in the hum-
blest atom and the most brilliant star, in the lowest insect
and the finest intelligence, there is the radiant smile and
thrill of the same Absolute. It is to this Absolute alone that
we have to cling, giving ourselves to it directly and with a
penetration that can see through even the most substantial
determinations of the real, and rejects them as superficial
appearances.[39]

Teilhard is clear that the Absolute, the divine ground, is none
other than the depths of matter, and he sees the work of redemption as divinely entangled evolution: "For there lay matter, and
matter was calling me ... it was begging me to surrender myself
unreservedly to it, and to worship it."[40] His ideas, like Jung's, were
based on the incarnation understood in its most radical sense.

Teilhard's theology is thoroughly incarnational and materialis-
tic. Although less developed than Tillich's theology, his insights are
similar. "From the moment when we say God is Being," he wrote,
"it is clear that in a certain sense God alone is."[41] Judeo-Christian

---

39. Teilhard de Chardin, *Writings in Time of War*, 28.

40. Teilhard de Chardin, *Writings in Time of War*, 29.

41. Pierre Teilhard de Chardin, *Christianity and Evolution: Reflections on
Science and Religion*, trans. René Hague (New York: Harcourt Brace Jovanovich, 1971), 23.

thinking is haunted by the threat of acosmism. To posit God as being is to bring about a negation of the world; it is to say that the rest of the world is not God. But God is not known apart from experience; we take hold of God in the finite. Being is not mere existence but existence toward the more, reflected in the process of evolution. Teilhard writes: "What comes first in the world for our thought is not 'being' but 'the union which produces this being.'"[42] Being must first be a "we" before it can become an "I." Relationality is the basis of all that exists, including God. He continues: "The problem of the co-existence and the complementarity of the created and the uncreated is undoubtedly solved in part:...The two terms that are brought together, each in its own way, have an equal need both to exist in themselves and to be combined with each other, so that the absolute maximum of possible union may be effected *in natura rerum* (in the things of nature)."[43] He writes:

> Let us in fact forget about *Ens a se* (Being in itself) and *Ens ab alio* (Being from another) and go back to the most authentic and most concrete expressions of Christian revelation and mysticism. At the heart of what we can learn or drink in from those, what do we find but the affirmation and the expression of a strictly bilateral and complementary relationship between the world and God?...In truth it is not the sense of contingence of the created but the sense of the mutual completion of the world and God which gives life to Christianity....What comes first in the world for our thought is not "being" but "the union which produces this being."[44]

He opposed the idea of an absolutely gratuitous creation because it makes creation independent of God, that is, there is no real relation between God and cosmos.[45] This was Thomas Aquinas's

---

42. Teilhard de Chardin, *Christianity and Evolution*, 227.

43. Teilhard de Chardin, *Christianity and Evolution*, 227.

44. Teilhard de Chardin, *Christianity and Evolution*, 226–27.

45. Donald Gray, *The One and the Many: Teilhard de Chardin's Vision of Unity* (London: Burns and Oates, 1969), 127.

idea: God bestows being to being. We participate in God's life because creation depends on God; however, we have no real relationship to God. Teilhard thought otherwise. Evolution toward greater
unity rests on the involvement of God in creation. The world is
coming to be because God is coming to be, and God is coming to
be because the world is coming to be. The complementarity of the
created (matter) and the uncreated (the numinous) means that
the two terms are brought together, each in its own way, and have
an equal need both to exist in themselves and to be combined
with each other. The two terms—God and world—are intertwined in such a way that the emergence of new being is the
emergence of a new "cosmotheandric" wholeness, where cosmos
(world), theos (God), and anthropos (human) are entangled or entwined. Nature's dynamic becoming is God's dynamic becoming;
as nature becomes something new, God becomes new. Teilhard
wrote: "All around us and within our own selves, God is in process
of 'changing,' as a result of the coincidence of his magnetic power
and our own thought."[46] God is creating the world and the world
is creating God by giving birth (theogenesis) to God: "God fulfills
himself, he in some way *completes* himself, in the pleroma," he
states.[47] Elsewhere he wrote: "As a direct consequence of the unitive process by which God is revealed to us, he in some way 'transforms himself' as he incorporates us."[48] As we come to a higher
consciousness of a point of unity, God rises up in us; God becomes
actualized in us.

GOD IS LOVE

If God is the numinous depth of all that is, we might think of the
numinous depth as the core energy of love. Teilhard posited love
as the core energy of the universe, the energy of the whole in evo-

46. Pierre Teilhard de Chardin, *Hymn of the Universe*, trans. Gerald Vann
(New York: Harper and Row), 53.

47. Teilhard de Chardin, *Christianity and Evolution*, 178; emphasis added.

48. Pierre Teilhard de Chardin, *The Heart of Matter*, trans. René Hague
(New York: Harcourt Brace Jovanovich, 1979), 53.

lution. Love is not sentiment or emotion alone. Rather, love is the affinity of being with being. It is the dynamic energy of all life and embraces all the forms successively adopted by organized matter. If there were no internal inclination for unitive life, even at the basic level of molecules, it would be physically impossible for love to appear higher up, in this human form. It is love that draws together and unites. Teilhard wrote that "love is the most powerful and still most unknown energy in the world."[49] Only love has the power of moving being toward something more creative and unified. He held that the ultimate source and object of love is within and ahead of the evolutionary process. It is not something (an impersonal numinous or field of potentials) but a supreme Someone (the ecstasy of love at the heart of the psyche), the Great Presence, moving evolution toward the fullness of conscious life. Love changes the impersonal fields of information into personal, subjective moments of care and concern. It is the inexplicable core energy that gives one identity and deep purpose. We do not train our minds to attain that which is impersonal; we train our minds to attain that which is most deeply personal, for only personal love can make us whole. The ultimate object of love can only be a personal God. Divine love is an inexhaustible energy deep within the field of our infinite potential of Self. When we listen to the depth of our hearts, we awaken to our soul's desire, break through our fears, and embrace the adventure of life. Love transforms because love unites. Love pierces through the veil of divine mystery and enters into personal union with the ground of life. What begins in this life endures for all eternity, for God's love is an everlasting love (Jer 31:3).

---

49. Pierre Teilhard de Chardin, *The Activation of Energy*, trans. René Hague (New York: Harcourt Brace Jovanovich, 1963), 120.

6
Trinitization

The new theology offered by Jung and Teilhard undoubtedly revolutionizes Christianity, indeed, all monotheistic faiths, by claiming that God is entangled with materiality. There is no "sky God" or supernatural God. There is the supra-natural God, the infinite depth and ground of what exists, the infinite transcendent potential of the psyche, the Whole of all wholes symbolized by Omega. Even these symbols of Omega and psyche, however, do not fully convey the mystery of God, for the divine symbols themselves are self-transcendent. The infinite potential can never be grasped or defined because it is inexhaustible. God is the un-graspable whole at the heart of matter, not other than matter and, yet, more than matter. God is the name of elusive mystery. Human logic can be easily deceived by the sheer presence of God unless, of course, it is the logic of the heart. We humans have the potential to enflesh this divine mystery because we are, in our root reality, fractals of the mystery. By "fractal," I mean repeated patterns of divine wholeness radiating different frequencies of divine light. The God-matter relational whole is the core of our being. To live in this entangled mystery is the focus of God's inexhaustible creative delight. And it should be our delight as well. However, our frenzied, scattered, information-driven world cannot comprehend the entangled God, and we continue to search without for that which is already within.

The mystics have known about the secret of God for centuries. God is that experience of ineffable oneness, the source of inner freedom and joy. A mystic knows God not as an object outside oneself but as another "myself." Any conceptual talk of God is not God-talk but ego-talk, a projected ideal of God. The great Dominican mystic, Meister Eckhart, knew that the experience of God cannot be confused with the *idea* of God, as he prayed: "I pray God to rid me of God."[1] Thomas Merton grasped the import of Eckhart's prayer as a spiritual-psychic unity:

> He [Eckhart] parted with god for God's sake and God remained in him as God is in his own nature—not as he is conceived by anyone to be—nor yet as something yet to be achieved, but more as an is-ness, as God really is. Then he and God were a unit, that is, pure unity. Thus one becomes that real person for whom there can be no suffering, any more than the divine essence can suffer.[2]

Eckhart prefigured what has become, in our own time, the return of the apophatic God, the unsayable divine mystery, what John Caputo calls "weak theology" or what Richard Kearny calls the new theology, *anatheism*, "God without God." The death of the supernatural God is the new birth of God and world.[3] God is the experience of matter's infinite goodness. Unless we return

---

1. Franz Pfeiffer, ed., *Meister Eckhart: Sermons and Collations; Tractates; Sayings; Liver Positionum* (Plum City, WI: J. M. Watkins, 1924), 220.

2. Thomas Merton, *Zen and the Birds of Appetite* (New York: New Directions, 1968), 10.

3. See Catherine Keller and Mary-Jane Rubenstein, eds., *Entangled Worlds: Religion, Science, and New Materialisms* (New York: Fordham University Press, 2017).

God to matter, an incarnational God, we live with a functional atheism. We may talk *of* God, but only experience of the ineffable *reveals* God. Divine light stuns the ego into silence, drawing one beyond oneself into the mystery of the whole.

Jung contributes to the new theology by helping us understand that access to the entangled God of matter is the journey of consciousness. According to Jung, the self is an archetype that represents the unified unconsciousness and consciousness of an individual, often represented as a circle, square, or mandala. As the ego is transformed into the self, God "appears" ever more real as the true self. This is the process of conversion, from lower levels of consciousness to higher levels of unified or Christ consciousness. Without connecting the constricted ego to the psyche, the self remains fractured, disconnected, and the world is in a thousand pieces. Awakening to a new divine reality at the heart of life, a new pantheism or divine entanglement, is the only real way to heal our earth of its wounds. Without a living God entangled with the heart of our lives, we will destroy ourselves and our planet, because without a divine depth, nothing matters.

THE CLASSICAL TRINITY

It may not seem obvious at first, but Jung and others point to an open and relational God, a God who is Trinity. The term "open theism" was coined in the twentieth century to describe a new understanding of God in relation to the world. In 1994, a group of evangelical scholars formed a symposium, and later published a book entitled, *The Openness of God: A Biblical Challenge to the Traditional Understanding of God.* Their contributions explored the topic of God's relation to the world with five specific concerns in mind —biblical, historical, theological, philosophical, and practical aspects of biblical faith. God is "open and relational," a God of covenant who is truly with us and for us.

Theologians of the early Church recognized a God of deep relationality because they realized there cannot be an incarnation without a relational or self-communicative God: without the Trinity, there is no Christ. The earliest Christians had to cope with the implications of Jesus as the Messiah and the power of God among them. They reasoned that God could not communicate God's life in a finite way if God was not communicative in Godself. Hence, God must be relational. Neither the word "Trinity" nor the explicit doctrine of the Trinity appears in scripture. Furthermore, neither did Jesus nor his followers intend to contradict the Shema in the Hebrew Scriptures: "Hear, O Israel: The Lord our God is One Lord" (Deut 6:4). The early Church reflected on the experience of Jesus and developed an understanding of God that broke new theological ground. God was not only a deeply personal God (indicated by the proper name of "God"), but God was a deeply relational God, a Trinity of persons. This was a radical departure from the earlier Abrahamic theological understanding of God and unlike the later understanding of the prophet Mohammed.

The doctrine of the Trinity emerged from the need to make sense of God acting in Christ. Following the Council of Nicaea (325 CE), trinitarian doctrine was developed in the West by Augustine and in the East by the Cappadocian Fathers. Augustine distinguished the persons of the Trinity according to relations: the Father is the Father of the Son, the Son is Son of the Father, and the Holy Spirit is the bond between Father and Son and proceeds from the Father and Son. God, however, is a mystery, and describing the relations of the divine persons is a way of understanding God's activity in creation, not God's inner life.

The Cappadocian Fathers were the first to define God in terms of personhood. Each divine person is the divine nature; God's *ousia* or common nature is distinguished by persons. Since God is expressed in a personal way, God must be personal. Catherine LaCugna writes: "A person is not an individual but an open and ecstatic reality, referred to others for his or her existence. The actualization of personhood takes place in transcendence."[4] God's ultimate reality is not found in substance but only in personhood, that is, what God is toward another. Personhood is defined by relationships. God exists as the mystery of persons in communion. "Only *in communion* can God be what God is, and only

---

4. Catherine LaCugna, *God for Us: The Trinity and Christian Life* (New York: HarperCollins, 1991), 260–61.

as communion can God be at all. Since love produces communion among persons, love causes God to be who God is."[5]

To be a person is to be defined by where a person comes from (that is, one's primary relationship) because what a person is in oneself cannot be determined. The Father comes from no one and thus is the fountain fullness; the Son is begotten by the Father and is image and Word of the Father; the Spirit who proceeds from the Father and Son is the bond of love between them. The idea of relation of origin makes it impossible to think of a divine person "unto itself," as a single, distinct entity or disconnected from other persons or from the divine essence. In other words, *it is impossible to think of the divine essence in itself or by itself,* and it is impossible to think of the divine persons in an entirely abstract way disconnected from their presence in salvation history.[6] The unknowable God (Father) dwells in light inaccessible and is made known by the Son and Spirit. Bonaventure said that God's inner life (immanent Trinity or *theologia*) and outer life (economic Trinity or *oikonomia*) are one and the same life. There is only one ecstatic movement of God outward, and that is the begetting of the Son and spirating of the Spirit in creation. The Trinity makes sense only in the history of the world.

DYNAMIC AND HISTORICAL

Twentieth-century theologian Karl Rahner once remarked that one could dispense with the doctrine of the Trinity as false and the major part of religious literature could well remain virtually unchanged.[7] The Trinity, he continued, had become a doctrine in name but not in practice. He speculated that announcing a fourth person of the Trinity would make no real difference in the way the faith is lived except that a meeting would have to be called to discuss how to add the fourth person to the sign of the cross. Rahner's

---

5. Michael Aksionov Meerson, *The Trinity of Love in Modern Russian Theology* (Quincey, IL: Franciscan Press, 1998), 4.

6. LaCugna, *God for Us*, 69–70.

7. LaCugna, *God for Us*, 6.

remarks somewhat humorously describe the virtual disappearance of the Trinity from Christian theology in modernity. Inresponse to this disappearance, Trinitarian theology witnessed a strong revival in the twentieth century. To say God is Trinity is to speak of a God who is involved in the life of the world in a deep and personal way. Despite the neglect of Trinitarian theology in practice, the cornerstone of Christian faith is fundamentally Trinitarian.

Lutheran theologian Jürgen Moltmann reflected on the triune God in view of the atrocities of war and the Holocaust. What kind of God could allow such profound suffering? An apathetic, self-sufficient God cannot be the God of Jesus Christ. Rather, God is constituted by openness. The Trinity symbolizes a deeply relational God who is open to new life. In his book *The Crucified God*, Moltmann insists that we cannot say of God "who he is of himself and in himself; we can only say who God is for us in the history of Christ which reaches us in our history."[8] The Christian message brings about something new and strange, culminating in a mysterious turn of events: the suffering and death of Jesus on the cross. While Jesus experiences the abandonment of God ("My God, my God, why have You abandoned me?"), he also makes a total act of faith and surrender ("Father, into Your hands, I commend my spirit"). A theology that understands the relationship between God and world to be a rational relationship but not a real relationship will frame the sufferings of Jesus as human sufferings that are unable to affect God. Without a real relationship between God and world, God does not experience the sufferings of Jesus, let alone those of each person and fragile creature of the earth. A real relationship between God and world is a relationship of mutuality and involves the suffering of God. Not only is God deeply affected by the sufferings of the world, but God empties Godself of all power to be with the suffering one. God's self-emptying is the openness of God to be affected by what is not God; this is the basis of the world's empowerment. In Jungian terms, all creation is potentially God waiting to be fully incarnated or actualized.

---

8. Jürgen Moltmann, *The Crucified God* (Minneapolis, MN: Fortress Press, 1993), 83.

Moltmann understands the cross of God's self-revelation as love. Simply put, a God who cannot suffer cannot love. Developing the theme of kenosis from Paul's Letter to the Philippians, Moltmann's open and suffering God abandons and contradicts classical theistic concepts of divine immutability, impassibility, and timelessness. Instead, he emphasizes divine love as a power that can suffer in the face of death and not be vanquished. God, then, is to be found amid the violence of the world, not as an overpowering ruler but as One who, out of unconditional love, suffers with all those who are crushed, trampled upon, broken-hearted, or defeated. God's gives one the power to rise from the ruins of defeat into the dawn of new life. In this way, strength is found in the midst of suffering, for the cross is key to God's own life, as Walter Kasper wrote:

> On the cross the incarnation of God reaches its true meaning and purpose. The entire Christ-event must therefore be understood in terms of the cross. On the cross God's self-renouncing love is embodied with ultimate radicalness. The cross is the utmost that is possible to God in his self-surrendering love; it is "that than which a greater cannot be thought"; it is the unsurpassable self-definition of God. This self-renunciation or emptying is therefore not a self-abandonment and not a self de-divinization of God... but the revelation of the divine God.... God need not strip himself of his omnipotence in order to reveal his love. On the contrary, it requires omnipotence to be able to surrender oneself and give oneself away; and it requires omnipotence to be able to take oneself back in the giving and to preserve the independence and freedom of the recipient. Only an almighty love can give itself wholly to the other and be a helpless love.[9]

The cross, therefore, belongs to the inner life of God as the structure of God's desire to love and to be reconciled. God's being is in suffering because God is love; the willingness to suffer begins

---

9. Walter Kasper, *The God of Jesus Christ* (New York: Continuum, 2012), 194–95.

in love, and only out of love can one suffer with joy because of the hope of new life. God is involved in the struggles of history, allowing suffering and death to affect God's own life in order to heal, liberate, and draw forth new life through the power of love.

Like Moltmann, Lutheran theologian Eberhard Jüngel developed a theology of the Trinity based on the inner relational structure of God's life and the self-relatedness of God. There cannot be relationality in the incarnation, he thought, without there being antecedent relationality in the life of God. Hence, Jüngel explores the idea that God's being is constituted by God's temporal relations with the world. He argues that the unity of the immanent and economic Trinity is found in the identity of God as love: "God has shown himself as love . . . in the unique event of the surrender of Jesus Christ to death."[10] God's being is God's action in Jesus Christ. In other words, "the eternal Word of God from the beginning . . . is to become incarnate."[11] He introduces the eschatological notion of divine becoming because God has already, in freedom, taken up historicity into the divine life. God does not become other than what God has always been from eternity. God's being is defined eschatologically as a becoming, a dynamic process in which the fullness of divine being is expressed in his determination to fulfill his eternal purposes for humanity. Ted Peters remarked: "If Jüngel is really serious when he says that the historical event of Jesus Christ means that God has defined himself as a human God, then why not make *God's ongoing incarnation part of the ongoing process of divine self-definition?*"[12] This is an interesting question that Teilhard addressed in his own way.

Wolfhart Pannenberg, another prominent twentieth-century Lutheran theologian, also held that the Trinity is historically and not ontologically determined. The life of God is not autonomous and self-sufficient, independent of creation; rather, God's life depends on creation for its unfolding identity. God's transcendent

---

10. Eberhard Jüngel, "The Relationship Between 'Economic' and 'Immanent' Trinity," *Theology Digest* 24 (1976): 182.

11. Jüngel, "The Relationship Between 'Economic' and 'Immanent' Trinity," 182.

12. Ted Peters, *God as Trinity: Relationality and Temporality in Divine Life* (Louisville, KY: Westminster/John Knox Press, 1993), 96.

unity-in-divinity finds its fullest expression only when history has been finally and completely embraced within the divine life, that is, when time has been assumed into eternity. Only then will the existence of God be "conclusively decided."[13] God has chosen from eternity to make Godself dependent upon his creation for his identity. Within this framework of the history of creation, Pannenberg's trinitarian construction assumes both the work of the Spirit and the finality of the history of the world. God, the Father, has made Godself dependent on the course of history, in which the Son's obedience to death on the cross and the Spirit's work in consummating the kingdom reflect the dependence of the trinitarian persons on one another in the history of the world.[14] Peters suggests that the "picture one gets here is of a God who jeopardizes his own divinity in order to engage in historical intercourse with created reality."[15]

For Pannenberg, the divine adventure of God's involvement with history is the exegesis of the phrase "God is love." Expressed in God's self-dedication in the history of the world, trinitarian love will find its eschatological completion through the activity of the Spirit in the world. The Holy Spirit is the power that transcends and operates within nature, guiding it to its destiny. The Spirit expresses the ecstasy of divine life, the overabundance of joy that gives birth to the universe and ever works to bring about a fullness of unity. Thus, history determines God's divinity, such that the unity of God can be finally established only eschatologically, when the kin-dom of God is fully realized. God's true identity is set in the future; only at the end of history do we find the meaning of history and the meaning of God.

TRINITY AND PSYCHIC UNITY

While twentieth-century theology aligned the Trinity with the course of history, further development on the psyche and entan-

---

13. Peters, *God as Trinity*, 140.

14. Peters, *God as Trinity*, 141.

15. Peters, *God as Trinity*, 141.

gled relationality can help integrate the Trinity into the life of the world. The Trinity symbolizes a relational God in history, and Christ signifies a relational God brought to the highest level of nondual consciousness. The Trinity and Christ are interrelated mysteries and symbolically undergird the entangled mysteries of divinity and humanity.

In Jungian terms, the world is not an accumulation of things but one interrelated whole grounded in the infinite field of the psyche, the unconscious. We can say that our world, at its deepest level, is marked by the radical potential to reveal the mystery of divine love within it. The relational God seeks fulfillment in that which is not God to make Godly that which has the potential for divinity, namely, matter. Divinely entangled matter is nothing other than incarnation, the root reality of life. The Trinity signifies that matter has never been outside the scope of divine life. As Saint Paul wrote, Christ is in the heart of God since the foundation of the world, "the mystery hidden from all eternity" (Eph 3:9). The theory of special relativity states that matter and energy are equivalent. Energy is neither created nor destroyed but can change from one form to another. In this respect, energy is infinite and God is infinite. If Trinity is what God is in relation to matter, and Trinity is eternal, then is matter eternal? If matter expresses divine love, then the starting point for reconceiving God in an age of entanglement is matter. Matter is the mirror of God.

In the fourteenth century, the Franciscan theologian Duns Scotus argued against Anselm's doctrine of satisfaction, or what has come to be known as "atonement theology." Anselm said that the incarnation took place to repay the debt incurred by human sin. Scotus rejected this position. Rather, he said, creation and incarnation are two interrelated mysteries of divine love. The reason for all divine activity is found in the very nature of God as love. The Trinity is a communion of love. God desires to be loved by another who can love God as perfectly as God loves Godself. The reason for the incarnation, then, is not sin but love. Christ is first in God's intention to love. The Incarnation is the unrepeatable, unique, and single defining act of God's love. Thus, even if sin had not entered the universe through the human person, Christ would have come.

The Scotist doctrine of the primacy of Christ situates Christ at the center of creation, predestined to grace and glory. The incarnation shows divine freedom for self-revelation and relationship to humanity, without regard to human sinfulness. The unfolding love of the Trinity, incarnate from all eternity, is the Christ. Christ is first in God's intention to love. Jesus Christ, therefore, is the model of divine-human communion who exemplifies the meaning and purpose of all creation, namely, the praise and glory of God in a communion of love. In Scotus's view, every creature is made in the image of Christ. Every leaf, cloud, fruit, animal, and person is an outward expression of the Word of God in love.

Understanding the Trinity within the paradigm of relational holism, we can say that the Trinity signifies unity in love; love is the energy of entangled bodies. Teilhard spoke of communion with God through matter. God is not found in opposition to matter but through matter. God is the divine energy of love that gives form to matter; matter, informed by the energies of love, gives birth to God. The union of God and matter in love is symbolized by the Christ. As Scotus realized, God's vision for this unfolding universe is *personal union in love.*

Although Jung did not expound on the Trinity of love, his theology helps us understand the personalization of love as the movement of the mind into higher realms of consciousness. We can read a classic passage from the fifth-century Neoplatonic writer Pseudo-Dionysius and interpret the mystery of the spiritual journey as the opening up of the mind to the infinite field of the unconscious psyche. Dionysius writes:

> Trinity!! Higher than any being, any divinity, any goodness!
> Guide of Christians in the wisdom of heaven!
> Lead us up beyond unknowing and light,
> Up to the farthest, highest peak of mystic scripture,
> Where the mysteries of God's Word
> Lie simple, absolute and unchangeable
> In the brilliant darkness of a hidden silence.[16]

---

16. Colm Luibheid, trans., *Pseudo-Dionysius: The Complete Works* (New York: Paulist Press, 1987), 135.

Seeing the Trinity within the context of Jung's psychosomatic unity reveals the process of individuation: the infinite field of the psyche is analogous to the "Father"; the actualizaiton of the psychic potential, the "Word"; and the energies of love that actualize the potential into existence, the "Spirit." As the mind makes the journey inward and ascends to higher levels of consciousness, the God within awakens to a new reality of the whole. This awakening is a dynamic movement of love toward the actualization of potential life brought about by the expansion of consciousness on the level of integral wholeness or unity. The Trinity, therefore, symbolizes the psychosomatic relationships that give rise to wholeness and personhood, as divinity is incarnated at the highest level of Christ consciousness.

Teilhard and Trinitization

Teilhard was a process thinker who thought in terms of biological relationality and wholeness. Whereas Jung used terms of personal formation to describe psychic unity, Teilhard thought in terms of the evolutionary formation of biological personhood. Each thinker expressed an aspect of Christ in evolution, since the unity of the self and the emergence of self on a higher level of conscious life reflects the rise of the Christic. The Trinity is not the final definition of God but the starting point for God's becoming, that is, God's interpersonal relatedness in history based on the relationships of persons in love. God expresses a "Word" of love when we attend to and respond in love. The world is the ongoing dynamic activity of events, the Word of divine love entangled with space-time-mattering. To awaken to this reality is to open up the mind to the deeper truths within us, to realize that we have an unquenchable capacity for love expressed in wholeness and beauty. Love is the energy of life's evolution toward greater unity.

In a world of entanglement, numbers signify relationships of complexity. The Law of Three is an esoteric principle formulated by the Armenian George Gurdjieff (1890–1912) who traveled extensively in the Far East and was impressed by the cosmogeny of the East. He developed the "Law of Three" or the "Fourth Way" as a means of describing humanity's place in the universe.[17] The Law of Three posits a set of relationships that differ from binitarian relationships, with the interplay of two polarities calling forth a third, a "mediating" or "reconciling" principle between them. In terms of relationships, the number three stipulates a third force that emerges as a necessary mediation of opposites. The third force is the openness of opposites to reconciliation on a whole new level. It is a dialectic of which resolution simultaneously creates a new realm of possibility. While binary systems seek completion in a "reabsorption into the Whole," complex or ternary systems seek completion in *the drive into a new dimension*."[18]

The Law of Three helps us to reconceive the Trinity as divine relationships of complexifying love. Love, as the highest form of divine creativity, is an eternal movement from potentiality to act: the fountain fullness of love overflows into new life. Whereas binitarian Trinitarian theology sees the trinitarian relationships as Father and Son, Son and Spirit, Father and Spirit, the Spirit sharing life with the Father and Son, the Law of Three suggests that the Spirit is the coincidence of opposites of self-donation and receptivity. The generativity of the Father and the receptivity of the Son is resolved in a third Person, the Spirit who reconciles the opposites in the openness to new life. God's openness is consistent

---

17. For a detailed discussion on Gurdjieff and the Law of Three, see Cynthia Bourgeault, *The Holy Trinity and the Law of Three: Discovering the Radical Truth at the Heart of Christianity* (Boston: Shambhala, 2013), 22–37. Bourgeault notes that "the most important thing to keep in mind here is that this third force is an independent force, coequal with the other two, not a product of the first two as in the classic Hegelian "thesis, antithesis, synthesis" (26). The interweaving of the three creates a fourth, a whole new dimension "that transforms the triangle into a pyramid" (28). In a recent article on Hegel and the Trinity, Peter Benson claims that "Hegel himself never used the words 'thesis, antithesis, synthesis' to characterize the dialectical process," although the word "antithesis" occasionally appears in his writings. Benson suggests that Hegel's emphasis on the philosophy of three is more closely aligned to the biological concept of emergence and, I would suggest, shares an affinity with Gurdjieff's notion of the Law of Three. See Peter Benson, "Hegel and the Trinity," *Philosophy Now* 42 (2003), https://philosophynow.org/issues/42/Hegel_and_the_Trinity.

18. Bourgeault, *The Holy Trinity and the Law of Three*, 19.

with divine love because God's nature is love.[19] The Trinity symbolizes the openness of divine love to personalization in created reality. In this respect, the Trinity is the first expression of God's creative love, that is, the dynamism of intersubjectivity, the communication of Being and the community that emerges from it. God is a community of persons-in-love, a community that continues to grow in and through the world into ever greater unity.

The threefoldness of divine life symbolizes an asymmetrical-complexified relationship projecting love outward and calling new forms of being into existence. Each new existence is marked by a pattern of divine relationality, so that the trinitarian dynamic "is a repeated pattern on every scale of the cosmic order."[20] While we are used to thinking of the Trinity as just three Persons, this is only the minimum for community because of the nature of love. The divine community is continuously self-making, since love constantly flows as a center of activity in the perichoretic flow of shared life. There is nothing to say that there could not be more persons, perhaps an infinite number of persons, as persons seek fullness through the actualization of divine love. If God is all possibilities for the fullness of life, then the trinitizing dynamism of divine love in evolution is the energy that converts the potentials of matter into actual material expressions of beauty, good, unity, and truth. Transpersonalized cosmic life is symbolically trinitarian.

Teilhard grasped this new understanding of God by speaking of the trinitization of evolution. In his view, evolution is the movement from potentiality to act, as divine love creates, incarnates, and draws together in greater unity. This trinitizing process is the rise of God in evolution or "theogenesis":

We might say that for the discursive reason two phases can be distinguished in "theogenesis." In the first, God

---

19. Joseph Bracken, *Divine Matrix: Creativity as Link Between East and West* (Eugene, OR: Wipf and Stock Publishers, 2006), 34.

20. Beatrice Bruteau, *God's Ecstasy: The Creation of a Self-Creating World* (New York: Crossroad, 1997), 14. On the notion of "memes," see Limor Shifman, *Memes in Digital Culture* (Cambridge, MA: MIT Press, 2013), 2. The word "meme" was coined by Richard Dawkins in 1976 to describe small units of culture that are spread from person to person by copying or imitation.

posits himself in his Trinitarian structure (fontal being reflecting itself, self-sufficient, upon itself): "Trinitization." In
the second phase, he envelops himself in participated
being, by evolutive unification of pure multiple (positive
non-being) born (in a state of absolute potency) by antithesis to pre-posited Trinitarian unity: Creation.[21]

In the nineteenth century, F. W. Schelling spoke of religion in
history as a "theogonic process," in which human consciousness
completes the progressive revelation and earthly realization of a
personal God. Teilhard contributed to the new myth of theogenic
holism. He believed that, without creation, something would be
absolutely lacking to God, not in the fullness divine being but in
the divine act of union. He wrote: "If God was not triune, we
could not conceive the possibility of his creating (by being incarnate) without totally immersing himself in the world he brings
into being."[22] The theory of creative union was not so much a
metaphysical doctrine as a sort of empirical and pragmatic explanation of the universe. He wrote: "[T]his theory came to birth
out of my own personal need to reconcile, within the confines of
a rigorously structured system, the views of science respecting
evolution... which have driven me to *seek out the presence of God,
not apart from the physical world, but rather through matter and in a
certain sense in union with it.*[23] The evolutionary pressure is the
presence of God at every stage, helping, driving, drawing. We always assumed that God could be located "above," he said, but
now we realize that God is "ahead" and "within," as well. As
God "metamorphizes the world from the depths of matter to the

21. Pierre Teilhard de Chardin, *Christianity and Evolution: Reflections on
Science and Religion,* trans. René Hague (New York: Harcourt Brace Jovanovich, 1971), 178. It is interesting to note that Bourgeault (*Trinity and the Law
of Three,* 21) states that the Trinity should be approached "in its cosmically
subtle role as an ordering and revealing principle, of which Christ is its culminating expression," an idea consonant with Teilhard's insights.

22. Teilhard de Chardin, *Christianity and Evolution,* 157–58.

23. Donald Gray, *The One and the Many: Teilhard de Chardin's Vision of
Unity* (London: Burns and Oates, 1969), 34.

peaks of Spirit, so too the world 'endomorphizes' God."[24] As we are incorporated into the life of God, so too God's life is incorporated into us; God is transformed as we are transformed.

In this respect, creation, incarnation, and redemption are three aspects of the same fundamental process, namely, the self-creating and self-involving love of God. Teilhard identified creative union as a *fourth* divine mystery, "the mystery of the creative union of the world in God, or pleromization."[25] It is a *fourth mystery* because it is not merely divine-created union; rather, the union of divinity and materiality is an entirely new union.

COSMIC PERSONALIZATION

Teilhard claimed that love undergirds a fundamental law of attraction in the universe and that this force of attraction is the basis of personal being. In this respect, trinitizing the universe is the flow of love, which gives rise to personhood. Personhood, in turn, forms community, and community grows as divine love is continuously hybridized and transcended in love. In this way, everything that exists is integral to the ever-growing unity of God as love; evolution is the actualized personalization of divine love.

Teilhard described this dynamic love of God incarnate in evolution as the birthing of the Christ or Christogenesis. The Spirit's creative love is the personalization of being-in-love. The hybridization of divine love expressed in cosmic personalization (Christogenesis) is the "fourth" dimension of Trinitarian life (pleromization), insofar as God's personalizing love finds its fullest meaning in openness to new life. The emergence of Christ in evolution is divine love trinitizing the universe; that is, divine love draws created reality into personhood and ever more unified personal relationships. Trinitizing the universe, therefore, is the rise of the cosmic person, in which God and world evolve into ever greater

---

24. Pierre Teilhard de Chardin, *The Heart of Matter*, trans. René Hague (New York: Harcourt Brace Jovanovich, 1979), 52.

25. Teilhard de Chardin, *Christianity and Evolution*, 183.

unity, symbolized by the mystical body of Christ. This union is the differentiation of God and world.[26] Bracken writes: "God, as the primordial subject of the never-ending act of existence, is a determinate reality here and now, but with the unlimited capacity to acquire further determinations in later moments of the divine existence."[27]

Created life is potentially divine life waiting to be brought to conscious expression. As Teilhard suggests, without creation, something would be absolutely lacking to God in his act of union.[28] God is ever newness in love and is creatively expressed in the evolution of personhood. God rises up in evolution as God for evolution. As divine ecstatic love is actualized, evolution is pleromized and becomes increasingly filled with God. Yet, God is always the transcendent more of love, from fountain fullness to receptivity; from expressive love to receptive love; from donative-receptive love to ecstatic love. God is thus the future of creation, drawing created reality into increasingly new levels of personal, unified love. Divine love bubbling up from the ground of matter evolves into the fullness of God and world. The complexified God-world relationship is an ever-ascending wholeness in love, in which Christ symbolizes what the actualization of divine love can become.

Teilhard's new language of Christogenesis and trinitization is an attempt to signify the energetic dynamism of divine love and created reality. Something vital is taking place in our midst: we are moving toward something more. Consciousness is increasing as we converge into new pluralities. If we look around the planet we realize we are shifting from separate continents and nation-states to interconnected fields of shared concerns. If we can realize the root meaning of our religious lives and reconcile ourselves in love,

---

26. In *The Phenomenon of Man*, trans. Bernard Wall (New York: Harper and Row, 1959), Teilhard writes that union differentiates: "[T]he more 'other' they become in conjunction, the more they find themselves as 'self'" (262). While he is speaking of unitive entities on the level of physical evolution, the same principle can also be applied to God and world insofar as the incarnation of God is the personalization of God which rises to explicit consciousness in the person of Jesus Christ.

27. Bracken, *The Divine Matrix*, 34.

28. Teilhard, *Christianity and Evolution*, 182.

then we can evolve toward the fullness of the Body of Christ or pleroma.

Openness to pleroma or fullness is pleromization, and such fullness is not possible without interpersonal relationships. Hence, pleromization *is* trinitization and trinitization is the evolution of cosmic personalization, signified by the Christ. The unification of divine and human natures emerges in a third nature—the Christic —which opens up to a new type of person in creation.[29] If creativity is the essence of divinity and the highest expression of divine creativity is incarnate love, then the Trinity's creative love is openness to creative personhood-in-love. God's love is an eternal movement from potentiality to act; from nonbeing to being; from interiority to expression. For God *is* love, and it is love that makes personhood possible. God is always becoming God, as love deepens personhood. Christ symbolizes the unitive and unconditional love of a relational God, rendering all reality personal and creative in love, oriented toward communion. In this way, the history of the world in all its suffering and sorrow is a sign of openness, a sign that love is not fully realized, for the world is aimed toward the fullness of love.

---

29. Teilhard spoke of a "third nature" of Christ. In his writings, he describes this nature as follows: "Between the Word on the one side and the Man-Jesus on the other, a kind of 'third Christic nature' (if I may dare to say so) emerges...that of the total and totalizing Christ." Teilhard spoke of a third aspect of the theandric (divine-human) complex as "the *cosmic nature*," which, in his view, has not been sufficiently distinguished from the other two natures (divine and human). See Teilhard, *Christianity and Evolution*, 179; J. A. Lyons, *The Cosmic Christ in Origen and Teilhard de Chardin: A Comparative Study* (London: Oxford University Press, 1982), 183–96.

7

The Individuation of God

Jung attempted a re-reading of the New Testament because the old myth that Jesus saves us neglected the psychic dimensions of human life. He reinterpreted the Chalcedon formula as a description of individuation brought to full consciousness. Divinity and humanity are not unique to Jesus, he claimed; rather, the two natures are present in everyone. By saying this, Jung implied that divinity is not ontologically distinct from created being. Jung correlated instead humanity and divinity with consciousness and unconsciousness, and he identified both levels of consciousness in every human person. Divinity, he suggests, is the realm of the transcendent psyche, the inner infinite potential that undergirds the field of the unconscious and the openness of the unconscious to wholeness. The unification of personal consciousness works toward the divinization of the person. The simple awareness of divinity in the individual, the transcendent ground of the psyche, marks the point to which the religious instinct has currently evolved. By saying that all individuals are to realize their natural divinity, Jung democratized and universalized the Christian meaning of incarnation, which he thought had been greatly constricted by its application to one outstanding historical individual. Uniting the depths of the mind with the depths of matter could effectively enact a new religious myth of divine and human entanglement. For Jung, the incarnation, thus understood, is the source of both the sacramental (the holy) and the iconoclastic (the critique of the holy). He wrote: "It was only quite late that we realized (or rather, are beginning to realize) that God is Reality itself and therefore—last but not least—man. This realization is a millennial project."[1]

What is Individuation?

Jung held that religion is a natural process of individuation. Humanity's relation to divinity corresponds to the relationship between personal consciousness and the collective unconscious (cosmic plenum) as the ground of consciousness and meaning. Individuation means becoming a single, integrated person, and, insofar as "in-dividuality" embraces our innermost, last, and incomparable uniqueness, it also implies becoming one's own self. We could, therefore, translate individuation as "coming to selfhood" or "self-realization."[2] Individuation, Jung contends, is a force of nature within the human that cannot be denied:

> The urge and compulsion to self-realization is a law of nature, and thus of invincible power. Who will undertake the task of individuation? Who will hear and respond to the inner voice? Only the man who can consciously assent to the power of the inner voice becomes a personality.[3]

---

1. Carl Jung, "Answer to Job," *Collected Works* 11 (Princeton: Princeton University Press, 1952), para. 631.

2. Carl Jung, "The Function of the Unconscious," *Collected Works* 7 (Princeton: Princeton University Press, 1938/1940), 266.

3. Carl Jung, "The Development of Personality," *Collected Works* 17 (Princeton: Princeton University Press, 1954), 308.

Individuation is the process of becoming a "person," a fully integrated and relational being. It is not an option, in Jung's view. It is our only hope for the welfare of the planet: "The psychological rule says that when an inner situation is not made conscious, it happens outside, as fate. That is to say, when the individual remains undivided and does not become conscious of one's inner opposite, the world must perforce act out the conflict and be torn into opposing halves."[4] Jung held to the same principle of wholeness that Teilhard and Bohm espoused. Matter and mind form an integral whole that must be actualized for the realization of humanity's wholeness. Alfred North Whitehead's philosophy of organism is a metaphysical description of wholeness that supports the psychogenic process of relational holism. God is creating through matter and, in a certain sense, in union with it, and the creativity of matter imparts newness to God's life.[5] While Jung's position is sympathetic to cosmic wholeness, he explicitly identifies the role of consciousness for the actualization of wholeness.

Jung considered individuation to be fundamentally a spiritual development. Christ is not a unique savior figure but a universal archetype. Jung spoke of Christ as the "Self," a cosmic archetype, the Self of every person. Jesus lived from the depths of his Christ consciousness. Christ symbolizes the psychic totality of the individual. He shows us that the birth of God is possible in a union of opposites. Jung's ideas resonate with the medieval insights of Bonaventure and Nicholas of Cusa, both of whom spoke of Christ as the coincidence of opposites. In his *Soul's Journey into God*, Bonaventure said that, in Christ, heaven and earth, eternity and time, beginning and end are reconciled. Ewert Cousins identified opposites as mutually affirming complements; opposites are incomplete in relation to each other until brought into a complementary whole.[6] The revelation of God is a union of opposites.

---

4. Carl Jung, "Christ, Symbol of the Self," *Collected Works* 9 (Pt. 2) (Princeton: Princeton University Press, 1951), 126.

5. Alfred North Whitehead, *Process and Reality*, ed. David Ray Griffin and Donald W. Sherburne (New York: The Free Press, 1979), 349.

6. See Ewert Cousins, "The Coincidence of Opposites in the Christology of Saint Bonaventure," *Franciscan Studies* 28 (1968): 27–45.

Jung suggested that God is like a patient in analysis for whom consciousness needs to be brought into its unconscious darkness in a self-transformative process, one of individuating and becoming whole. According to Peter Todd: "[I]t is precisely this expanded and higher consciousness which Jung believes God acquires through incarnation in humankind."[7] The union of opposites, God and human, are united in the person; the "self" is an ongoing, dynamic conjunction of opposites. Jung wrote: "One should make it clear to oneself what it means when God becomes man. It means nothing less than a world-shaking transformation of God."[8] God becomes human, and the human becomes God. Jung's idea of natural religion is summed up in this way: The many gods become one; the one God becomes human; every human is to become God.

CHRIST, AN INCOMPLETE SYMBOL

Jung reflected on Christ not as a divine savior but as the exemplary archetype of the human person. He claimed the symbol of Christ is incomplete as a symbol of absolute wholeness because the doctrinal Christ, the Christ of the Creed, has no dark side; its dark side has been split off, leaving only an all-good Christ. When Jung says that Christ is the archetype of wholeness, he is not making a statement about God; he rejects any type of ontological God. Rather, he sees Jesus as living from the infinite potential of love within him, able to ascend into this love by going into the desert and facing his own conflict and darkness.

Jung claims that the Church's doctrine of the *privatio boni,* that is, evil as the absence of good, is flawed, if not dangerous. Pseudo-Dionysius claimed that God knows evil under the form of the good; that is, all goodness is in God while all evil is in

---

7. Peter Todd, "Teilhard and Other Modern Thinkers on Evolution, Mind, and Matter," *Teilhard Studies* 66 (2013): 5.

8. Carl Jung, "Answer to Job," *Collected Works* 11, para. 631; cited in Todd, "Teilhard and Other Modern Thinkers," 6.

humans.[9] Jung takes passionate and lengthy issue with this idea and argues that this proposition fails to recognize the reality — and the power — of evil as the dark side of God within the human. The darkness of God is the shadow of our unreconciled self. This split in the Christ symbol (ignoring the darkness of God) prevents — or protects — us from facing and assimilating our own evil and leads instead to the projection of evil onto the world. In other words, if we never face the darkness of God within us, the unreconciled God, we will project that chaotic darkness into the world. Unless we make peace with the inner ground of God, God is not made whole, we are not made whole, and the world remains divided. Hence, we must go into the desert of our minds and hearts, like Jesus, and confront our darkest (and fractured) selves.

The wholeness of God emerges through the healing of opposites. In a sense, we have to "go against" our self to find our true self. This "going against the self" (*agere contra*) means embracing the suffering of our unreconciled lives as the path to wholeness. The most difficult journey to make is the journey within. Without this journey, Christ is not born in us, God remains incomplete, and the world remains in partial darkness. Saint Paul writes: "[We] make up in our bodies what is lacking in the sufferings of Christ" (Col 1:24). The Cistercian monk Isaac of Stella said that "our salvation is necessary for the completion of Christ."[10] Saint Teresa of Avila confessed that Christ has no body now on earth but ours. Traditionally, the Church has interpreted these ideas in terms of participation, that is, our own sufferings participate in building up the body of Christ. Jung reverses this and puts the emphasis on participation in the self, doing the "hard work" of inner reconciliation. Only then is Christ born within. Merton wrote:

> At the center of our being is a point of nothingness
> which is untouched by sin and by illusion

---

9. See Jijimon Alakkalam Joseph, "Dionysius on the Problem of Evil: Lessons One Can Learn," *Tattva-Journal of Philosophy* 7, no. 2 (2015): 79–95.

10. Caroline Walker Bynum, *Jesus as Mother: Studies in Spirituality of the High Middle Ages* (Berkeley: University of California Press, 1982), 95.

a point of pure truth, a point or spark
which belongs entirely to God.... This little point of nothingness
in us, as our poverty, is the pure glory of God in us....[11]

To enter the God-self, the Christ, is to face the opposites that exist between the ego and the self, and which one experiences as inner conflict. As Saint Paul confessed: "I don't really understand myself, for I want to do what is right, but I don't do it. Instead, I do what I hate" (Rom 7:15). Reconciling the opposites within is to hold the opposites in tension, which involves suffering and accepting the limits of our lives. Jung's spirituality is similar to the Twelve Steps program of Alcoholics Anonymous, namely, facing the truth within oneself and realizing there is a greater power within. Such realization begins the process of individuation. The healing process of the self begins with acceptance and surrendering to a "higher power" by which the inner conflicts of the self are eventually reconciled. If we do not do this, we run the risk of depriving ourselves of our true self, living unfulfilled lives of quiet desperation. Without the process of individuation, we can project the fractured inner soul of darkness onto others and identify the other as the problem, when in fact the problem of division lies within us. Those who live from a reconciled heart see every situation as an invitation to love in a new way, even in the face of rejection. Every moment becomes an invitation to creative love in the flow of life.

Jung points to the quest for perfection, citing Matthew 5:48: "Be you therefore perfect." Perfection here means wholeness. To strive for wholeness is to encounter, accept, and reconcile our inner opposites. Jesus reflects a wholeness born from the heart; thus, Jung concludes, Christ is our nearest analogy of the self and its meaning.[12] He writes:

If one inclines to regard the archetype of the self as the real agent and hence takes Christ as a symbol of the self, one must bear in mind that there is a considerable difference

---

11. Thomas Merton, *Conjectures of a Guilty Bystander* (Melbourne: Image Books, 1968), 158.

12. Carl Jung, "Christ, Symbol of the Self," *Collected Works* 9 (Pt.2).

between *perfection* and *completeness*. The Christ-image is as good as perfect (at least it is meant to be so), while the archetype (so far as known) denotes completeness but is far from being perfect. It is a paradox, a statement about something indescribable and transcendental.[13]

Christ is archetypal to a high degree, but this archetype is the unconscious precondition of every human life. This, too, is what Raimon Panikkar suggested. He describes a deep inner center in the human person with the capacity to manifest Christ, what he calls "Christophany."[14] The term has as its root the *phaneros* of the Christian scriptures: a visible, clear, public manifestation of a truth: "Christophany stands for the disclosure of Christ to human consciousness and the critical reflection upon it."[15] God is not an idea to be proved or even believed, but a psychological fact of immediate experience:

> The Christian Incarnation is a universal human event unless we reduce Jesus Christ to a mere historical being. If we sever Christ from his humanity, he becomes a platonic ideal of perfection and an instrument of dominion and exploitation of others. If we break his humanity from his historical walking on earth and his historical roots, we convert him into a mere Gnostic figure who does not share our concrete and limited human condition. In Jesus, the finite and infinite meet; the human and divine are united; the material and spiritual are one. Whoever sees Jesus Christ sees the prototype of all humanity, the *totus homo*, the full man—the new Adam.[16]

Panikkar states that the task of Christians (today)—"perhaps even our kairos—may be the conversion...of a tribal Christology

---

13. Jung, "Christ, Symbol of the Self," 123.

14. Raimon Panikkar, "A Christophany for Our Times," *Theology Digest* 139, no. 1 (1992): 5.

15. Panikkar, "A Christophany for Our Times," 5.

16. Panikkar, "A Christophany for Our Times," 20.

into a christophany less bound to a single cultural event."[17] What happens in the life of Christ happens always and everywhere; the Christic signifies a life open to divinity, inherent in everyone. Each person lives out an archetypal life.

It takes a lifetime to become conscious of this Christic reality. Jung contends that God needs the human to show God to Godself. He wrote: "Existence is only real when it is conscious to somebody. That is why the Creator needs conscious man."[18] As Dourley points out, "for Jung, the drive to individuation is the empowering telos of life, a holy task in which the human rediscovers her or his nature as image of God."[19] Jung spoke of the unconscious as the image of God, indicating that God is always transcendent wholeness, beyond what can be fully actualized. His real concern is saving the human person from the existential dread of nothingness.

THE INDIVIDUATION OF GOD: JUNG AND TEILHARD

Monotheistic religions have avoided the psychic dimension of human personhood. Christians, in particular, have excluded the psychic or conscious dimension of Jesus's life from any doctrinal consideration, but this is exactly what is distinct about Jesus of Nazareth, a new awareness of God's immanent presence. By focusing on substance and nature, Christianity has excised the core of the New Testament and forged it into a juridical religion in which abstract philosophical concepts replace the role of the mind. One has only to note how the liturgy, beautiful as it is in its patristic prayers and rituals, exteriorizes the mind, as attention is drawn toward the altar and the priest who stands in the place of Christ.

Jung may have disclosed the truth of the New Testament by universalizing the incarnation; human individuation is integral to

17. Raimon Panikkar, *Christophany: The Fullness of Man* (Maryknoll, NY: Orbis Books, 2004), 162.

18. Jung, "Answer to Job," *Collected Works* 11, para. 575.

19. John Dourley, *The Psyche as Sacrament: A Comparative Study of C. G. Jung and Paul Tillich* (Ontario: Inner City Books, 1981), 78.

God's own life. New Testament spirituality is a transformative process, an alchemy of the spirit. Jung and Teilhard share a view of basic reality as that which does not consist of parts but is one unfragmented whole, the *unus mundus*, based on the complementarity of mind and matter. Jung, like Teilhard, maintained that religion is not a special act of divine grace but a natural process of individuation. In his essay, "The Spirit of the Earth (1931)," Teilhard wrote that the true function of religion is "to sustain and spur on the progress of life."[20] The religious function increases in the same direction and to the same extent as "hominization," that is, the emergence and growth of religion corresponds to the growth of the human person. The emergence of the human person *in nature* as a conscious, self-reflective being brings about the emergence of a divine pole, a direction toward what lies up ahead. The purpose of religion, therefore, is to sustain the "human zest for life."[21] Teilhard wrote that religion is primarily "on the level of consciousness and human action, rather than on the level of institutions or belief systems, except insofar as these systems manifest and give direction to the former."[22]

Both Jung and Teilhard thought that consciousness is the mirror of the universe and has evolved to a complex level of reflection in which consciousness itself is revealed. Consciousness and religion are correlative to each other in the progression of human evolution, from preaxial to axial and second axial periods. Religion is a function of consciousness and consciousness of transcendent reality is the basis of religion. The integral relationship between consciousness and religion led Jung and Teilhard to claim that religion, as most of the Western world knows it, has ended. Religion is not due to supernatural grace or special revelation but is a natural process of development. Jung introduced the concept of the psyche as central to the religious self and proposed

20. Pierre Teilhard de Chardin, *Human Energy*, trans. J. M. Cohen (New York: Harcourt Brace Jovanovich, 1979), 44.

21. Ursula King, *Teilhard de Chardin and Eastern Religions: Spirituality and Mysticism in an Evolutionary World* (Mahwah, NJ: Paulist Press, 2011), 186.

22. Pierre Teilhard de Chardin, *Activation of Energy*, trans. René Hague (New York: Harcourt Brace Jovanovich, 1963), 241.

that the evolution from the ego to the "self" as the stabilizing center of the personality has up to now produced what he called the "modern human." The human person has emerged "as individual" in the proper sense.[23]

We are now in the midst of the second axial period, an age of ecological consciousness and intersubjectivity. The individuation of God may seem *prima facie* to reflect first axial consciousness, but it connotes deep relationality. The more one is reconciled inwardly on the level of Christ consciousness, the more one lives by the life of the whole. To "put on the mind of Christ" is to live from a new awareness of interbeing, what is termed today "posthuman" or "rhizomic subjectivity," the interweaving relationships of shared life.

Interbeing and individuation are related. The path to self-realization or individuation requires one to plunge into the depths of God and into the depths of darkness. The Franciscan theologian Bonaventure wrote: "There is no other path than through the burning love of the Crucified."[24] There is no path to God without passing through the struggles, sufferings, and failures of life. This being the case, one must train the mind for higher things. Consciousness acts like an "agential cut"; one can experience God as the infinite horizon of goodness, beauty, and truth, or one can refuse to acknowledge the experience of anything. The more human consciousness awakens to God and lives from an integrated center of wholeness, the more one becomes "person." A person is a deeply relational being who lives by the life of the whole, and one who lives by the life of the whole lives a Godly life.

The Eastern Church uses the term "divinization" (or *theosis*) to describe the process of becoming Godly by the Spirit of divine energy or divine love. The Spirit of God grows us *from the inside out*, physically, emotionally, and mentally. Reconciling the inner Spirit of God with the opposites and tensions of the self is a growth in

---

23. William M. Thompson, *Christ and Consciousness: Exploring Christ's Contribution to Human Consciousness* (New York: Paulist Press, 1977), 21.

24. Bonaventure, *Itinerarium Mentis in Deum* 7.6. Engl. trans. Ewert H. Cousins, *Bonaventure: The Soul's Journey into God, The Tree of Life, The Major Life of Saint Francis* (New York: Paulist Press, 1978).

the energies of love, which leads to a more explicit expression of our divine entanglement. Such inner growth brought to the level of conscious action is expressed in personal transformation which energizes the world. This is what Teilhard anticipates by using the term, "zest for life," an energy of life that enkindles and furthers evolution.

THE DEVELOPMENT OF THE GODSELF

Twentieth-century studies in depth psychology and levels of consciousness have made tremendous development since Jung and Freud. There are different schools of thought on how consciousness develops in the human person, but the basic trajectory is a movement through stages from the isolated ego to the self as a fully integrated person. These stages of consciousness are heuristics or models of development, especially in light of what we know today about the brain and its capacity for change, described by the term "neuroplasticity." The process of conscious maturation is complex, and various sciences, such as quantum physics, chaos theory, and emergence, are helping to define the mysterious workings of the mind. While I do not subscribe to any particular model of conscious growth, I do think such models are helpful in understanding the evolution of the human person. Here I rely on the stages of conscious growth described by Jim Marion, whose work on Christ consciousness was inspired by Jung. The following is a brief summary of each stage:

Archaic Consciousness:
This stage begins with the infant's differentiation of its own body from that of its mother, and, second, the differentiation of the infant's emotions from those of the mother. This level is primarily a physical (and later emotional) level of consciousness, one ruled by sensations and impulses. According to Jung, human beings begin life in a state of original wholeness in our earliest infancy, when neither ego nor consciousness formally exist; however, the latent ego is in complete identification with the structures of the unconscious. The infant experiences him/herself "quite literally as the center of the universe." The earliest encounters with reality fracture this orig-

inal unity as the infant's demands eventually begin to be rejected by the world. This limitation displaces the child from its place of privilege. The child is thus exiled from paradise, and a permanent wounding and separation occur. Jung calls this wounding alienation.

Magical Consciousness:
This level of consciousness is the level of magical thinking in a young child, usually between the ages of two to seven years old. In the state of magical consciousness the child cannot clearly distinguish between its own emerging mental images and symbols and the external world. On the level of culture, magical consciousness is the average and dominant consciousness of most tribal cultures. With respect to religion, this is the level of animism, which sees the sky, thunder, and other natural phenomena as "alive" and controllable by magic words and ceremonies.

Mythic Consciousness:
This is the level of consciousness that emerges around age seven and continues to adolescence, around age fourteen. Here, the mind begins to grasp and understand general rules. The child also begins to realize the importance of specific cultural roles, such as mother and father. This is a conformist "law and order" stage of development. Confusion can arise by opposing laws or rules. The inner world at this level is popularized by cultural gods, such as Santa Claus and the Easter Bunny. On the institutional religious level, it is the stage of the "sky God" who can rearrange the world, works miracles, and punish, if necessary. Religious people who are stuck in mythic consciousness will see the followers of other religions as "evil" or "heretics." People at this level are psychologically incapable of thinking "globally." Marion states that this is the level of monotheistic religions, in general.

Rational Consciousness:
This level of consciousness is more or less attained by the average adult in contemporary society. The passage from mythic into rational consciousness is the primary spiritual task of adolescence. A person who thinks on the lower level of rational consciousness usually has few original thoughts or insights. A higher level of rational consciousness seeks to expand the mind to embrace

complex ideas. To be reborn into rational consciousness, one must die to the mythic worldview, which can be difficult. Higher-level rational consciousness dominates the world in terms of education, government, science, technology, business, and politics.

Vision-Logic Consciousness:
This is the highest of the three mental levels of consciousness and is associated with the abstract mind. At this level, persons are more grounded within themselves and unafraid to take bold steps or advance original ideas. This is the level of the integrated personality. At this level, we have a global perspective, and no longer define the self in narrow terms of race, color, gender, sexual orientation, or national origin. Tolerance and appreciation for diversity also mark this level.

Psychic Consciousness:
At this level, one no longer identifies the self with the rational mind. Instead, one identifies the self with the inner witness that observes body, emotions, and mind. Evelyn Underhill called this level, the "awakening of the self," that is, awakening to the deeper part of the self, the psyche that transcends space and time. We awaken to the energies of the psyche and astral body; we awaken to the energies of the soul. This stage is the beginning level of mystical knowing, clairvoyance, religious intuition, energy alignment, and prophecy.

Christ Consciousness:
As one progresses through the depth of psychic consciousness, one encounters the dark night of the soul, including the stripping of senses and emotions, the feeling of abandonment and darkness. However, a small wisp of inner light can hold the traveler through this rugged terrain of the soul, as one plods on through darkness, strengthened by faith and hope. Eventually, there is a breakthrough or a piercing of the veil that hides the infinite ground within. Meister Eckhart advised emptying yourself of everything, that is to say, emptying yourself of your ego and all things and of all that you are in yourself, and consider yourself as what you are in God. God is beyond being, a paradoxical allness

and nothingness beyond being. Therefore, be still and do not flinch from this emptiness.[25]

The progression of consciousness *is* the evolution of the self. Every person has the capacity for change and growth. As Charlotte Tomaino writes, "when inner reality is stronger than outer reality one can act from choice, creating one's own life."[26] Jung thought that the process of individuation was integral to history itself. He said that God and human are to be united in human consciousness as the depth meaning of history, both personal and collective. This historical process is at once redemptive of the divine ground and of human consciousness. Hence, the meaning of the Christ is not merely a religious idea but a historical and cosmic one; divine immanence is a universal power underlying all that is. To be reconciled with God as person is to live a Christic life.

As one approaches the ground of the psyche, the chaos of darkness dissolves into the light of God; one attains a level of Christ consciousness. Merton writes: "It is here, in this poverty, that man regains the eternal being that once he was, now is and evermore shall be."[27] At this level of the soul, one experiences unitive love and true compassion. Often there is a great peace at this level, as well; nothing disturbs the soul, whether having to do with sorrow or with joy. One who reaches this level attains non-dual consciousness whereby one ascends into the "kingdom of heaven," that is, the nondual vision of the world, the divine milieu in its radiance, the ineffable level of the selfless-self, where "self" is the experience of the All. As Marion states: "[A] person with nondual consciousness is a liberated soul" (cf. John 8:32).[28]

The stage of consciousness at which God is fully transparent in the person is that of Christ consciousness. This is the level,

---

25. Matthew Fox, *Breakthrough: Meister Eckhart's Creation Spirituality in New Translation* (Garden City, NY: Image Books, 1980), 104, 178, 242.

26. Charlotte Tomaino, *Awakening the Brain: The Neuropsychology of Grace* (New York: Atria Books, 2012), 52.

27. Thomas Merton, *Zen and the Birds of Appetite* (New York: New Directions, 1968), 23.

28. Jim Marion, *Putting on the Mind of Christ: The Inner Work of Christian Spirituality* (Charlottesville, VA: Hampton Roads Publishing Company, 2011), 214.

according to Todd, where the divinization or resacralization of the world is realized. As we become whole with the aliveness of God, our lives become holy and divinely radiant. The world too becomes holy and sacred. To reframe the incarnation as a process of divinization and individuation is to awaken to the holiness of everything, the divine milieu. Todd states: "The human evolves from an incomplete whole to a new level of completion and thus a *new vision*, a new knowing and new acting in the world."[29] We begin to see things the way *they are*, not as we are. Teilhard put it this way: "One can say that the whole of life lies in seeing—if not ultimately, at least essentially....Unity grows...only if it is supported by an increase of consciousness, of vision."[30] He adds that "if we lack these qualities of sight, no matter what anyone does to show us, the human being will indefinitely remain for us...an erratic object in a disconnected world."[31] A widened vision brings the whole into a new field of conscious reality. By bringing consciousness into unconscious darkness through a confrontation of the self; by facing our fears, failure, and anxieties, the unresolved darkness of God within, our inner chaos and confusion is confronted and reconciled, releasing us from separation and bringing us into light. We are liberated from being something in particular, with an identity is defined by our profession or lifestyle, and become united with the ALL, seeing in all things the light of divine love. As we come to a higher consciousness of God and thus wholeness in love, God *becomes* God in us. This "becoming God in us" is incarnation. Christ is not the great exception to humanity; Christ is every person who makes the journey in love.

The individuation process passes through the stages of the ego until we recognize the next stage of human becoming which, increasingly, is God's becoming. Indeed, without the process of individuation, God remains simply a possibility, an unresolved potential. The individuation process of incarnation is no longer

29. Todd, "Teilhard and Other Modern Thinkers on Evolution, Mind, and Matter," 5.

30. Pierre Teilhard de Chardin, *The Human Phenomenon*, trans. Sarah Appleton-Weber (Brighton: Sussex Academic Press, 1999), 3.

31. Teilhard de Chardin, *The Human Phenomenon*, 5.

an idea but a reality, personally actualized, and makes a difference to what the world becomes. The inextricable relationship of God and world is the full meaning of the divine Word incarnate.

THE INDIVIDUATION OF GOD AS A CO-CREATIVE PROCESS

Jung, like Teilhard de Chardin, was a process thinker. He maintained that God and humanity are in an entangled state and the individuation of each is inextricably bound with the other. *The evolution of God and the evolution of humanity cannot be separated.* God and human form a whole, and the whole is the Christic, the person who is more God than self and more self than God. Every human person has the potential to manifest Christ, because every person is divine and entangled with the energies of divine love. Teilhard's thought is complemented by Jung's insights. Since Christ symbolizes the capacity of the human for divine wholeness, every person can realize their capacity for infinite love. Christ symbolizes the archetypal "self," the psychic totality of the individual. As the one who reconciles the darkness of evil with the light of truth, Christ is the symbol of wholeness and unity. Without the integration of evil, there is no totality. Since the goal of psychological and biological development is self-realization, the process of individuation *is* incarnation and undergirds the openness of God to *pleroma*.

It is in the evolution of God and humanity together that beauty unfolds. Beauty is the "harmony of contrasts," according to Whitehead. Beauty is the myriad fractals of divine light radiating through thousands upon thousands of colored, gendered human Christic faces, each a unique face of God. In the infinite beauty of the human person, we see the infinite beauty of God. *The flesh that weeps and laughs; the mother weeping for her lost son, the child dancing with bare feet on the wet grass, filled with joy—in the many events of our lives, God springs up from within and is overflowing with life.*

As we awaken to the God-depth of our own lives, we become more than shadows of our true selves, merely human; we become light-filled human, ultrahuman. We see the whole in a flash of the eye and abound with love-energy, even in the midst of uncertainty. In Teilhard's view, we must aim beyond the "ego" toward the "superego," the "hyperpersonal," whereby shared life is the life of the self in union with others. "Union differentiates," Teilhard wrote. Whether it is the cells of the body or the members of a society, single lives are perfected and fulfilled in union with others.[32] When consciousness draws together and deepens, love unifies. Shared life is the entangled Godself. Every act of shared life forms the soul in a new way. When we share life, we no longer covet life for the self; we surrender it in order to find it on a deeper level. Shared life means we no longer have complete control over the self; rather, we live in openness to the possibilities of more life; we take risks by opening up to the potentials of new relationships. Shared life is love in action. We become more human because we live from a deeper center of God life, the life of the whole. We arrive at our deepest humanity, which is divine.

We are inextricably bound up with God and we help complete God by realizing the potential of our created existence in its divine reality.[33] Every single person has the divine light within; every single person radiates the life of God. When we awaken to the reality of God as the deepest center of our existence, we live in hope that the world can be recreated in justice, that the future will be different. When we live in God, we live in the future; we dream, hope, create, and travel lightly on this cosmic journey. The future depends on our choices in the moments we are given. We can help build up this world in love and radiate the glory of God or we can tear it into pieces in a bloody battle for survival. What Jung and Teilhard help us realize is that God's life and our lives are a single entangled life. We are bound up with each other, our lives with God, God's life with ours, and our lives with each another and with every living creature. Our task is to actualize this entangled whole by making the inner journey in the flow of evolution. Wholeness beckons us because it is already within us. We potentially have the life we are looking for.

---

32. Teilhard de Chardin, *The Human Phenomenon*, 262.

33. Pierre Teilhard de Chardin, *The Heart of Matter*, trans. René Hague (New York: Harcourt Brace Jovanovich, 1979), 53.

8

Christ as Archetype

When the early Church Fathers gathered in Nicaea to discuss the divinity of Jesus Christ, psychology was not factored into the discussion. The mind was unknown territory for these early theologians; the disciplines of modern science had not yet been born. The Fathers tried to reason out Jesus's divinity on the basis of several different concepts, using Greek philosophy to help understand the union of divine and human natures. A creed of faith was promulgated, and, to this day, a fourth-century confession of faith continues to dominate the liturgy. Through a rather turbulent history of development, the doctrine of Christ was officially formulated at the Council of Chalcedon, which took place in the fifth century. At this council, both the East and West agreed that Jesus Christ is true God and true man (*sic*), without change, division, confusion, or separation. Divine and human natures, they claimed, are in perfect agreement. Let us look at this history in more detail to assess the problem of an outdated Christology.

DOCTRINE AND CHURCH POLITICS

The Council of Nicaea in 325 CE was pivotal for the development of Christology. The events surrounding the council, however, were politically tumultuous. The Christian problem of God's incarnation began with Arius, who held to the transcendence of God as absolute. Arius, a priest in Alexandria, proposed a unitarian monotheism rooted in the absolute self-sufficient God. Apparently, he had heard a speech by the new Pope of Alexandria as being a revival of Sabellianism, which basically taught that the Father, Son, and Spirit were three modes of the same God, rather than three divine persons in one common nature. Arius opposed this view and argued that "if the Father begat the Son, he that was begotten had a beginning of existence: and from this it is evident that there was a time when the Son was not. It therefore necessarily follows, that he [the Son] had his substance from nothing."[1] Arius retained the absolute unity and immutability of God by relegating the Logos and Spirit to the domain of the finite and intermediary.

At the heart of the Arian debates was the question of suffering. If Jesus is *homoousios* (one in substance) with God, then God would suffer like Jesus. For the Greeks, God could not be passible; that is, God could not be affected by something else or "suffer" (*paschein*). Divine impassibility was also closely connected with other aspects of the Greek understanding of God, such as immutability and omnipotence, whereas suffering is connected with time, change, and matter, which mark the material world. However, theologians held that God is eternal in the sense of being outside time; furthermore, God is incorporeal, absolute, fully actualized perfection. Therefore, God is simply Being itself and cannot change, because any change could only be change for the worse. Arianism was rooted in the idea of an absolutely self-sufficient God, one who is immutable and outside time.

---

1. Socrates, "The Dispute of Arius with Alexander, His Bishop," *The Ecclesiastical Histories of Socrates Scholasticus*. Retrieved May 2, 2022, https://www.ccel.org/ccel/schaff/npnf202.ii.iv.v.html.

Arius held that the Son was the firstborn of the Father and thus not equal to God. He and his followers taught that Jesus Christ is not true God. The basic argument was simply that the divine Father cannot become man and suffer. Rather, the Father is God in the highest sense and is impassible, that is, he cannot suffer. The bishop of Alexandria, Athanasius, argued that Jesus Christ is truly God by nature. The Son to whom is communicated the entire essence of the Father proceeds from the Father but is unoriginate in the sense of being one with the Father in substance. While Arius sought to retain a strict distinction between God's inner life and God's action in creation, Athanasius said that God became human so that the human could become God.[2] The Council of Nicaea in 325 CE affirmed that Jesus Christ is consubstantial —"of the same substance" (*homoousios*)—with the Father; however, it was unclear how the constituent person of Jesus Christ was human and divine. It took another century of heated discussions to arrive at a consensus of doctrine.

The Council of Chalcedon was convened in 451 CE and brokered a political compromise between the Eastern Church, represented by Cyril of Alexandria, and the Western Church, represented by Nestorius. According to the Eastern Church, Christ had one divine nature (monophysitism), while according to the Western Church, Christ had two natures, divine and human (dyophysitism). A compromise between the polarized positions was drawn up by the bishops attending the Council. It was agreed that Christ had two complete but distinct natures: divine and human, and that these operated together in one person. According to the decree:

> Therefore, following the holy fathers, we all unite in teaching that we should confess one and the same Son, our Lord Jesus Christ. This same one is perfect in deity, and the same one is perfect in humanity; the same one is true God and true man, comprising a rational soul and a body. He is of the same essence *(homousios)* as the Father according to his deity, and the same one is of the same essence *(homousios)* with us according to his humanity,

2. Saint Athanasius, *De Incarnatione*, 54.3.

like us in all things except sin. He was begotten before the ages from the Father according to his deity, but in the last days for us and our salvation, the same one was born of the Virgin Mary, the bearer of God *(Theotokos)*, according to his humanity. He is one and the same Christ, Son, Lord, and Only Begotten, who is made known in two natures *(physeis)* united unconfusedly, unchangeably, indivisibly, inseparably. The distinction between the natures *(physeis)* is not at all destroyed because of the union, but rather the property of each nature *(physis)* is preserved and concurs together into one person *(prosopon)* and subsistence *(hypostasis)*. He is not separated or divided into two persons *(prosopa)*, but he is one and the same Son, the Only Begotten, God the Logos, the Lord Jesus Christ.[3]

The Council proceedings were highly charged and bitterly polemical; however, the solution sought at Chalcedon affirmed the unity of Jesus's person and the duality of his natures. The four essential factors needed for an accurate understanding of Jesus, called "the Chalcedonian box," were: divinity, humanity, the unity of one person, and the distinction of the two natures. Jesus Christ is "one person, who is both divine and human." Nevertheless, Chalcedon created "the problem of Christ" in a way that was foreign to the New Testament.

First, it did not define its key terms, "nature" (φύσις, physis) and "person" (πρόσωπον/ὑπόστασις, prosöpon/ hypostasis), leaving them open to speculation. Second, it did not specifically articulate Christ's preexistence in any way, such as in the Divine Logos. Third, it made no reference to Jesus's historical, public life, not even to his birth, crucifixion, and resurrection, leaving the impression that the incarnation alone accomplishes all of Christ's mission. Fourth, it did not come to terms with how this overlapping of natures might actually operate in one person.

Chalcedon resolved the dilemma about the two natures of Christ by appeasing political factions, but the resolution functionally created an insoluble problem. How can two distinct natures

---

3. See Donald Fairbairn, "The Chalcedonian Definition: Two Natures," *Credo* (February 18, 2021).

be united in a single person? By "nature," the Council meant a set of essential properties that distinguish what sort of thing an individual substance is. The early Church did everything possible to preserve the divinity of God in light of the Arian heresy, while affirming the two natures of Christ. What the Church sought to avoid at all costs was the possibility of hybridity that would result in a *tertium quid*, a third thing, or a kind of "third nature." It also sought to avoid any type of pantheism or Gnosticism. Jesus had the divine properties of perfection, omniscience, and omnipresence, yet he was a fully human being. The Church eventually settled on a doctrinal resolution, namely, that Christ has two natures and operates with two wills. In this resolution, the Church used the phrase *communicatio idiomatum*, or "communication of properties," to artificially bridge an ontological gap between the two natures. This effort reconciled the differences between those who held to a single divine nature in Christ (the Alexandrians) and those who maintained two distinct but interactive natures (the Antiochenes).

F. LeRon Shults quipped: "Divinity is not a substance that 'fills' other things by fitting into their boundaries, and humanity is not a substance whose boundaries are threatened by such filling."[4] But this is exactly how the early Church formulated an understanding of Jesus Christ, as one filled by the substances of divinity and humanity. Chalcedon was essentially a power game and play on language. It explained how to speak of Jesus Christ without saying anything about the significance of Christ; hence, we might say it was politically correct but theologically superficial. Putting the person of Jesus Christ into a philosophical straitjacket has enervated the significance of Christ and the mystery of God.

JESUS, THE NEW PERSON

Monotheistic religions have avoided the psychic dimension of human personhood. Christians, in particular, have excluded the psychic or conscious dimension of Jesus's life from any doctrinal

---

4. F. LeRon Shults, *Christology and Science* (London: Taylor and Francis, 2021), 57.

consideration. Christian doctrine has been taught and memorized by millions of people throughout the ages and has been the bedrock of Christian faith. The belief that Jesus Christ is true God is a confession of faith, rendering Jesus the great exception to humanity. According to doctrine, Jesus is distinguished as the unique and absolute savior, the axis of universal salvation, the foundation of the Church. Yet consciousness is what distinguishes Jesus of Nazareth. He was a faithful Jew who had a new awareness of God's immanent presence. By focusing on substance and nature, Christianity ignored the role of the mind in Jesus's experience of God. Substance-language came to define the natures of Christ.

In the early nineteenth century, the Protestant theologian Friedrich Schleiermacher (d. 1834), in reaction to the formula of Chalcedon, developed a Christology based on consciousness. His protests were aimed at the terminology of "two natures in one person." The single term "nature," he argued, ought not to be used for both the divine and the human in Christ. Schleiermacher said it is inappropriate to speak of God as having a "nature," since the term "nature" (in his view) refers to a limited existence, conditioned and divided and corporeal, subject to the flux of activity and passivity, while God is unconditioned, absolute, pure activity and beyond time. Worse still, he claimed, the relation between "nature" and "person" in the two-natures doctrine is nonsensical. In general, "nature" is a universal term that includes many individuals; but, in the two-natures doctrine, one individual has two natures. Similarly, Schleiermacher noted that assigning a duality of natures to the person of the redeemer contradicts the very life-unity that the word "person" describes. Confusingly, the two-natures doctrine speaks of a unity of nature while the doctrine of the Trinity speaks of a unity of essence. He wondered if the second person of the Trinity has a divine nature of its own (which is united to the human nature in Christ) in addition to its participation in the divine essence.

The inconsistency between the language of the doctrines of Christ and of the Trinity compromised the clarity of the dogmatic system. For Schleiermacher, the main problem with the two-natures doctrine is its lack of connection to Christian life. Its formulation is problematic and cannot give any guidance to the proper preaching of Christ. Furthermore, it has failed to serve as a guide for understanding the relation between the divine and human in Christ.

To avoid the problems of the two-natures doctrine, Schleiermacher gave Christ a full human constitution and posited God in Jesus as a continual living presence or power of God-consciousness, not as an alleged divine property or nature. For Schleiermacher, God-consciousness and the existence of God in Jesus are exactly the same thing. Jesus is fully human, with all the limitations of embodiment and finite consciousness. Yet, in Jesus, each moment of self-consciousness expresses the divine in virtue of his absolute dependence upon God while being fully active in relation to world. What makes Jesus unique is that his God-consciousness is constantly and fully active and powerful, unlike that of all other humans, whose God-consciousness is clouded and inhibited. Since God-consciousness itself is part of human nature, one can reasonably say that there is nothing in the constitutional makeup of Jesus that cannot be found in all other humans. Jesus has what other humans have (a God-consciousness), but in a perfectly ordered and complete way. Since he has perfect God-consciousness in a human nature, Jesus is a new creation—a "new implanting" of the God-consciousness in human nature—in a way that is understood as God's being through his perfection and steadiness.

Writing in a different age and through a critique of power, Beatrice Bruteau describes Jesus as one who showed a "neofeminine" consciousness, a consciousness of connectivity, mercy, passion, and freedom. This new consciousness evoked a genuine revolution, a "whole new way of seeing our relations to one another," changing our behavior patterns from the inside out. Jesus offered a new vision, "a consciousness of the whole where each person is valued equally."[5] His consciousness of wholeness evoked a genuine revolution in cosmic and social relations, a new creativity, a new structure of existence based on community and shared values. He constantly challenged others to "see," to awaken to the presence of God and to be part of an undivided

---

5. Beatrice Bruteau, *The Grand Option: Personal Transformation and a New Creation* (Notre Dame, IN: University of Notre Dame Press, 2007), 28.

whole, the "kin-dom of God," where Jew and Gentile, rich and poor, male and female are invited as equals to the divine banquet. He lived from his deep oneness in God by going "all over Galilee, preaching the Good News of the Kingdom, and healing people from every kind of disease and sickness" (Matt 4:23). He knew God as the source of wholeness and life. He challenged those who wanted to maintain fixed doctrines and beliefs that thwarted the in-breaking presence of God. His new religious consciousness called for a new way of understanding an immanent God: "No one tears a piece out of a new garment to patch an old one. Otherwise, they will have torn the new garment, and the patch from the new will not match the old. No, new wine must be poured into new wineskins" (Luke 5:36–38).

The most significant aspect of the life of Jesus is the role of the new mind in shaping the new person. The mind is the place of knowing, feeling, emotion, and intuition, the place of the heart: "Where your treasure is, there your heart will be also" (Luke 12:34; Matt 6:21). Saint Paul said we are to be transformed by a new mind (Rom 12:2). The new religious consciousness ushered in by Jesus called for a new type of worship: "Destroy this temple and I will raise it up in three days" (John 2:19). Jesus identified the temple with his own body, indicating that the living God dwells in the living person, not in concrete walls or buildings (John 2:21; 1 Cor 3:17). Language of mind and temple, body and spirit, suggests something radically new breaking in through the life of Jesus of Nazareth. Acquiring a new religious consciousness means that the human person discovers a new locus of sacred meaning—the world—the place where God is emerging. Matter, mind, person, community, all form the matrix of the living God. Consciousness brings the living God into the personal expression of active engagement.

THE HUMAN PERSON 2.0

Jesus's Godly life takes on new meaning in our own age of quantum physics and evolution. Christology is a function of anthropology. How we understand the human person is how we interpret the significance of Jesus of Nazareth. Clearly, a narrow understanding of the human person does not allow us to interpret the radical transformation of Jesus's life in terms of quantum reality. Either Jesus shows us the full capacity of cosmic human life, or he is the great exception to all humanity. To engage a new Christology, we must update our understanding of the human person.

Evolution opens a new window to the human person. We humans are not fixed or biologically static; we do not appear on earth as fully formed rational subjects. Rather, we are dynamic becomings, like eddies in the flowing stream of life. With Katherine Hayles, we must regard the category of person as historically contingent, rather than stable, in our ontology; we have not always been the way that we currently are. Quantum physics suggests that we humans are matter-energy constellations, more like dynamic and complex systems than individual parts. Today, the term "posthuman" signifies the rise of a new understanding of subjectivity. Deep relationality marks the holism of nature, and since humans are a complex facet of nature, deep relationality distinguishes human identity. We have a transpersonal capacity for new life that rejects universalism. Rather, we are grounded in the radical immanence of a sense of belonging and being accountable to a community. Relationality, not betterment, is the operative word of posthuman life. Humans are part of a deep relational wholeness that is characteristic of nature itself. Humans belong to nature; we are part of nature's becoming. Humans are part of the surrounding world, including culture, other creatures, plant life, animal life, solar life, and elemental life.

Complex dynamical thinking impels us to think of humans as integrated into wider systems of relationality. Donna Haraway expounds deep relationality in a way that reflects the posthuman concern. The term *poiesis*, or the artistic ability of nature to craft (techne) relationships into particular forms, means that humans are never an isolated or special species, but a species being formed in relationship with all other forms of life; we are part of "sympoietic systems," that is, we "become-with" other forms of life in the ongoing emergence of life. The sympoietic human is relational being, a "we" in which the "I" is constantly emerging through the construction and reconstruction of relationships. Michael Burdett and Victoria Lorrimar put it this way: "We are but the inheritors of an entwined history and actors within a present biological-social-cultural-technological system and, as such, are a being-in-relation."[6] That is, we are part of an intrinsically connected whole.

The posthuman is a hybrid creature emerging in an information-rich, computer-driven, networked world. The term "cyborg," borrowed from the information sciences, is an abbreviation of "cybernetic organism" and expresses the capacity of biological nature to be joined to or hybridized with non-biological nature, such as a prosthetic device. Haraway used the symbol of the cyborg to define the emergent boundaries of personhood. The basic idea of the cyborg is that a human can fuse or be merged with something other than human in a way that optimizes function. Cyborgs appear where boundaries are transgressed. The cyborg disrupts persistent dualisms and challenges us to search for ways to study human identity as a cultural construction rather than a given. The emergence of the cyborg as a hybrid organism tells us something about nature that jars our prevailing understanding of nature as fixed and inert. Nature is not dead but a vital flow of living processes. Biological boundaries are not essential or universal but local; boundaries can change as living entities form new relationships. The concept of hybridity destabilizes a concept of human personhood as bounded substance. We cannot assume to know what constitutes human nature, because what counts as human or nature is not self-evident.

The notion of human personhood must shift to a broader conceptualization of the person. The cyborg offers a way out of the maze of dualisms (for example, male/female, black/white, divinity/humanity) with which we have identified ourselves. Boundaries are imprecise and, as such, are giving rise to a new understanding of social subjectivity. Boundary-crossing changes human identity, opening up new and positive conceptions of social subjectivity. To consider the human person as cyborg is to understand personhood as open, emergent, and capable of hybridization—aspects of per-

---

6. Michael Burdett and Victoria Lorrimar, "Creatures Bound for Glory: Biotechnological Enhancement and Visions of Human Flourishing," *Society for the Study of Christian Ethics* 32, no. 2 (February 8, 2019): 11.

sonhood that are not found in the classical notion of personhood. The classical definition of the human person was formulated by the sixth-century writer, Boethius, who defined the person as "an incommunicable substance of rational nature."[7]   Today we know that personhood is not only an emergent process but is itself a process of emergence. Bruteau writes that a person is "the creative activity of life as it projects itself to the next instant."[8] If personhood is defined in and through relationships, then the posthuman is the epitome of relationality. John Johnston suggests that, in our networked internet age, the term "human" may come "to be understood less as the defining property of a species or individual and more as a value distributed throughout human-constructed environments, technologies, institutions and social collectivities."[9] The fragility of boundaries and the recursive loop of identity construction through biological emergence means that no category can ontologically define personhood in a final and universal manner; rather, the self is an ongoing dynamical process.

JESUS AS CYBORG

Anne Kull posits the cyborg as a symbol of the incarnation. Two radically different natures are united in a single union symbolized by the person of Jesus Christ. To appreciate Kull's insights is to realize why the Chalcedonian formula of two distinct natures existing in one person *without change or confusion* contradicts the "plasticity" of human personhood. The cyborg signifies that biological essentialism no longer holds true; the individual is not "an individual substance of rational nature." Personhood is not fixed or substantive; rather, biological boundaries can change. The human person is

---

7. This definition is given in Boethius, *Liber de Persona et duabus naturis*, chap. 3.2.

8. Bruteau, *The Grand Option*, 142; cited in Ilia Delio, "Evolution Toward Personhood," *Personal Transformation and a New Creation*, ed. Ilia Delio (Maryknoll, NY: Orbis Books, 2016), 141.

9. John Johnston, *The Allure of Machinic Life: Cybernetics, Artificial Intelligence, and the New AI* (Cambridge, MA: MIT Press, 2008), 7.

constantly formed and reformed by the constitutive relationships of family, culture, genetics, history, and the ongoing development of self-identity in which consciousness plays a fundamental role. Whereas substances require fixed boundaries, relationships require ongoing negotiation of boundaries.

The incarnation can be understood as neither a biological nor a sociological category but as a point of overlap among divine, physical, symbolic, and material social conditions. Jesus as cyborg refers to a human being in a particular relationship to divinity. Instead of essence and substance, the cyborg's "ontology" is defined in categories of relationality, even hyper-relationality, in which the subject is embedded in multiple, overlapping, shifting relationships. When the human person is seen as part of an entangled system, full expression of human capability can be seen to depend on the splice, the shared space of relationality between natures or relata, rather than being imperiled by it. The cyborg is a way of speaking about Christ as a theandric whole; that is, the intermingling of divine and human energies, a *tertium quid* in evolution. The full expression of Christ's person can be seen precisely to depend on the theandric "splice," the inextricable union and shared life between divinity and humanity.

Jesus is the one who comes in many guises, and who can be represented neither once and for all nor for everybody's satisfaction. Raised in a Jewish household and formed according to Jewish law and customs, Jesus was a faithful Jew and showed no signs of converting to a new religion. He was born of a woman, in time, meaning that Jesus was a physical human being. He seemed to have a deep awareness of God from an early age, since we are told he engaged in temple discussion with the rabbis at only twelve years of age. As he grew in wisdom, he experienced a divine lure to go into the desert and confront the darkness and confusion of Satan: "Jesus, full of the Holy Spirit, left the Jordan and was led by the Spirit into the wilderness, where for forty days he was tempted by the devil" (Luke 4:1). This interestingly suggests that Jesus faced his own darkness in a solitary way; he confronted the demons that challenged his total reliance on God. He faced his own temptations of the flesh and reconciled them with the power of God's Spirit. Bringing the darkness of God to light within himself, Jesus was empowered to return to Nazareth and enter the temple, where he stood up before the rabbis and read from the Torah:

> The Spirit of the Lord is on me,
> because he has anointed me
> to proclaim good news to the poor.
> He has sent me to proclaim freedom for the prisoners
> and recovery of sight for the blind,
> to set the oppressed free, to proclaim the year of the Lord's
> favor. (Luke 4:18–19)

These words were startling to those around him: "Isn't this the carpenter's son?" they asked. Jesus began his public ministry by revealing a new awareness of God's imminent presence. This announcement was shocking for the Jews who awaited the Messiah: "The coming of the kingdom of God is not something that can be observed, nor will people say, 'Here it is,' or 'There it is,' because the kingdom of God is in your midst" (Luke 17:21). He challenged Jewish customs and laws that put law before spirit, excluding those who did not conform. Jesus showed a new sense of relatedness that clearly upset the Pharisees and teachers of the Law: "This man welcomes sinners and eats with them" (Luke 15:2). Jesus internalized the Torah and challenged those who were addicted to power, those who were blind to the needs of others, leading them to "bind up heavy loads and put them on the shoulders of men and women" (Matt 23:4). He chastised those who substituted legalism for charity or looked down on others, or separated themselves from others, as if being superior (cf. Luke 18:9–11) or of greater authority.

Instead, he ate with outcasts and sinners (Mark 2:15) and, revealing God's merciful love, he accepted as friends those who were declared untouchable. Jesus saw that there was no separation between himself and any other person. He saw all human beings (and, indeed, the whole created universe) as part of himself and called his disciples to a new future. His identity was performative. It was precisely by engaging with others that his own sense of self and mission rose to explicit self-awareness.

He introduced a new pattern of order into the Jewish milieu, a pattern marked by God's immediacy, a new vision for the future, a new type of person. He realized that this new way of life would not come about easily because it called for a whole new way of living into the future. This is the paradox of incarnation, the power of divine love showing up in ordinary people doing ordinary things in an extraordinary way. While Jesus's intimate relationship with God was scandalous, even more so was his acceptance of death as an act of obedience to the will of God. The figure of the suffering servant in Isaiah has long been associated with Jesus's acceptance of death:

> He had no form or comeliness that we should look at him, and no beauty that we should desire him. He was despised and rejected by men; a man of sorrows, and acquainted with grief, and as one from whom men hide their faces he was despised, and we esteemed him not. Surely, he has borne our griefs and carried our sorrows; yet we esteemed him stricken, smitten by God, and afflicted. But he was wounded for our transgressions, he was bruised for our iniquities; upon him was the chastisement that made us whole, and with his stripes we are healed. (Isa 53:2–4)

In this passage from Isaiah, Haraway recognizes multiple stagings of a figure of suffering humanity. Here, the figure of the Incarnation can never be other than a trickster, a check on the arrogances of a reason that would uncover all disguises and force correct vision of a recalcitrant nature in her most secret places. The suffering servant is a check on our hubris; the suffering servant is the paradoxical figure associated with the promise that "the desolate woman will have more children than the wife."[10]

Christians confess belief in the union of humanity and divinity in a universal salvation narrative. Far from the paradoxical figure of the suffering servant, Jesus was forged into a divine universal

---

10. Donna Haraway, *The Haraway Reader* (London: Routledge, 2004), 51.

savior by welding the New Testament with Greek philosophy. But the figure is complex and ambiguous from the start, enmeshed in translations and stagings that are deceiving to the eye. The cyborg exemplifies the fact that we do not have a clearly defined, exhaustive concept of humanity, let alone divinity. Kull states: "[T]he concept of cyborg urges us to see in the Incarnation, and generally in embodiment of any kind . . . emancipation and choice."[11] It also means that life's lawfulness is not binary or dualistic (heaven and hell; matter and spirit; body and soul; God and human). In traditional terms, when the divine Word becomes flesh (Incarnation), God traverses the boundaries of separation (between divinity and creation) to become something new. God enters into bounded existence, yet these boundaries are not fixed, because God constantly transcends each creative moment by taking up the choices or decisions of creaturely life into the divine life and returns them as possibilities in pursuit of new life. Jesus is fully divine and fully human, and yet his person cannot be reduced to either divinity or humanity. As a hybrid creature, Jesus shows the arbitrariness and constructed nature of what is considered the norm. His life and ministry disrupted traditional values. Jesus as cyborg means that no one person or existent can exhaust the presence of God. God is always the more of anything that can exist. Transcending boundaries and forming new relations define the person of the cyborg Christ.

The openness of the cyborg to further relationships more coherently explains the subversive activity of Jesus of Nazareth. He is not the universal man of the enlightenment but a suffering servant whose broken body disrupts our assumptions of what it means to be religious and human as well as our assumptions about God. Asian theologian Kwok Pui-lan claims that Jesus as cyborg is the most hybridized concept in the Christian tradition. The human/divine boundary is unfixed and fluid, contested and constructed, rendering New Testament Christology inclusive and pluriform.

---

11. Anne Kull, "Cyborg Embodiment and the Incarnation," *Currents in Theology and Mission* 28, nos. 3–4 (2001): 284.

The vibrancy of the Christian community is diminished when the space between Jesus and Christ is fixed and rigidly defined. In shifting from a classical Chalcedonian Christology to "Cyborg Christology," the central Christological question shifts as well. The question is not "How can two natures coexist in one person?" but "How does the symbol of Christ affirm life, dignity and freedom?" The cyborg's hybrid ontology points us toward our kinship with the nonhuman and the necessity of constructing a world in which the life, dignity, and freedom of all God's hybrid creatures may be affirmed. To say that Jesus Christ is the exemplary cyborg means that God is to be found in a life recognizably like our own yet also uniquely other. To live within fixed boundaries of the expected that seem to provide stability, security, and certainty is to be dead even while alive; persons who live this way are withered trees and barren soil. In the evolutionary flow of life, we let go of isolated existence in order to flow into new life.

CHRIST AS ARCHETYPE

In the midst of the war-torn twentieth century, Jung challenged the whole Christological infrastructure. Jung may have disclosed the truth of the New Testament by universalizing the incarnation: individuation is integral to God's own life. There is no doubt that Jesus enacted a deep awareness of a Godly-human life. Jung, like Schleiermacher, thought that Christianity had become a "dead system" imprisoned in its dogmatic certitudes. Religion had become a matter of the head, not of the heart. Teilhard, too, thought that the overly rigid dogma of Catholicism paralyzes the human spirit. The power of religion to change the world has in fact divided the world. Clearly, something is off.

However, Jung, like Teilhard, thought Christianity held the key to a renewal of religion in the modern era. Jung's discovery of the psyche as the collective unconscious is a starting point for rethinking religion. It is the prime matter of archetypes and the basis of consciousness. The psyche is where the principal archetype of the self originates. "The self is not only the center but also the whole circumference which embraces both consciousness and unconsciousness."[12] The self is so integrally bound to the psyche that it is difficult to distinguish them. In his essay on "Psychology and Religion," Jung wrote:

> Indeed, it is quite impossible to define the extent and the ultimate character of psychic existence. When we now speak of man we mean the indefinable whole of him, an ineffable totality, which can only be formulated symbolically. I have chosen the term "self" to designate the totality of man, the sum total of his conscious and unconscious contents.[13]

Whereas official Church doctrine developed the doctrine of Christ according to Greek philosophical concepts of nature, Jung spoke of Christ as a symbol to describe the complex depths of the human person. A symbol, Jung states, "is the best possible expression for an unconscious element, whose nature can only be guessed, because it is still unknown."[14] In his essay on the "The Undiscovered Self," Jung elaborates on the pre-existence of the psyche as the ground of the individual:

> Without consciousness there would, practically speaking, be no world, for the world exists for us only in so far as it is consciously reflected by a psyche. *Consciousness is a precondition of being.* Thus the psyche is endowed with the dignity of a cosmic principle, which philosophically and in fact gives it a position co-equal with the principle of physical being. The carrier of this consciousness is the individual, who does not produce the psyche of his own volition but is, on the contrary, preformed by it and nourished by the gradual awakening of consciousness during childhood.

---

12. Carl Jung, "Psychology and Alchemy," *Collected Works* 12 (Princeton: Princeton University Press, 1953), para. 44.

13. Carl Jung, "Psychology and Religion" (The Terry Lectures), *Collected Works* 11 (Princeton: Princeton University Press, 1938/1940), para. 140.

14. Carl Jung, "The Archetypes and the Collective Unconscious," *Collected Works* 9 (Princeton: Princeton University Press, 1969), 9i; 7nl0.

If therefore the psyche is of overriding empirical importance, so also is the individual, who is the only immediate
manifestation of the psyche.[15]

Thus, the psyche is the mother and the maker, the subject, and
even the possibility of consciousness itself. According to Jung,
Christ is not a unique savior figure but a universal archetype, an
idea that corresponds to religion as a cosmic phenomenon.

Jung's position is clearly at odds with that of the Church. The
encyclical issued by Pope Saint John Paul II, *Dominus Iesus*, affirmed the Nicene Creed:

Jesus Christ is the only Son of God, eternally begotten of
the Father, God from God, Light from Light, true God
from true God, begotten not made, consubstantial with
the Father, through whom all things are made...who for
us men [*sic*] and our salvation came down from heaven
and became man.[16]

The very first paragraph of the encyclical (elaborated in para.
15) affirms that, from the beginning, the community of believers
has recognized in Jesus a salvific value such that he alone is the
source of revelation and divine life. He is uniquely Son of God
made man, crucified and risen, and by the mission received from
the Father and in the power of the Holy Spirit, is divine. As the
Catholic Church holds to the present: Jesus Christ has a significance and a value for the human race and its history. This significance and value are unique and singular, proper to him alone,
exclusive, universal, and absolute. Jesus is the Word of God made
man for the salvation of all. In expressing this understanding of
faith, the Second Vatican Council affirmed that salvation comes
through Christ, although the spiritual wisdom of other religions
is to be acknowledged. Hence, the Church adheres to the belief

---

15. Carl Jung, "The Undiscovered Self," *Collected Works* 10 (Princeton:
Princeton University Press, 1931), 528.

16. Pope Saint John Paul II, *On the Unicity and Salvific Universality of Jesus
Christ and the Church* (August 6, 2000), para. 1.

in a transcendent (or supernatural) God who became flesh and exists as a unity of divine and human natures in one single person, Jesus Christ, Savior of the world.

Jung dismissed Church doctrine as a deadly enemy of the soul. He felt that, instead of allowing personhood to flourish, the Church suppressed the human spirit and thus the human potential for growth. Teilhard felt the same way and lamented:

> Our Christology is still expressed in exactly the same terms as those which three centuries ago could satisfy those whose outlook on the cosmos it is now physically impossible for us to accept.... What we now have to do without delay is to modify the position occupied by the central core of Christianity—and this precisely in order that it may not lose its illuminative value.[17]

Teilhard was clear that evolution changes theology in a radical way. His dismissal of divine participation and creation out of nothing were not mere rejections of the past. His lament of an antiquated Christology was not meant to be antagonistic. Rather, he was pointing out that scientific insights invite us to reconsider what we mean by the tremendous word, "God," and the presence of God in matter. The scholars of the past, such as Athanasius, Augustine, and Aquinas, wrote within the philosophical constructs of their age. Their ideas on divine participation, creation out of nothing, and the notion of salvation expressed the relational holism *of their time.* They pondered the truths of faith according to the whole, as they understood it, which makes them truly "catholic" thinkers. By "catholicity" I mean "having a consciousness of the whole."[18] Teilhard also was a "catholic" thinker and realized that we must consider the whole God-world complex within our own scientific understanding of the world, that is,

---

17. Pierre Teilhard de Chardin, *Christianity and Evolution: Reflections of Science and Religion,* trans. René Hague (New York: Harcourt Brace Jovanovich, 1971), 77.

18. Ilia Delio, *Making All Things New: Catholicity, Cosmology, Consciousness* (Maryknoll, NY: Orbis Books, 2015), 1–2.

as a relational paradigm. Hence, he was keenly aware of the ways evolution changes the doctrine of Chalcedon:

> 1. There are no fixed essences, so it is impossible to talk about divine essence and human essence as substantial entities. Rather, we can posit a cosmotheandric wholeness of nature undergirding the process of nature's becoming.

> 2. If God is at the heart of evolution as divine empowerment, then the emergence of the human person, including Jesus, must include physical nature itself. Jesus emerges by way of evolution.

> 3. Evolution is an incomplete process open to the future, which means that humans are incomplete and open to completion in the future.

Teilhard's understanding of Christ in evolution reflects the fact that incarnation and creation are integral to one another. God and matter form a complementarity pair and are brought into a personal unity in Christ. Because of this integral unity, a world without Christ is an incomplete world. In other words, the whole world is structured Christologically. This is not to say that everyone is to become Christian; it is to say that every person bears the ground of divine love within and has the capacity to actualize divine love and express divine love in the world. Every person can radiate the Christ because every person illuminates divine love incarnate. Panikkar expressed a similar idea when he said: "Christ is not only the name of a person but the reality of our own lives; that is, Christ does not belong only to the Jesus of history but symbolizes the Living human Person united with God at the heart of the universe."[19] In this respect, the universe is oriented toward the fullness of divine love radiating throughout all cosmic life.

Jung, Teilhard, and Panikkar each perceived the significance of Christ for all humanity, without reducing Christ to any indi-

---

19. Raimon Panikkar, *Christophany: The Fullness of Man* (Maryknoll, NY: Orbis Books, 2004), 21.

vidual religion. Teilhard described Christ as the symbol of evolution while Jung spoke of Christ as the symbol of the Self. By "Self," Jung meant the cosmic archetype, the Self of every person. Christ is the archetypal person who actualized the Self; for Teilhard, Christ is the person of evolution; for Panikkar, Christ is the icon of divinity found in everyone. Jung summed up the significance of Christ in this way:

> [H]e is the living myth of our culture. He is our culture hero, who, regardless of his historical existence, embodies the myth of the divine Primordial Man, the mystic Adam. It is he who occupies the center of the Christian mandala. He is in us and we in him. His kingdom is the pearl of great price, the treasure buried in the field, the grain of mustard seed which will become a great tree, and the heavenly city. As Christ is in us, so also is his heavenly kingdom.[20]

By saying that Christ is the symbol of the Self, Jung indicated that Christ symbolizes wholeness, the psychic totality of what it is to be human. Harald Atmanspacher writes: "Conceiving the psychophysically neutral domain holistically rather than atomistically, reflects the spirit of a corresponding move in quantum theory, which started out as an attempt to finalize the atomistic worldview of the nineteenth century and turned it into a fundamentally holistic one."[21] Jung sees Christ as unique in the perfection of wholeness. This apparently unique life became a sacred symbol, because it is the psychological prototype of the only meaningful life, that is, a life that strives for the individual realization—absolute and unconditional—of its own particular law.[22]

---

20. Carl Jung, "Christ, Symbol of the Self," *Collected Works* 9ii (Princeton: Princeton University Press, 1951), 69–70.

21. Harald Atmanspacher, "20th-Century Variants of Dual-Aspect Thinking," *Mind and Matter* 12, no. 2 (2014): 285.

22. Carl Jung, "The Development of Personality," *Collected Works* 17 (Princeton: Princeton University Press, 1954), 310. By using the word "unique"

TOWARD A NEW MYTH

Jung's insights reorient the "Christ Self" of every person as the primary work of spiritual development. Jesus is not the great exception to humanity but the norm. Whereas the Church holds that Christ is divine by nature and we become divine by grace, Jung maintained that all nature is endowed with infinite potential; all matter is deep grace. Every person has infinite potential and infinite love; hence, every person has a transcendent ground, a divine nature. Divinity is the depth dimension of all that exists, the wholeness of life, and all people have the capacity for wholeness through development of consciousness. Eastern religions have long espoused a divine nature at the heart of human nature, as in, for example, the Hindu *advaita* or nondual consciousness. What the Christian myth sees as the intervention of the divine into one human being, the Messiah, identified in Jesus Christ, Jung sees as an intervention from the collective unconscious of the archetypal Self that, he hypothesizes, all humanity shares. The consciousness of the human is to awaken to its own unconsciousness.

Myths are sacred stories that shape life, but myths can change. Jung thought that the Christian myth had lost its power to transform. The sense of divinity that is based in the collective unconscious of the archetypal self can escape the containment of the psyche and take on the form of transcendent gods or gods of political absolutes. When this happens, empathy is limited to members of specific devotional or tribal communities whose imperative then, too often, becomes the conversion or death of the differently-bonded.[23] We have seen this in our time with the politics of evangelical conservatives and the platforms of racism and white supremacy. Such atrocious acts bear witness to the tragedy of humanity's loss of its common ground, from which all the gods

---

here to describe Jesus, I am distinguishing his uniqueness as a person from the classical understanding of Jesus as a union of two natures. Jesus's uniqueness lies in his fully integrated self, rather than an ontological union of natures.

23. John Dourley, "Jung's Equation of the Ground of Being with the Ground of the Psyche," *Journal of Analytical Psychology* 56 (2011): 527.

and other absolutes derive. In a society widely removed from its roots, the question today is: How many are capable of relating to the common ground. At the societal level, when the symbols become literal, historical, and political, they block rather than mediate the energies that gave them birth.

Jung had great esteem for revelations and their symbols as valuable expressions of archetypal depths, but he rejected the interpretation of revelation as the proof for a transcendent God: "I cannot see that it proves the existence of a transcendent God."[24] He thought that the volatility and wealth of meaning expressed in defining revelation forced institutional religions into the inflexibility of dogma, killing their life in an effort to preserve it.[25] Neither Jung nor Teilhard thought that revelation is completed in the New Testament. Jung especially warned that, unless the West undergoes a "symbolic death," it will likely face the probability of a "universal genocide."[26]

The symbolic death must be a death of our current religious and political symbol systems, that is, the extant religions and their political equivalents. What we need, according to Jung, are symbols that enable the unity of religious opposites beyond their current implacable enmity. His penetrating analysis of the psyche challenged the world with the choice of losing its specific faiths or losing its collective life, a choice we are facing today. He contended that everything depends on humanity's response to the progressive birthing of its divine ground. He has put the ball squarely in the court of humanity. How it is played out remains to be seen.

---

24. Carl Jung, "Mysterium Coniunctionis," *Collected Works* 14 (Princeton: Princeton University Press, 1955), para. 785.

25. Jung, "Mysterium Coniunctionis," *Collected Works* 14, paras. 781, 786.

26. Carl Jung, "Jung and Religious Belief," *Collected Works* 18 (Princeton: Princeton University Press, 1957b), para. 1661.

9
Are We Saved?

The Bible presents salvation in the form of a story that describes God's eternal plan for God's people and the problem of human sin. The story is set against the background of the history of God's people and reaches its climax in the life, death, and resurrection of Jesus Christ. In Adam, all have died; in Christ, all are redeemed (cf. 1 Cor 15:22). Christ is the new Adam, the new Person. The Genesis story of the disobedience of Adam and Eve (cf. Gen 3:1–24) is the basis of explaining sin and its consequences, suffering, and death. Augustine wrote that sin is a universal condition of inherited guilt that can be overcome only by God's grace through the sacrament of baptism. The doctrine of a fallen creation in need of a Savior is a fundamental teaching of Catholic doctrine. "If Adam had not sinned, Christ would not have come," Anselm of Canterbury wrote.[1] Since all have fallen into sin, all are in need of redemption. For Christians, Jesus Christ is savior of the world:

---

1. See Saint Anselm of Canterbury, *Cur Deus Homo*, trans. Sidney Norton Deane (Fort Worth, TX: RDMc Publishing, 2005), 68–80.

Just as sin came into the world through one man, and death through sin, and so death spread to all men because all sinned . . . much more have the grace of God and the free gift by the grace of that one man Jesus Christ abound- ed for many. . . . For if, because of one man's trespass, death reigned through that one man, much more will those who receive the abundance of grace and the free gift of righteousness reign in life through the one man, Jesus Christ (Rom 5:12, 15, 17).

Taken in its widest sense, as deliverance from dangers and ills in general, most religions teach some form of salvation. In Chris- tianity, original sin becomes a fundamental power against which human power is helpless. Sin is a human predicament and con- sidered to be universal. For example, Saint Paul declared every- one to be under sin—Jew and Gentile alike. Salvation is related to "atonement" (Rom 1:18–3:29) or the act of sacrificial love that re- turns us to God. To be saved is to be reconciled to God.

Christian theories of salvation range from exclusive salvation, in which there is no salvation outside the church, to universal sal- vation concepts, in which the grace of salvation does not depend exclusively on faith in Jesus Christ. The Church holds that salva- tion is made possible by the work of Jesus Christ and is fulfilled by his death and resurrection. Anselm Min writes:

At the heart of Christian faith is the reality and hope of sal- vation in Jesus Christ. Christian faith is faith in the God of salvation revealed in Jesus of Nazareth. The Christian tra- dition has always equated this salvation with the transcen- dent, eschatological fulfillment of human existence in a life freed from sin, finitude, and mortality and united with the triune God. This is perhaps *the* non-negotiable item of Christian faith. What has been a matter of debate is the re- lation between salvation and our activities in the world.[2]

2. Anselm Kyongsuk Min, *Dialectic of Salvation: Issues in Theology of Liber- ation* (Albany: State University of New York Press, 2009), 79.

Salvation is a matter of faith. It begins with faith in Jesus Christ as true God, for salvation comes from God. The Nicene Creed is a confession of faith that underscores the belief that there is nothing we can do to save ourselves other than to have faith in Jesus Christ. Christians profess:

> I believe in one Lord Jesus Christ, the Only Begotten Son of God, born of the Father before all ages. God from God, Light from Light, true God from true God, begotten, not made, consubstantial with the Father; through him all things were made. For us men and for our salvation he came down from heaven and by the Holy Spirit was incarnate of the Virgin Mary, and became man....I believe in one, holy, catholic and apostolic Church. I confess one Baptism for the forgiveness of sins, and I look forward to the resurrection of the dead and the life of the world to come. Amen.[3]

Since its inception, the Catholic Church has defended the doctrine of salvation as a singular and exclusive act of divine grace and power. Thomas Aquinas developed a metaphysics that fit the Christian story: the one savior saves the many sinners. The doctrine of salvation is sacrosanct, and one must tread lightly when engaging theological questions about salvation.

However, we can no longer presume that a patristic-medieval doctrine can adequately direct human life in an unfinished universe of immense proportions. To begin, the question of salvation can no longer be an individual ideal. Theologians who favor universal salvation use ancient Greek philosophical ideas to support their arguments. To confess belief in Jesus is to be saved, as Saint Paul writes: "If you confess with your mouth that Jesus is Lord and believe in your heart that God raised him from the dead, you will be saved" (Rom 10:9). However, we emerge from a whole and we belong to a whole. Salvation (from the Latin *salvare*) is essentially the act of being healed and made whole. Can one unique

---

3. Abbreviated version of the Nicene-Constantinopolitan Creed, which is an expression of the fundamentals of Christian faith.

person save the entire species of *Homo sapiens*, a species that is in evolution? Where does salvation itself begin? Does it begin with *Homo erectus*, about 1.6 million years ago? With the life of the cosmos, about 13.8 billion years ago? Today, the story of salvation must be told from the perspective of the whole earth and all its creatures. The new story of salvation must be one of relational holism.

Twentieth-century theologian Karl Rahner recognized the importance of relationality when he argued that God creates humans to become ourselves by responding in freedom to God's self-communication. While persons are determined by cultural and biological factors (including interpersonal relationships), Rahner said that persons who possess reason ultimately have the transcendental and categorical freedom to realize who they will become before God. We must choose to accept or reject God's self-communication, to be attentive and open to that which is pulling us beyond ourselves. Rahner's position approximated what Jung and Teilhard perceived and what the new story of salvation must become today.

The human person has within oneself the capacity for God and, thus, the capacity to be made whole as an act of freedom; however, we must make a radical choice to be made whole, to be saved. Jung put the question of salvation in terms of choice and decision. He suggested that it is not God who saves but we who must choose to save ourselves by reconciling the inner darkness with divine light. That is, we must connect to our divine nature within. Salvation is a co-creative process of choice and decision, a cooperative relationship of divinity and humanity. The choice to become fully human is the choice for God, and the choice for God is the choice for wholeness. The decision to save oneself is the desire for life, the decision to overcome alienation and indifference. Salvation is not based on fallen human nature, unless we understand fallenness as the unreconciled and unfinished human. Salvation is the choice for wholeness, and we can become whole only when we heal our inner divisions in creative cooperation with God. The key to salvation lies within us.

JUNG'S REPRESSED GOD

Jung described a novel approach to the question of fallen nature and suffering from a psycho-religious perspective. His insights are at once alarming and provocative, an invitation to rethink the question of suffering in light of God's own trinitarian life. In his *Answer to Job*, he demonstrates an in-depth knowledge of the Bible. What makes the work remarkable is the fact that it is a personal and authentic exposition of human suffering as it relates to the Christian God. Jung wrote this book in his old age, when he was ailing and feverish. Its style is passionate, unrestrained, and he often repeats himself. It seems to emerge from the depths of his unconscious. He was facing his own set of personal, religious, and professional challenges and grappling with the idea of good and evil that he saw in himself and in the world around him.

Jung felt repressed anger toward God, and he seemed to wrestle with God the same way Jacob wrestled with the angel of God. The dynamics between Job and God can be equated to Jung's dynamics between the ego and the self. Job appears as the morally upright person while God seems to be the perpetrator. The text is an exploration of the unconscious, particularly the way that humans relate to the depths of religion. The story of Job's suffering serves as a metaphor for how one can correct the imbalance in the psychology of God and, at the same time, correct the imbalance in the way Christians have been formed to think of God as immutable and apathetic. Jung probes the source of evil in an original way, not as punishment for sin, but as the incompleteness of divinity and humanity in relation to one another. God must become human to become God because, without incarnation, God is unpredictable. That is to say that, for Jung, God is more real in "fallen" humanity than in Godself. [4] John Dourley explains:

> Only through the fall...can the divine idea of humanity
> move from its source in a divine dream into existential

---

4. John Dourley, "Jacob Boehme and Paul Tillich on Trinity and God: Similarities and Differences," *Religious Studies* 31, no. 4 (December 1995): 438.

but fallen human reality.... A God who had to create to know Godself could not create without creating evil as the unrelenting power of self-affirmation derivative of one side of the divine life itself.[5]

Jung relied on Job's relationship with God as a metaphor for humanity's relationship to suffering. God, he states, is insufficient as an answer to the question about evil in the world. Since the idea of God is based on unconscious aspects and relates to archetypal images, there is no "objective" God. Rather, God is the personal depth of the psyche. One's experience of God cannot be separated from the experience of oneself. Furthermore, if we are prepared to engage with the tensions within the lived experience of the psyche, we may be able to understand life in a spiritual context. Evil, then, is the result of the incomplete divine-human unity. God is unreconciled within the human, and the human is unreconciled within God. Since God and human need one another to be complete, the incompletion of God and human results in human evil and chaotic forces in the world.

Jung located the basis of conflict between archetypal opposites suffered by humanity in the ground itself. Humanity's universal task is to unify and make conscious a split divinity, and this task is the underlying meaning of human history.[6] By "split divinity," Jung was suggesting that the Trinity of opposites is unreconciled: source and receptivity, unoriginated and originate, power and meaning. Hence, the Trinity seeks its own reconciliation beyond itself, in human life. In other words, the healing of the world begins with the healing of God in the healing of the self.

For Jung, the dream becomes the medium through which the process of unification of the divine in the human takes place. Dreams are personal revelations in which the divine self-contradiction seeks resolution in the individual's life. Dreams allow aspects of the unconscious to enter consciousness in an unobtrusive way in which one can open up to new possibilities for

---

5. Dourley, "Jacob Boehme and Paul Tillich on Trinity and God," 438.

6. Carl Jung, "Answer to Job," *Collected Works* 11 (Princeton: Princeton University Press, 1952), paras. 739, 585, 567.

inner healing. One must be attentive to the invitation within, what is described as the movements of the divine Spirit or divine energy. The inner divine ground requires the ego to open up to the psyche and undergo the process of reconciliation, that is, the process of reconciling the opposites within oneself. This process undergirds the integration of the numinous whereby the ego comes to terms with the self. One must, like Job, contend with God.

Jung's novel, psychological approach to the question of evil, as the deepest question of religion, is worth serious consideration. Do we project our own deep, unconscious, and unreconciled anger onto God? Are we implicitly at war with God? Is God frustrated as well, angry that divine life cannot find completion in the human self? Is God's anger expressed in the rage of discontent? An unreconciled God is an unreconciled world; a wild and chaotic God is a wild and chaotic world. If God cannot rest or find completion in creation, it is because we cannot find rest or completion within ourselves. Jung's *Answer to Job* reveals a frustrated God. It is hardly a reassuring image, but Job surrenders to God, and God finds a good person in whom divine dwelling is expressed as renewed life. Job's choice is salvific.

EVIL AND EVOLUTION

Like Jung, Teilhard did not think we are born into sin because of some aboriginal sin of a primitive Adam. Rather, sin is the law of the universe, the cosmic condition of a world in evolution. In a universe this large, evil is statistically inevitable at every level of evolving life. The work of the unification of all things in Christ inevitably involves the pain of reconciliation. Teilhard called this the "creative pain" of unification, a necessary pain if we are to evolve and not regress to a lower state of existence that returns us to multiplicity or dissipated existence.

In his book *The Future of Wisdom*, the late Cistercian mystic Bruno Barnhart suggested that our modern Western world, in all of its sprawling untidiness, is not a deviation from the path of the crucified Christ but its legitimate and inevitable trajectory: "The unitive wisdom which has become manifest in Christ disappears into or metamorphoses into an immanent historical dynamism that transforms all of creative reality."[7] In the immanent historical dynamism of creativity, God suffers as God experiences the birth pangs of creation. God is ecstatically in pain, at once completely open, self-giving, outpouring, infinite love, and yet unrequited in the fullness of love. God's pain is the aching heart of absolute love longing for creative union.

Teilhard was somewhat more optimistic than Jung because of his belief in the power of Omega at the heart of evolution. Yet, he was sympathetic to Jung's concern. Everything now depends on the human person and how each of us grasps the reins of evolution and the evolution of God. If we misread the "signs of the times," we will annihilate ourselves. The presence of Omega does not guarantee a successful future; rather, the future fullness of life depends on how the human person sees the whole, which is why contemplation is essential to evolution. Mind and matter must work together in this holographic cosmos. Like Jung, Teilhard lamented that our religious symbols and language of God fail to provoke the self's discovery of the psyche; instead, religion paralyzes the mind. The human's inability to access the numinous seems to reverberate in projected anger. The frustrated religious ego becomes the warring ego, the wars within us become the wars among us; the violence within us becomes the violence among us; inner self-hatred becomes outer hatred of others; the inner war of rejection becomes the outer war of rejection. What we cannot realize within ourselves is projected onto others, often the innocent of the earth. God becomes a plaything of the isolated ego, crying out in agony on the cross of alienation and rejection.

Institutional religion wants to heal suffering and pain by the therapeutic transcendence of divine grace, as if supernatural power can eradicate the unresolved self. The struggle for the God-person to emerge is a constant challenge to the childlike dependency fostered by the institutional Church. Patriarchal power

---

7. Bruno Barnhart, *The Future of Wisdom: Toward a Rebirth of Sapiential Christianity* (New York: Monkfish Book Publishing, 2018), 186.

not only thwarts real personhood by cutting off the divine dimension of personhood, but it stifles the birth of God within and the need for God to be complete in us. The inability to reconcile the unfulfilled God with the unfulfilled self is a split between self and God, expressed in violence against the innocent.[8] If God is the ground of existence, then God remaining sterile as infinite ground leaves open all possibilities of chaos and destruction. Without the fulfillment of God, everything else remains unfulfilled. Without beauty, goodness, truth, and unity, nature withers. The promise of life abundant stands before us because it is within us: "I have come so that you may have life and have it to the full" (John 10:10). God needs the human person to realize the fullness of God's love, and the human needs God to be whole and complete.

There is no doubt that a frustrated and hollow human person with a beating heart is the most dangerous weapon around. Where there is profound sorrow, death is the only reprieve. Without God, we are a dissolute species bound for destruction, an earth hurtling into the great void. On the other hand, God without personalization is a thought without expression, a pure potentiality with no actuality. We hope because we experience a power of love within us, a power that defies logical explanation, a power that moves matter toward spirit, precisely because it empowers us to see what cannot be seen. Love dynamizes by putting into motion that which it touches. If faith is "the assurance of things hoped for" (Heb 11:1), then we live by faith when we live from a higher consciousness of knowing ourselves to be loved by an ineffable inner center of love. To live from the energy of *this* love is to risk everything for love, returning love for love.

MADE WHOLE BY LOVE

Teilhard wrote: "Nothing holds together absolutely except through the Whole; and the Whole itself holds together only through its

---

8. See René Girard, *The Scapegoat*, trans. Yvonne Freccero (Baltimore: The Johns Hopkins University Press, 1986).

future fulfillment."⁹ The Whole is Omega, and Omega reveals itself through the energies of love.¹⁰ God Omega is rising up
amidst the forces of evolution, showing us that love alone has the
power to endure into the future. Love, personally incarnate in
every aspect of matter, is the Christ. Christ is the one in whom
mind, body, and spirit are unified in love. Teilhard spoke of Christ
as a symbol of progress, the one who realizes the potential of evolution for pleroma or fullness. He writes: "If Christ is to be completely acceptable as an object of worship, he must be presented
as the savior of the idea and reality *of evolution*."¹¹ Christ is the
one who

> overcomes the resistance to unification offered by the
> multiple, resistance to the rise of spirit inherent in matter.
> ...He is the symbol and sign-in-action of progress. The
> complete and definitive meaning of redemption is no
> longer only to expiate [sins]; it is to surmount and con-
> quer. The full mystery of baptism is no longer to cleanse
> but (as the Greek Fathers fully realized) to plunge into the
> fire of the purifying battle "for being"—no longer the
> shadow, but the sweat and toil, of the Cross.¹²

As the exemplar of evolution, Christ does not save us from
sin but shows us how to rise above sin, that is, to rise above incompleteness, resistance, and apathy through the power of love.
Christ exemplifies the capacity of the human person for non-
dual consciousness. We are made whole by facing our difficulties and accepting the sufferings of life as opportunities to
transcend from that which is incomplete toward more completion. We are *not* saved by a Christ who is "master of the world"

9. Pierre Teilhard de Chardin, *Christianity and Evolution: Reflections on
Science and Religion*, trans. René Hague (New York: Harcourt Brace Jovanovich, 1971), 71.

10. See Pierre Teilhard de Chardin, "Centrology," *Activation of Energy*,
trans. René Hague (New York: Harcourt Brace Jovanovich, 1963), 111–15.

11. Teilhard de Chardin, *Christianity and Evolution*, 78.

12. Teilhard de Chardin, *Christianity and Evolution*, 85.

but by a Christ who is being born in evolution.[13] In a universe this old and this large, in which spacetime dynamically unfolds, there are no givens, no absolutes, which means that the only way to heaven is through the earth. Teilhard spoke of "communion with God, communion with the earth, and communion with God through the earth," or, as he states elsewhere, "communion with God through the world."[14] He wrote: "The truth about today's gospel is that it has ceased ... to have any attraction because it has become unintelligible."[15] The old "savior model" stifles us because it fails to enkindle God's super-abundant love within us, the same love moving the universe toward more life. The old savior model has created fearful, frightened, and guilt-ridden people, who are more concerned with going to heaven (and avoiding hell) than with the health of the planet, the atrocities of racism, the wounds caused by gender inequality, or just the importance of plain common courtesy without being overly judgmental. "We cannot be saved," Teilhard wrote, "except through the universe and as a continuation of the universe."[16] He also wrote: "I can be saved only by becoming one with the universe."[17]

Teilhard's soteriology requires faith in the world as well as faith in God, for one is not saved by "abandoning the world but in active participation in building it up."[18] Essentially, we are saved by the power of love. That is, we are saved by an option that chooses the whole or we are not saved at all. Salvation is the process of becoming whole by widening relationships through love. Jesus returned love for love unconditionally; so too must we. What good is it to love those who only love us? Such love is *quid pro quo*; it is no more than a business deal. If we hope in the future, we must risk loving those who are our enemies, loving to

13. Teilhard de Chardin, *Christianity and Evolution*, 89.

14. Teilhard de Chardin, *Christianity and Evolution*, 93.

15. Teilhard de Chardin, *Christianity and Evolution*, 91.

16. Teilhard de Chardin, *Christianity and Evolution*, 92.

17. Teilhard de Chardin, *Christianity and Evolution*, 128.

18. Pierre Leroy SJ, "The Man," *Letters from a Traveler*, ed. Bernard Wall (New York: Harper Torchbooks, 1962), 25.

the point of tears. Very few attain this level of love; hence we trust in the slow work of God which is also the slow work of humans.

Love is the core energy of the universe because love is the energy of attraction, union, and transcendence. If God is love and creates the world out of love, then the universe is in the process of *creating itself* through the energies of love. To exist is to live in the dynamism of love, always moving from potentiality to actuality. This ever-dynamic movement in love is God's infinite movement from potency to actuality in virtue of love's own intrinsic dynamism. God is always active as the subject of the ongoing act of existence or the ongoing subject of relationality. God is the wholeness of relational love so that, through the energies of love, God continuously comes into being as God.[19] Love is not something God has—love is what God is, God's very essence. God is not a separate existence and love is not an attribute. Rather, God is the divine wellspring of love and is actualized and personalized in and through our love for one another. Anthony Gittins writes that "revelation is God's way of opening up for us unbounded possibilities; it expands our horizons and calls us beyond rules and laws to love."[20] Since God's essential nature is love, God is most deeply actualized not simply in being human but in the multitude of loves that humans enact.

To say "God is love" is to realize a God who is deeply related to and concerned for the world; a God who suffers rejection (Gen 3), who gets angry, who shows deep tenderness and compassion and is willing to forgive at all costs. This is a God who is both a jealous lover and a tender parent; a God who bends down to find us in our darkness and isolation, to be with us, to comfort us and lead us onward toward the fullness of life. Early Jewish writers portray God in strikingly anthropomorphic terms: as a person encountered in history, the biblical God is one who has regrets and repents of his actions (Gen 6:61; Sam 15:11, 35); one who can be bargained with and cajoled (Gen 18:22–33; Exod 32:11–14); one

---

19. Joseph Bracken, *Divine Matrix: Creativity as Link Between East and West* (Eugene, OR: Wipf and Stock, 2006), 30.

20. C. A. J. Gittins, "Can We Get Beyond Religion? Revelation, Faith, and the Dignity of Difference" *New Theology Review* (April 15, 2013): 11.

who answers heartfelt prayers and listens patiently to complaints (2 Kgs 20:1–5; Jon 4); one who gathers Israel like a hen takes chicks under its wings (2 Esd 1:30); one who promises not to remember human sins (Isa 43:25); one who recoils from anger because of compassion (Hos 11:8–9); and one who deeply cares for the community of creation (Ps 65:9). In the words of Jonah and Joel, God is gracious and merciful, slow to anger, abounding in steadfast love and relenting from punishing. God is *not* the "unmoved Mover" but the "most moved Mover" of all life, in the words of renowned Jewish scholar Abraham Heschel.[21] As the human person becomes more aware of a deep presence of God, the human awakens to a new reality through the energies of love.

SALVATION AS INDIVIDUATION

Teilhard's ideas are consistent with Jung's, and it would take a much more thorough study to show the complementarity of these two thinkers. However, two things stand out clearly: first, the key to salvation lies within us, where God is "the total sphere that embraces all things—a center that itself is in process of formation;" and second, mysticism inevitably rises.[22] Christianity is not a rescue mission from a corrupt world but is "pre-eminently faith in the progressive unification of the world in God; it is essentially universal, organic and monist," Teilhard claims.[23] What Teilhard calls monism can be better described as relational holism or divine entanglement, in which God is integral to the whole in process.

One of the difficulties with Teilhard's writings is his use of theological language merged with novel ideas on religion in evolution. Jung is more explicit in reframing doctrinal beliefs in terms of psychogenesis and the essential role of consciousness in

---

21. Alan T. Levenson, *An Introduction to Modern Jewish Thinkers: From Spinoza to Soloveitchik* (Oxford: Rowman and Littlefield Publishers, Inc., 2006), 215.

22. Teilhard de Chardin, *Activation of Energy*, 383.

23. Teilhard de Chardin, *Christianity and Evolution*, 171.

personal formation. Teilhard speaks about God being born "from the welding together of the elements of the world," by which he means "a differentiating synthesis with the elements of the world."[24] Jung states more clearly that divinity is at the heart of humanity. God is the ground, the transcendent depth, where the unconscious dimension of the psyche exists in relation to the levels of consciousness that comprise the field of the mind.

Jung's God is the experience of divinity, wholly generated by intra-psychic forces, or more precisely, by the impact of numinous archetypal powers as they seek concrete expression in consciousness. He wrote: "These powers are numinous 'types'—unconscious contents, processes and dynamisms—and such types, if one may so express it, are immanent-transcendent."[25] Archetypes are immanent because they exist within the human psyche which, in turn, suggests an inexhaustible dimension of personhood. They are transcendent because they transcend the ego with which they are organically connected in the total psyche and in which they seek to become conscious. The creative potential of the archetypes is inexhaustible and resonates with Whitehead's idea that creativity is the fundamental principle of cosmic life, including the life of God who is most intensely creative.

While Jung conceived of the psychogenesis of divinity from within, it is not without a transcendent dimension. The fontal wealth of the archetypal realm will never cease the drive to fuller realization and will always transcend the present degree of its incarnation both in the individual and the species. Jung describes the surpassing plenitude of the creative energy of the unconscious as having no assignable limits.[26] The undefinable wealth of the psyche in which the creative potential for unity, truth, goodness, and beauty is open to actualization by the conscious self is comparable to what Teilhard conceives of as God in evolution. As

---

24. Teilhard de Chardin, *Christianity and Evolution*, 171.

25. Carl Jung, *The Collected Works of Carl Jung*, ed. Gerhard Adler, Herbert Read, and Michael Fordham (Oxfordshire, UK: Taylor and Francis, 1973), para. 1505.

26. Carl Jung, "Transformation Symbolism in the Mass," *Collected Works* 11 (Princeton: Princeton University Press, 1952), para. 390.

Teilhard writes: "God fulfills himself, he in some way completes himself, in the pleroma."[27] As divinity is individuated, brought to light through the realization of values that enlighten the world in hope and create the world in love, God is actualized, and the actualization of God is salvific.

Putting on Christ means actualizing God in the flesh; the personalization of God is salvific for the life of the planet. If faith is the basis of salvation, then we are to have faith in ourselves if we have faith in God. We must awaken to the vitality of divine love within, as Saint Paul wrote: "It is with your heart that you believe and are justified" (Rom 10:9). We are so sure divinity is *not* within us, however, that we are constantly searching outside ourselves to be saved. We have yet to realize that "the mystery we call God is personal rather than *a* person."[28] God is the personal divine depth immanently transcendent within every aspect of cosmic life. God is the personal mystery, the ground, of every single human person.

By placing the choice for salvation on the human person, both Jung and Teilhard indicated that Christianity needs a new birth if it is to survive. Christ must be reborn from within: "The Messiah whom we await...is...the Christ of evolution."[29] Love's actualization in the universe must become *personal*; the actualization of love requires the ego to dismantle its protective barriers and free the mind to embrace the difficult task of transformation that leads to Christ consciousness. Love is the basis of God's entangled reality open to completion through the human capacity to love. Love comes to expression when barriers break down and hearts are laid bare. To love is to live courageously by suffering through trials and failures into the promise of everlasting love. It is to let go into the wider flow of evolution, conscious that we are fractals of an immense reality, as if the entire universe is one magnificent stained-glass window radiating light through each beveled piece of glass. The beauty of light in a stained-glass window is the sum-

---

27. Teilhard de Chardin, *Christianity and Evolution*, 178.

28. Albert Nolan, *Jesus Today: A Spirituality of Radical Freedom* (Maryknoll, NY: Orbis Books, 2006), 146.

29. Nolan, *Jesus Today*, 95.

mation of many pieces of glass of various shapes and colors radiating light. Similarly, the radiance of love's energy forever exceeds our power to grasp and control, and it is the vital force within us:

> [An] aptitude for feeling and evolving—that I can claim as specifically my own: and yet although this force is indeed my own in the sense that it is I who concentrate it and experience it, I am quite unable to pin it down, whether I try to decipher any part either of its past or of its future. Behind the unity it assumes in my consciousness there lies hidden the dense multitude of all the succession of beings whose infinitely patient and lengthy labor has carried to its present stage of perfection the phylum of which I am for a moment the extreme bud. My life is not my own: I know this from the inexorable determinism contained in the development of overpowering emotions, in pain and in death. And I feel this, not only in my bodily members but in the very core of what is most spiritual in my being.[30]

Every person has a Christic center because every being has a divine root. When one strives to live in the archetypes of love, peace, compassion, forgiveness, and nonviolence, Christ is alive and active in that person, even if one has never heard of Jesus or accepts the Gospel. Such a person is a co-creative agent of salvation. Every person has a heart of love, open to the fullness of life; every person is oriented toward the absolute center of love, the heart of God. When we are caught up in the dynamism of love, we are engaged in the creative process of salvation by choosing the whole. We choose the whole of kindness; the whole of healing; the whole of forgiveness; the whole of listening and patience. Wholeness is the mind attuned to the heart by actualizing divine love within oneself and in others: wholeness heals. According to the Gospel of Luke (4:23), Jesus was known as the "great physician." Those who are whole do not need healing, Jesus said, "but

---

30. Pierre Teilhard de Chardin, *Writings in Time of War*, trans. René Hague (New York: Harper and Row, 1968), 26.

those who are sick do. I came not to call the righteous, but sinners" (Mark 2:17).

Jesus anticipated a new understanding of salvation by calling us to awaken to God within: "the kingdom of God is within you" (Luke 17:21). Jesus was a faithful Jew who entered into the depths of his own God consciousness. He spoke of a new law of love (John 15:12) and enacted a deep awareness of a Godly-human life. He was a deeply relational person and genuinely human. Jesus was an explosion of love in the midst of a politically chaotic situation: "I have come to cast fire on the earth and how I wish it were ablaze already" (Luke 12:49). His intimate experience of God and his unitive identity with God (John 10:30: "The Father and I are one") empowered him to act in the name of love, healing, and reconciling all that is unloved and unlovable. Throughout the New Testament, we see the explicit contrast between the mere religiosity of following the law and the consciousness of love that binds together and makes whole. For Jesus, deeply centered wholeness is everything. The mind directs the heart to see God in everything. Sin is a failure to see and thus a failure to love.

If God is love, then the Spirit is love's dynamic energy. Matter is spirit-energy moving slowly enough to be seen. But what type of spirit-energy is at play? Is it God's Spirit moving matter or is created matter moving God? Entanglement makes it impossible to distinguish the spirit-energy of matter, and the complexity of God and matter is enervated by language that separates and distinguishes these realities. What we can say is that incarnation is the Spirit-energy of divine love bringing matter to life. Teilhard wrote: "As a direct consequence of the unitive process by which God is revealed to us, he in some way 'transforms himself' as he incorporates us."[31] On the level of human life, God is transformed in us if we devote ourselves to the work of love, to be convinced not only of the merit of what we do but also of its value. We must believe in ourselves and in our actions. Teilhard wrote: "I feel that the more I devote myself in some way to the interests of the earth in its highest form, the more I belong to God."[32] If salvation is grace that

---

31. Pierre Teilhard de Chardin, *Hymn of the Universe*, trans. Gerald Vann, OP (New York: Harper and Row, 1965), 53.

comes from God, then we are already steeped in grace, for the love of God is the field of love energy seeking to expand into the widest embrace of life. We engage this field of energy within and without. In doing so, we build our souls unto eternal life. Soul expansion is salvific. By choosing the whole, we save ourselves, and by saving ourselves, we save God from oblivion. Salvation is a cooperative act of love. God cannot be saved without us, and we are not saved without the wellspring of divine love.

CHURCH AS THE PHYLUM OF SALVATION

One of the most enduring lines of Christian theology was written by Saint Cyprian of Carthage in the third century: *Extra ecclesiam nulla salus* (Outside the Church, there is no salvation). This means essentially that "all salvation comes from Christ the Head through the Church which is his Body."[33] In the twentieth century the Vatican II document *Lumen Gentium* confirmed this patristic belief: "The Church, now sojourning on earth as an exile, is necessary for salvation. Christ, present to us in His Body, which is the Church, is the one Mediator and the unique way of salvation."[34] If becoming whole and wholly united with God requires an institution, it is no wonder the Church is losing members. Many people today are discovering ways of connecting with God, one another, and the earth without relying on institutional religious norms. Should the Church rethink its mission?

Teilhard reframed theology for a world in evolution. The Church, in his view, exists to foster the energies of evolution. If it does not do so, it loses its reason for existence and diminishes with each passing age of evolution. He thought the future of the Church would depend on its ability to provide humanity with access to those energies that are working now to create the future. Teilhard envisioned a Church that could support a process of

---

32. Teilhard de Chardin, *Writings in Time of War*, 57.

33. "No Salvation Outside the Church," *Catechism of Catholic Church*, 2nd ed. (Vatican: Libreria Editrice Vaticana, 2012), 846.

34. Pope Paul VI, *Lumen Gentium* (November 21, 1964), para. 14.

Christogenesis in which the universe, unfolding in and through us, is God's becoming.

Each life process contributes to the mutual completion of God and humanity in the dynamic process of ongoing complexification, or what he called, "pleromization." Pleroma or fullness is synonymous with wholeness. The human evolutive effort toward personhood completes God in a very real sense; we help build up the pleroma by bringing Christ to fulfillment. Jung contends: "[O]nly those who are self-possessed or possessed by the self are in a position to give of themselves."[35] Personal and divine completion are two sides of the same process. Teilhard writes in a Pauline spirit: "He encompasses us on all sides, like the world itself. What prevents you, then, from enfolding him in your arms? Only one thing: your inability to see him."[36] As Dourley points out: "[T]he obstacle to seeing is uprootedness from the sense of the sacred energies of evolution around and within the individual. For those not so blind . . . nothing here below is profane for those who know how to see."[37] We are the New Creation in the active sense of being those who participate in the act of creating.

Teilhard spoke of the Church as a new Christic phylum that transcends *Homo sapiens*, a phylum of love that could spearhead evolution toward maximal wholeness, the Omega point. A phylum is a taxonomic term of biology to describe a group that has common characteristics or features. To speak of the Church as a "phylum" suggests that the Church could be a source of a new type of humanity, Christified humans, or *Homo Christus*. The Christic is the new God-person who lives from the deepest level of Christ consciousness. Such persons are dynamically engaged in holistic God-life, which springing from their own inner selves into the world. As a wholemaker, the Christic is being saved through the creative energies of love.

---

35. Carl Jung, "The Undiscovered Self," *Collected Works* 10 (Princeton: Princeton University Press, 1931), 525.

36. Pierre Teilhard de Chardin, *The Divine Milieu*, trans. unidentified (New York: Harper and Row, 1960), 46.

37. John Dourley, "Conspiracies of Immanence: Paul Tillich, Teilhard de Chardin and C. G. Jung, *Journal of Analytical Psychology* 60, no. 1 (2015): 89.

The Christic is a new complexified God life, one in whom the Holy Spirit is active and alive, living on the edge of change in the evolutionary flow. The Christic is the basis of the new community, the Church. It was this new type of Church that was at the heart of Jesus's message: "Destroy this Temple that is made with hands, and in three days I will raise it up" (John 2:19). This was shocking to his hearers because it took forty years to build the temple. But Jesus was speaking of a new temple of the human person, where the Spirit of God dwells. "Do you not know that you are God's temple and that God's Spirit dwells in you" (1 Cor 3:16)? Although theologians have done an awesome job filling in the gap between the New Testament and an overly juridical, patriarchal church, theology is a construction of ideas. When we return to the New Testament, we find a faith-filled Jew who spoke of a new path of salvation through the transformation of mind and heart and a new law of love. Jesus anticipated a new way of worship by becoming a new human person and living on a higher level of love.

Teilhard envisioned a living Church as the reflectively Christified portion of the world. The Church is to continue the dynamic activity of God's creative love in the world; it is the central axis of universal convergence and cosmic personalization. This new "phylum of salvation," according to Teilhard, is to spread its inner life and hyper-personalism in a movement of greater consciousness, always ascending until the completion of the Body of Christ. This "completion" of the Body of Christ is the Parousia, the moment when Christ appears in history again, that is, when divinity is completely incarnated in every person of the earth, and beyond the earth, on every conceivable planet with intelligent life; Christ will shine out in the brilliance of light, that is, all people will live with Christ consciousness, vitalized by the energies of love.

New Church?

As the Church struggles with the complexities of the world today, amidst the rise of the "Nones" and the forces of secularization, it would do well to consider aspects of process thought espoused by Jung, Teilhard, Whitehead, and others and develop an "open systems Church."[38] An open system is a self-organizing system: when the needs change, so, too, do the structures. Self-organizing systems require interior freedom to change. One of the paradoxes is that the more freedom in self-organization, the more order. Autonomy at the local level allows greater overall coherence and continuity. Self-organization is the basis of ongoing wholeness in evolution. In his 1950 talk to the World's Congress of Religions, Teilhard said: "[T]he various creeds still commonly accepted have been primarily concerned to provide every human with an *individual* line of escape" and, for this reason, they fail to "allow any room for a global and controlled transformation of the whole of life and thought in their entirety."[39] He pondered the need for a new creed that could enkindle the fire of evolution: "In a system of cosmo-noogenesis, the comparative value of religious creeds may be measured by their respective power of evolutive activation."[40] He continued: "Remain true to yourself but move ever upward toward greater consciousness and greater love."[41] What would Church look like if this were its main ideal?

Teilhard was distressed by the Church's refusal to accept evolution as descriptive of the the human person, much less the completion of God! The Catholic Church still holds to the 1950 decree of Pope Pius XII in his encylclical *Humani Generis*: the body may come about by means of evolution, but the soul is created immediately by God (para. 36). Teilhard's entangled holism means that faith in God must be faith in the world, for God is revealed in and through conscious material life. Liturgy, therefore, should be nurturing the consciousness of a cosmotheandric entanglement, nurturing our participation in creating toward Omega. Coming together in the name of the One who is the Whole, the

---

38. See Joseph Bracken, *Church as Dynamic Life-System: Shared Ministries and Common Responsibilities* (Maryknoll, NY: Orbis Books, 2019).

39. Teilhard de Chardin, *Activation of Energy*, 240.

40. Pierre Teilhard de Chardin, *The Heart of Matter*, trans. René Hague (New York: Harcourt Brace Jovanovich, 1979), 7.

41. Pierre Teilhard de Chardin, *The Phenomenon of Man*, trans. Bernard Wall (New York: Harper and Row, 1959), 64.

divine Trinity of love, should ignite in us our deepest vocation, to become new persons, Christics, those who live on a higher level of conscious divine life. To live a scramental life is to Christify the world.

SACRAMENTAL CHRISTIFICATION

If we are to progress toward greater holism, toward a deepening of Christ consciousness, then the sacraments are helpful for forming dynamic relations with the Risen Christ who is the symbol of cosmotheandric unity. Through the Body of Christified persons, Christ reaches humankind and, through humankind, the whole earth community. Teilhard spoke of baptism as the sacrament of fire, not a cleansing of original sin, but a plunging into the fire of Christogenesis. "To be baptized," he wrote, "is to be fully immersed in the trials and tribulations of evolution, a willingness to trust, create and risk going forth."[42] Eucharist incorporates us a little more fully on each occasion into Christogenesis, "which itself ... is none other than the soul of universal cosmo-genesis."[43] Emerging through Eucharist, we are to live out the transforming power of love in the world. If God is the divine energy of love, "the effect of love is to accentuate the individuality of the beings brought into union."[44] In other words, it is to move from our divine, sacramental lives to the sacrament of the universe. Teilhard thought that the modern human is uprooted from nature and thus unconscious of the deep connection with all matter that comprises "nature." In his *Mass on the World*, he beautifully brings into focus the mystery of God-matter entanglement celebrated by the sacrament of the Eucharist:

> Since once again, Lord ... I have neither bread, nor wine, nor altar, I will raise myself beyond these symbols, up to the pure majesty of the real itself; I, your priest, will make

---

42. Teilhard de Chardin, *Christianity and Evolution*, 85–86.
43. Teilhard de Chardin, *Christianity and Evolution*, 166.
44. Teilhard de Chardin, *Christianity and Evolution*, 171.

the whole world my altar and on it will offer you all the labors and sufferings of the world. Over there, on the horizon, the sun has just touched with light the outermost fringe of the eastern sky. Once again, beneath this moving sheet of fire, the living surface of the earth wakes and, once again, begins its fearful travail. I will place on my paten, O God, the harvest to be won by this renewal of labor. Into my chalice I shall pour all the sap which is to be pressed out this day from the earth's fruits. My chalice and my paten are the depths of a soul laid widely open to all the forces which in a moment will rise up from every corner of the earth and converge upon the Spirit.... Over every living thing which is to spring up, to grow, to flower, to ripen during this day, say again the words: This is my Body.[45]

The Eucharist is to be a celebration of *holiness* and *wholeness*; matter, life, and spirit woven together into one divinely centered cosmos, enriched by the energies of love. The fruits of nature and the work of human creativity are to be integrated into the cosmic flow of God's life, as God's life grows into greater fullness in and through this wide, wonderful, and mysterious world of matter. Teilhard is clear that Christ's cosmic Body extends throughout the whole universe. He writes:

If we read Scripture with openness and breadth of mind, if we reject the timid interpretations of the narrow common-sense that is ready to take the words of Consecration literally.... The Incarnation is a making new, a restoration, of all the universe's forces and powers; Christ is the In-strument, the Centre, the End, of the whole of animate and material creation; through Him, everything is cre-ated, sanctified, and vivified.... The mystical Christ has not reached the peak of his growth—nor, therefore, has the cosmic Christ. Of both we may say that they are and at the same time are becoming: and it is in the continua-

---

45. Teilhard de Chardin, *Christianity and Evolution*, 119-21.

tion of this engendering that there lies the ultimate driving force behind all created activity. By the Incarnation,
which redeemed man, the very Becoming of the Universe,
too, has been transformed. Christ is the term of even the
natural evolution of living beings; *evolution is holy*. There
we have the truth that makes free... faith in the world
and faith in God.[46]

The key to cosmic wholeness is awakening to the realization that evolution is holy. Everything, Teilhard said, "every ex-
halation that passes through me, envelops me or captivates me,
emanates, without any doubt, from the heart of God.... Every
element of which I am made up is an overflow from God."[47] Incarnation calls for participation in the world's becoming. We
are to throw ourselves into the creative energies within us,
around us, and before us, for these energies are of God and are
divinely aimed toward the maximization of love and all that
love entails—beauty, goodness, truth, justice. This is Teilhard's
mantra: We are saved by an option that has chosen the whole.
To do so is to accept the cost of unification, the trials and tribulations of a world in movement. The cross, then, symbolizes the
creative effort needed to move to a higher level of life. As Teilhard states:

> The one who has determined to admit love of the world
> and its cares into his interior life finds that he has to ac-
> cept a supreme renunciation. He has sworn to seek for
> himself outside himself, in other words, to love the world
> better than himself. He will now have to realize what this
> noble ambition will cost him.... In the first place he must,
> in any case, work to drive things, and his own being, up
> the steep slope of liberation and purification, he must dis-
> cipline or conquer the hostile forces of matter.... The mul-
> titude of the dead cry out to him not to weaken, and from
> the depths of the future those who are waiting for their

---

46. Teilhard de Chardin, *Writings in a Time of War*, 59.
47. Teilhard de Chardin, *Writings in a Time of War*, 60.

turn to be born, stretch out their arms to him and beg him to build for them a loftier nest, warmer and brighter.[48]

We are saved, made whole, not as individuals but as a collective community, a body imbued with a living Spirit of life, the pulsating energies of love. We are made whole for the future of those who will follow us and continue the work of wholeness in the pursuit of Omega. The Christian is one who is connected through the heart to the whole of life, attuned to the deeper intelligence of nature, and called forth irresistibly by the Spirit to creatively express one's gifts in the evolution of God, self, and the world.

The universe is unfinished, we are unfinished, the earth is unfinished, and, much to our amazement, God is unfinished, as well. We are co-creators of the great movement toward Omega, the complexified wholeness of empowered life. We do not save ourselves without God, not by money or power or self-preservation. We are saved by our reconciliation with God within and without, by making a conscious option for the whole. As we are brought into wholeness, God too is made whole. Our lives and God's life are an inextricable whole, separated by the illusion of matter, united by the evolution of mind. The symbols of the Church can hold value if we read them in a new light of the evolving mind. As Thomas Berry wrote: "The human community and the natural world must be seen as a unified, single community with an overarching purpose: the exaltation and joy of existence, praise of the divine, and participation in the great liturgy of the universe."[49] We will go into the future together or not at all.

---

48. Teilhard de Chardin, *Writings in a Time of War*, 66.

49. Thomas Berry, *The Christian Future and the Fate of Earth*, ed. Mary Evelyn Tucker and John Grim (Maryknoll, NY: Orbis Books, 2009), 66.

10
Quaternization and the Not-Yet God

Carl Jung was intrigued by the notion of quaternity, the idea that God is a symbol of four interrelated persons rather than the three or Trinity. He was influenced by the sixteenth-century Lutheran mystic Jacob Boehme, who espoused the idea of quaternity in his writings, as well as Meister Eckhart, who speculated on the idea of quaternity. While Jung was inspired by these mystics, it was Teilhard who, without using the word "quaternity," described a new understanding of God in evolution that yields to a new "fourth" person, the Christic. Trinitization is the openness of divinity to become something more in human evolution. Teilhard's complexifying God is brought into quaternity through the process of Christogenesis. I would summarize Teilhard's quaternity this way: Trinity (3) enfolded into humanity (1) on the level of unitive consciousness is the Christ (4); Christ is the complexifying Whole, and this Whole is the emerging new person who is no longer the individual but the collective or cosmic Person.

To enter more deeply into the idea of quaternity, it is helpful to realize that, in ancient history, quaternity dominated Greek philosophy and science because it represented the number of completion or wholeness, such as in the four elements (earth, air, fire, and water), four directions (north, south, east, and west), as well as the number of dimensions in the space (length, width, height, and depth). Jung regarded quaternity as the most important symbol, even more important than trinity: "The quaternity is an archetype of almost universal occurrence.... There are always four elements, four prime qualities, four colors, four castes, four ways of spiritual development, etc. So, too, there are four aspects of psychological orientation.... The ideal of completeness is the circle sphere, but its natural minimal division is a quaternity."[1] In fact, Dante's final vision in the *Paradiso* captures the mystical vision of quaternity, the mandala, the human person in the cosmic divine heart:

> As the geometer who sets himself
> To square the circle and who cannot find,
> For all his thought, the principle he needs,
>
> Just so was I on seeing this new vision
> I wanted to see how our image fuses
> Into the circle and finds its place in it,
>
> Yet my wings were not meant for such a flight —
> Except that then my mind was struck by lightning
> Through which my longing was at last fulfilled.
>
> Here powers failed my high imagination:
> But by now my desire and will were turned,
> Like a balanced wheel rotated evenly,
>
> By the Love that moves the sun and the other stars.[2]

The square within the circle, humanity in divinity, divinity in humanity is the inextricable mystery of divine love in the heart of

---

1. Carl Jung, "Psychology and Religion" (The Terry Lectures), *Collected Works* 11 (Princeton: Princeton University Press, 1938/1940), para. 246.

2. Dante Alighieri, *The Divine Comedy*, trans. Henry Wadsworth Longfellow (Philadelphia: National Library Company, 1909), Canto XXXIII: 130–45.

matter: quaternity symbolizes the dynamic mystery of incarnation. Three divine persons embracing one human nature gives rise to a blinding vision of a new person in whom divinity is entangled. What was envisioned by Dante in the fourteenth century was brought to light in the twentieth century in the thought of Jung and Teilhard.

JUNG AND DIVINE QUATERNITY

Jung shifted the religious matrix from a two-tiered system of God and world to a relational holism in which divinity is integral to the whole: "[D]ivinity approaches consciousness from no other source than... one's own being."[3] As we have said many times throughout this book, God and humanity are entangled or, in Jung's words, "functions of each other."[4] This is a critical realist approach that places consciousness as the axis of the God-human whole. For Jung, the Trinity is not reconciled within itself but in the process of history and, in particular, the human person, in whom divinity dwells as ground, depth, and light. The human person does not dwell *in* God and God does not dwell *in* the human; rather, God and human are correlative and require each other for completion. God completes the human, and the human completes God. The completion of God and human is the cosmic joy of the earth; all nature resounds with the glory of God.

Jung thought "out of the box" primarily because he found the human mind to be an endless wellspring of possibilities. He saw the divine capacity of the human person and he saw the human capacity for God. He had no regard for the fallen human in search of the perfect God; rather, he espoused the entangled God and the co-redemptive need of God and human for each other. In this respect, one can understand his ideas on the Trinity as a tension of opposites, a divine self-contradiction, seeking to be resolved in

---

3. John Dourley, "Jung's Equation of the Ground of Being with the Ground of the Psyche," *Journal of Analytical Psychology* 56 (2011): 520.

4. Dourley, "Jung's Equation of the Ground of Being with the Ground of the Psyche," 521.

humanity. A God of inner opposites (power and receptivity; source and servant) cannot be the fullness of love unless opposites are reconciled; otherwise, God's life is chaotic and imbalanced and, in Jung's view, a chaotic God can allow evil. Hence the incomplete God and the unreconciled power of evil can be resolved only in the human person who can actualize God's love.

None of the monotheistic faiths have challenged the integrity of God, much less posited an internally conflicted God. Such ideas seem absurd, if not outright scandalous. Theology developed a medieval wall around an omnipotent and omniscient God. Jung, however, treated God as a patient in need of inner healing, showing the vulnerability of God in light of the human person. The cure for God and the human, he said, is to connect the mind with its own transcendent depth and allow the truly humanizing religious experience to surface. This "therapy" is needed, in his view, to progress toward a more just and peaceful world. Jung's radical ideas on the incarnation as a psychic integration, however, have been met by obstinate resistance, especially from uncompromising theologians. John Dourley writes:

> Theologians have contributed greatly to the demise of such a perspective with their conception of transcendent and wholly other Gods entering into arbitrary covenants or agreements with a variety of peoples set apart. Such theologies never realized that Gods without a natural and experiential presence and stake in humanity and its outcome render human life meaningless and themselves irrelevant. Today's theological tragedy consists largely in the systematic extirpation of humanity's universal and natural sense of the divine in the interests of commending one or other divinity as the answer to the resulting emptiness. The deliberate inoculation of the mind against its native religious instinct backfired. Religion as a humanizing factor died and with it the credibility of its institutional variants. [5]

---

5. Dourley, "Jung's Equation of the Ground of Being with the Ground of the Psyche," 526.

Jung saw the urgent need to reconcile the ego with the psyche if we are to aspire to wholeness; in religious terms, if we are to be saved. While this approach seems to compromise divine transcendence, he was clear that the ground of the psyche cannot be transcended and remains ever transcendent to all. The infinite potential of the ground, however, impels it to an ever-fuller birth in history, which is the meaning of incarnation. By equating divinity with the ground of psychic existence itself, Jung proposed a new religious myth that speaks to every person because every person is capable of divinization. Dourley sums up Jung's Neo-Christian myth:

> The Council of Chalcedon's description of Christ as possessed of two natures in one person becomes a description of the process of individuation brought to full consciousness in Jung's psychology. The two natures present in everyone when taken out of Greek substantive categories are those of consciousness and the unconscious whose unification works toward the divinization of the person to the extent their unification is approximated in the person.[6]

Jung's holistic God is open to new and fulfilling life, to quaternity. Jung spoke of the feminine and bodily polarities that long to be included in divinity in order for divinity to fulfill itself. In Jung's view, the Assumption of the Blessed Virgin Mary, which was made a dogma of the Catholic Church in 1950, was a step in the right direction toward wholeness, that is, masculine and feminine, matter and spirit, body and soul are reconciled as mutually affirming opposites in God's own Trinitarian life. The Catholic Church does not consider Mary as a divine figure, but the Assumption does suggest a goddess figure as part of divine reality. Jung wrote: "I consider the declaration of the Assumption the most important symbological event since the Reformation."[7] In

---

6. Dourley, "Jung's Equation of the Ground of Being with the Ground of the Psyche," 524.

7. Murray Stein, *Jung on Christianity* (Princeton: Princeton University Press, 1999), 274.

his letter on "The Missing Element in Christianity," he notes that the feminine and bodily elements build upon Jacob Boehme's insight on quaternity. Unless God's life is reconciled with opposites, such as evil, matter, the feminine, and all other opposites, there is no resolution to evil. This is not an effort to break with tradition or challenge orthodoxy; rather, it is an effort to reconcile God and the human psyche. As Jung said: "I do not fight for a recognition of the "fourth" (that is, quaternity). . . . I only fight *for* the reactivation of symbolic thinking, because of its therapeutic value, and *against* the presumptuous undervaluation of myth."[8] By reframing theology as a function of the psyche, Jung proposed everything the Church rejects: monism, pantheism, and quaternity. His insights impel us to take seriously the role of the mind as the co-redemptive field of divine and human energies. This is what Teilhard thought, as well.

THE CHRISTIC FOURTH

While Jung explored the fields of the mind, Teilhard wrote on the depths of matter in evolution. He saw that a new spirit of the earth is needed, a new connection to the whole, a new religious consciousness, born out of the wisdom of the past but refashioned for a convergent future. God and world are complementary opposites: God and world belong together and complete one another in mutually affirming union. God and humanity are in an entangled state and the individuation of each is inextricably bound with the other.

The entanglement of God and world is symbolized by the concept of Omega. God becomes God in union with what is not God, because the nature of God is to become what it is not in order to reveal what it is.[9] Through ongoing incarnation, God is completed by humankind in directed evolution. The evolution of God and

---

8. Stein, *Jung on Christianity*, 275.

9. Peter Todd, "Teilhard and Other Modern Thinkers on Evolution, Mind, and Matter," *Teilhard Studies* 66 (2013): 5.

the evolution of humanity cannot be separated. Todd states: "It is as an archetypal and cosmic reality rather than a purely theological concept."[10] What Todd means, in my view, is that the notion of God is more than faith in a divine reality. Rather, "God" is the name that points to the Whole of the cosmic whole. The name "God" speaks of the infinite depth of all that exists. Hence God is a cosmic name before it is a religious one, which is why the incarnation is the fulfillment of natural evolution. God enfleshed (divine wholeness) is what empowers evolution, so that incarnation becomes explicit when consciousness awakens to this divine immanent power. "This transformation in consciousness," Todd writes, "is the divinization or resacralization of the world."[11] As God emerges through higher levels of consciousness, the human evolves to a new level of completion, a new vision, a new way of knowing and acting in the world.

The incarnation is typically described as the Word made flesh, but this simple statement does not do justice to the power of the divine mystery. Teilhard recognized that incarnation is the radical transformation of God and the radical transformation of embodied life. God becomes something new, and the human person becomes something new. "As God metamorphizes the world from the depths of matter to the peaks of Spirit," he wrote, "so in addition the World must inevitably and to the same degree 'endomorphize' God."[12] The metamorphosis of God, in the Jungian sense, is God's individuation in us which undergoes growth and development as a result of divine magnetic power and our own thought. An entangled relationship with God means that one nature cannot be changed without affecting the other. If God were not personal entangled love, incarnation would not be possible; if matter were not formed by mind, God would be without a per-

---

10. Todd, "Teilhard and Other Modern Thinkers on Evolution, Mind, and Matter," 8.

11. Todd, "Teilhard and Other Modern Thinkers on Evolution, Mind, and Matter," 8.

12. Pierre Teilhard de Chardin, *The Heart of Matter*, trans. René Hague (New York: Harcourt Brace Jovanovich, 1979), 52–53.

sonal form. The God-human is a holon, a whole within a larger whole. Teilhard poetically describes the process of cosmic personalization in his *Hymn of the Universe:*

> A Being was taking form in the totality of space; a Being with the attractive power of a soul, palpable like a body, vast as the sky; a Being which mingled with things yet remained distinct from them; a Being of a higher order than the substance of things with which it was adorned, yet, taking shape within them. The rising Sun was being born in the heart of the world.[13]

Something is going on in this chaotic world of struggle and suffering, and it can easily escape the physical eye unless one sees from a deeper center. God and the world are in the process of becoming *something more* together because the universe is grounded in the Personal center of divine love.

Teilhard celebrated the spiritual power of matter and spoke of it as the source of all energy and the crucible of the Spirit. His attraction to matter was strong, almost ecstatic. For him matter was ensouled, divinized, and holy—and he wrote a hymn of praise to "The Spiritual Power of Matter." The heart of matter—the heart of reality—is infused with divine power and presence; it is "the hand of God, the flesh of Christ."[14] The power of matter was real and impelled him to embrace the universe in an act of communion and union. Matter expresses the spiritual power of God: "I bless you, matter. . . . I acclaim you as the divine *milieu,* charged with creative power, as the ocean stirred by the Spirit, as the clay molded and infused with life by the incarnate Word."[15] Teilhard's entangled God is the energy of divine love giving matter its morphogenic power, its future.

---

13. Pierre Teilhard de Chardin, *Hymn of the Universe*, trans. Gerald Vann, OP (New York: Harper and Row, 1965), 68.

14. Teilhard de Chardin, *Hymn of the Universe*, 64.

15. Teilhard de Chardin, *Hymn of the Universe*, 65.

The Third Nature

By reflecting on the incarnation within an unfolding spacetime universe, Teilhard considered that divinity cannot unite with humanity without first being united to cosmic nature. Hence, he spoke of the "third nature" of Christ without which the other two natures cannot be fully united. The idea of a "third nature," or entangled divine-created energies, can be traced back to the patristic era, especially in Orthodox theology, where the idea of theandric nature emerged. In one of his letters to the monk Gaius, Pseudo-Dionysius wrote:

> For, if I may put the matter briefly, he [Christ] was neither human nor nonhuman; although humanly born he was far superior to man, and being above men, he yet truly did become man. Furthermore, it was not by virtue of being God that he did divine things, not by virtue of being a man that he did what was human, but rather, by virtue of being God-made-man he accomplished something new in our midst—the activity of the God-man (literally, the "theandric" activity).[16]

David Coffey states that "the single activity of Christ should be characterized neither as simply divine nor simply human, but as something unique, divine-human, theandric."[17] Coffey follows the patristic notion that theandrism results in the uniqueness of Christ's person, who was considered "monoenergetist" or "monophysite" (one nature). This notion of the theandric Christ was condemned by Pope Saint Martin I in 649 CE and the condemnation was confirmed by the Third Council of Constantinople in 681.[18] The relation of these two operations was expressed by

---

16. Colm Luibheid, trans., *Pseudo-Dionysius: The Complete Works*, Classics of Western Spirituality (New York: Paulist Press, 1987), 265.

17. David Coffey, "The Theandric Nature of Christ," *Theological Studies* 60 (1999): 407.

18. Coffey, "The Theandric Nature of Christ," 407.

John of Damascus in the following way: "Being God made man, he manifested a new, strange, and theandric operation: divine but working through the human, human but serving the divine and exhibiting the tokens of his conjoined divinity."[19] And because of their unity in the divine person, the two natures operated in "communion" with each other.[20] Thomas Aquinas put it this way: "Dionysius places in Christ a theandric or divine-human operation ... because his (Christ's) divine operation uses his human operation (that is, via his obedience), and his human operation participates in the efficacy of the divine operation."[21] Reflecting on the theandric nature of Christ, the contemporary theologian Edward Schillebeeckx spoke of Christ as being a special type of human because the mystery of God lies in his being human:

> The divine nature of Jesus is relevant to the saving mystery only insofar as it alters and elevates the human nature. And whatever that is must be called a new mode of being man. We keep turning around in the same circle: the divine nature is here irrelevant except insofar as it elevates the human nature. To the extent that it does this, it puts us in contact with a *human* reality. When one says, "Jesus is, besides man, also God," such an "also God" cannot form part of the salvation reality. The mystery borrows its whole reality from what belongs to the human sphere.[22]

In a similar but more definitive way, Karl Rahner said that "the incarnation of God is the uniquely highest case of the perfection of the human reality, which consists in the fact that man *is* insofar as he gives himself up."[23] What Rahner suggested is that

---

19. Coffey, "The Theandric Nature of Christ," 408.

20. Coffey, "The Theandric Nature of Christ," 408.

21. Coffey, "The Theandric Nature of Christ," 408–9.

22. Edward Schillebeeckx, "Persoonlijke openbaringsgestalte van de Vader," *Tijdschrift voor Theologie* 6 (1966): 275.

23. Karl Rahner, "Zur Theologie der Menschwerdung," *Schriften zur Theologie* 4 (Einsiedeln: Benziger, 1964): 142–43.

"human nature, though created, is potentially divine, and, in the case of Christ, actually so."[24] Christ's human nature is genuinely human, but more so, it is divinely human, or human in a divine way. This is a way of speaking about Christ's theandric nature. It is not purely divine nature nor is it mere mortal matter. It is an entangled relation of natures.

To say that Christ's natures exist "without confusion or change" is to use obsolete terms to describe a wondrous mystery. The basis for Rahner's insight is that human nature has an intrinsic openness to God, what he called *obedientia potentialis,* and this openness is realized in the person of Jesus Christ, without exhausting the human capacity for God. Coffey argues that Rahner's position is not some kind of *tertium quid*; it is human, but it is the human at the limit of its possibility under grace. He interprets Rahner by saying "there are two ways of being divine: the simply given divinity of the transcendent God, and the divinity achieved by divine grace in humanity."[25] This notion of grace-filled nature is based on Scholastic notions of substance and accident. Divinity may be substantial, as in the case of Christ, or "accidental," that is, by habitual grace, as in the case of other human beings, Coffey writes.[26]

The effort here is to interpret the theandric nature of Christ in a way that is faithful to the norms of Chalcedon, that is, the unity of Christ without change, confusion, separation, or division. The notion of the theandric nature, according to classical philosophical notions of substance and accidents, however, contradicts one of the most significant aspects of modern science, namely, change. Matter does not simply mean a plurality of forms; rather matter itself is constantly forming or coming into being. All matter is in search of a form, Teilhard thought, and the evolution of matter toward greater complexity and consciousness is the emergence of form. The form of matter is how Teilhard conceived of the *symbol* of the Christ, a concrete reality that takes on definite shape in the life of Jesus of Nazareth. He recognized a unifying influence in

---

24. Coffey, "The Theandric Nature of Christ," 412.
25. Coffey, "The Theandric Nature of Christ," 413.
26. Coffey, "The Theandric Nature of Christ," 413.

the whole evolutionary process, a centrating factor that continues to hold the entire process together and move it forward; this centrating factor is Christ Omega.

In his essay on "The Christic," Teilhard states that "energy is presence."[27] The energy of the incarnation is present in a physical —not a metaphysical—way because God is born in time and *of* time, in matter and *of* matter.[28] Christ is more God than "God" and more human than "human." He wrote: "There is more in the total Christ than Man and God. There is also He who, in his 'theandric' being, gathers up the whole of creation: *in quo omnia constant.*"[29] Christ is the whole space-time-matter evolution in a personal union entangled with God. Teilhard spoke of a third nature of Christ, indicating that divinity, humanity, and cosmos are three interlocking realities united in a single reality. He describes this nature as follows: "Between the Word on the one side and Man-Jesus on the other, a kind of 'third Christic nature' (if I may dare to say so) emerges...that of the total and totalizing Christ."[30] He spoke of a third aspect or the theandric (divine-human) complex as "the *cosmic nature*" which, in Teilhard's view,

---

27. Teilhard de Chardin, *Heart of Matter*, 99.

28. Teilhard de Chardin, *Heart of Matter*, 48.

29. Teilhard de Chardin, *Heart of Matter*, 93.

30. Pierre Teilhard de Chardin, *Christianity and Evolution: Reflections on Science and Religion*, trans. René Hague (New York: Harcourt Brace Jovanovich, 1971),179; cited in J. A. Lyons, *The Cosmic Christ in Origen and Teilhard de Chardin: A Comparative Study* (Oxford: Oxford University Press, 1982), 183–96. The concept of a "third nature" is difficult to grasp if we conceive of nature as substantial being. Although Teilhard's insight is more mystical than scientific, we can describe this third nature along the lines of what science is telling us today about matter, namely, that it is thoroughly relational. There is no part that is not related to other parts and every part is the result of its relationships. Hence, the whole is in every part and every part represents the whole. If Christ is the divine Word truly incarnate, then every aspect of matter is truly Christ and Christ is every aspect of matter. The humanity of Christ symbolizes the meaning of Christ not only for humanity but for the entire creation. In short, the cosmic or third nature that Teilhard describes is not a figurative description but a literal one. It underlies his "Mass on the World," in which he could offer up all his activities and all creation "through him, with him, and in him" to the glory of the Father.

has not been sufficiently distinguished from the other two natures (divine and human).

The apprehension of a third nature of Christ means that the
whole physical world has a spiritual nature that attains its full
consciousness and openness to God in the person of Jesus Christ.
By using the term "third nature," Teilhard suggested that Christ
is related organically—not simply juridically—to the whole cosmos. If evolution is the process of emerging life, a process that
eventually discloses God to the human mind, then the third nature is the evolving nature of Christ, in which humanity opens
up to divinity. The third nature, the cosmic nature of Christ,
emerges from an entangled God-world relationship and is cosmotheandric. In this respect, cosmogenesis (the birthing of cosmos) is Christogenesis (the birthing of Christ).[31]

James Lyons states that Christ, in his third nature, is the orga-
nizing principle in Teilhard's evolving universe. Whereas the
Alexandrian Logos was the organizing principle of the stable
Greek cosmos, today we must identify Christ with a "new
Logos"; the evolutive principle of a universe in movement. Christ
in his third nature is the prime mover of the evolving universe.[32]
Teilhard saw himself in the tradition of the Greek Fathers, especially Irenaeus and Gregory of Nyssa. He believed his concept of
Christ the evolver should have the effect of "giving traditional
Christianity a new reinforcement of up-to-dateness and vitality,"[33]
presumably in the same way the theology of the Greek Fathers
did. He found the Latin Fathers and Western Christology in general far too juridical: "[T]he Christian history of the world has assumed the appearance of a legal trial between God and his
creatures."[34] Teilhard envisioned a Christology for a new evolutionary world. He wrote: "Since, in fact, only one single process of
synthesis is going on from top to bottom of the whole universe,

---

31. Teilhard de Chardin, *Christianity and Evolution*, 181.

32. Lyons, *Cosmic Christ in Origen and Teilhard de Chardin*, 185–86.

33. Henri de Lubac, *Teilhard de Chardin: The Man and His Meaning* (New
York: New American Library, 1967), 49.

34. Teilhard de Chardin, *Christianity and Evolution*, 89.

no element and no movement can exist at any level of the world outside the informing action of the principal center of things."[35] He insisted that it is time to return to a form of Christology which is more organic and takes more account of physics. We need a Christ "who is no longer master of the world solely because he has been *proclaimed* to be such," he wrote, "but because he animates the whole range of things from top to bottom."[36] Teilhard's insight into the mystery of Christ lies in the organic nature of Christ as the heart of change in the universe: "If we are to remain faithful to the gospel," he says,

> We have to adjust its spiritual code to the new shape of the universe. It has ceased to be the formal garden from which we are temporarily banished by a whim of the Creator. It has become *the great work* in process of completion *which we have to save by saving ourselves.*[37]

The geologian Father Thomas Berry highlighted the "great work" as the work of our own time. Following the insights of Teilhard, Berry advocated for conscious involvement in the healing of the earth, since "nothing is itself without everything else ... the universe remains a single multiform reality."[38] We cannot remain passive in the hope of salvation; rather, it is our active involvement in the fate of the earth and the formation of the human community that is our salvation. We are saved by our awareness of belonging to a whole.

CHRISTOGENESIS

Teilhard's notion of the third nature of Christ shifts the meaning of the Christ from a single personal savior to pleromizer, the sym-

35. Teilhard de Chardin, *Christianity and Evolution*, 88.

36. Teilhard de Chardin, *Christianity and Evolution*, 89.

37. Teilhard de Chardin, *Christianity and Evolution*, 91–92.

38. Mary Evelyn Tucker and John Grim, eds., *The Christian Future and the Fate of the Earth* (Maryknoll, NY: Orbis Books, 2009), 53.

bol of vital fullness. Christ is seen as integral to the process of evolution itself. The ultimate mover of the entire cosmogenesis, he indicated, is something that is simultaneously *within* the sequence of beings as tendency, desire, and purpose, and *in front* of the advancing wave of development, beckoning it, as its ideal culmination. Teilhard identified this Mover with God. The whole history of the universe, and particularly the history of biological life on earth, has been characterized by the steady emergence of complexity. Teilhard described evolution as a "biological ascent," a movement toward more complexified life forms which, at critical points in the evolutionary process, qualitative differences emerge. He extended the term "evolution" beyond its biological meaning and applied it to the whole cosmic process. This progressive evolutionary movement is one in which the consistence of the elements and their stability of balance lie in the direction not of matter but of spirit.[39] Thus, he concluded, "there is only one real evolution, the evolution of convergence, because it alone is positive and creative."[40] We always assumed that God could be located "above," he said, but now we realize that he can also be situated "ahead" and "within," as well. His faith in Christ led him to posit Christ as the future fullness of the whole evolutionary process, the "centrating principle," the "pleroma" and "Omega point" whereby the individual and collective adventure of humanity finds its end and fulfillment. The universal Christ could not appear at the end of time at the peak of the world, if he had not previously entered it during its development. Christ is key to evolution's direction.

For Teilhard, the entire universe can be seen as a vast transhuman body in the process of formation. Individuals are like partially separable cells that comprise the cosmic Body, the great Being, that is coming to be. Ultimately, the Self of Christ is the soul of the world. The cosmic Person, the Christ, is the form or organic

---

39. See Pierre Teilhard de Chardin, *Activation of Energy*, trans. René Hague (New York: Harcourt Brace Jovanovich, 1970), 387–403; Pierre Teilhard de Chardin, *The Phenomenon of Man*, trans. Bernard Wall (New York: Harper & Row, 1959), 46–66.

40. Teilhard de Chardin, *Christianity and Evolution*, 87.

life emerging in evolution. The world falls forward in the direction of Spirit through the energies of love, which is why nature appears as an "almost heart-rending effort towards light and consciousness."[41] The chaotic appearance of matter and the dark shadow of the future is due to our seeing the development of the universe "from the underside," which is dark, fearful, and fragmented. The harmony of events or the possibility of union must be viewed in descending order, beginning with the cosmic Christ, the risen Christ, and working backward to the beginning of evolution. Only then, Teilhard claims, can we know what God is doing in evolution and what we are created for in this process of Christogenesis.

Teilhard used the term *Christogenesis* to indicate that the biological and cosmological genesis of creation—cosmogenesis—is, from the point of faith, Christogenesis. The genesis of Christ, the cosmic person, is the core of Teilhard's thought. As we are incorporated into the life of God, so too God's life is incorporated into us; God is transformed as we are transformed. By saying that cosmogenesis is now Christogenesis, Teilhard indicated that the very being of the world is being personalized. The emerging Christic is the Personal center of a personalizing universe. Raimon Panikkar wrote:

> *If the Christian message means something, it is this experience of the cosmotheandric reality of all being,* of which Christ is the paradigm. Christ symbolizes that matter is not on its own, nor is the human on one side and God on the other; none of these intrinsically united dimensions surpass the others, so that it does not make sense to affirm that Christ is more divine than human, more worldly than heavenly, or vice versa. The veil of separation has been torn, and the integration of reality begins with the redemption of man.[42]

To say that Christ is more God than God and more human than human is to affirm that something new emerges in the

---

41. Thomas King, *Teilhard's Mysticism of Knowing* (New York: Seabury Press, 1981), 21.

42. Raimon Panikkar, *Culto y secularización. Apuntes para una antropología litúrgica* (Madrid: Marova, 1979), 37.

Christ event. By bringing together the birth of God in time and the emergence of Jesus, the Christ, Teilhard brings together the Christian hope of new creation and the evolution of complexity-consciousness. We are not outside God's becoming. On the contrary, we are integral to the convergent and emergent process of theogenic evolution. God is being born from within. God emerges in the form of a person and has a personality marked by love. Such a position does not diminish God but "contributes something that is vitally necessary to God."[43] God's self-sufficiency is paradoxically God's dependency. God does not need matter to be God; yet, without matter God cannot be God. God is entangled with created being and created being is entangled with God. This dynamic unitive becoming is the inextricable wholeness, the third nature of Christ. The emergence of the Christ is the process of quaternization or the movement toward fullness (*pleroma*). Thus, Teilhard states: "As God fulfills himself, he in some way completes himself, in the pleroma."[44]

A Christogenic universe calls us to recognize that connectedness is a basic reality of our existence. We are wholes within wholes. All we do affects all the other wholes of which we are a part and all the other parts that make us whole. Seeking wholeness as a way of life—becoming Christified—means traversing the levels of consciousness that keep us bound within a constricted ego. It is the path of the mystic. It is a difficult path as one confronts one's own fractured ego: the walls of ego protection, the defenses of ego security, and the power of ego control. To seek the higher power within is to enter into the place of the unknown, the darkness or the shadows within blocking light. This is the risky business of exposing oneself to oneself, for one enters the place of spiritual poverty where one relies on nothing but the power of God and the infinite field of divine potentials that undergird the divine energies of love. One must approach life *sine proprio,* without possessing anything, unafraid to enter within. To enter the place of unspoken love and to find oneself in love is the birth of

---

43. Panikkar, *Culto y secularización,* 177.
44. Panikkar, *Culto y secularización,* 178.

the Christic, the New Person. This birth changes everything: life is changed, and a new power is unleashed in the world. One becomes a *person* as one progresses from an isolated and protected ego to an open, relational, and connected person belonging to the whole. One is connected to the widest fields of life. A person is one who freely lives by the life of the whole. In this respect, the Christic becomes the *terrestrian*, one who is at home in every land and with every person, of every color, gender, and language; with every rock, mountain, and star. The Christic gives glory to God in the cathedral of the universe. In her book *The Grand Option*, Beatrice Bruteau writes:

- To be "in Christ" is to accept the offer that Jesus makes, to be food for his friends. One must renounce the lordship pattern of organizing social relations. One must forsake being either dominant or submissive. One must undergo this "particular mutation in consciousness."

- To be "in Christ" is to enter into the revolutionary events of Holy Thursday by...letting an old modality of consciousness die and seeing a new one rise to life.

- To be "in Christ" is to abandon thinking of oneself only in terms of categories and abstractions by which one may be externally related to others and to coincide with oneself as a transcendent center of energy that lives *in* God and *in* one's fellows—because that is where the Christ lives, in God and in us.

- To be "in Christ" is to experience oneself as an initiative of free energy radiating out to give life abundantly to all, for that is the function of the Christ. To be "in Christ" is to be an indispensable member of a living body, which is the Body of Christ.[45]

---

45. Beatrice Bruteau, *The Grand Option: Personal Transformation and a New Creation* (Notre Dame, IN: University of Notre Dame Press, 2001), 173.

Bruteau reveals that the Christ is all of us, the *totus Christus,* as Saint Augustine wrote. To live "in" Christ is to "experience oneself as a center of free energy," to "let an old modality of consciousness die," to "accept the offer of Jesus and undergo a mutation of consciousness." She finally discloses that Christ is the whole, and the whole is the Church. As we enter by our transcendent freedom into Christ, as the ego is reconciled with the deeper levels of the psyche, as the mind integrates its activities through consolidation of consciousness, one becomes a new creation. On this level of Christic life, we "enter by faith into the future of every person and into the very heart of creativity itself, into the future of God."[46] We become the Christ in evolution:

> If I am asked, then, "Who do you say I am?" my answer is: "You are the new and ever renewing act of creation. You are all of us, as we are united in You. You are all of us as we live in one another. You are all of us in the whole cosmos as we join in Your exuberant act of creation. You are the Living One who improvises at the frontier of the future; and it has not yet appeared what You shall be."[47]

To enter into the Christ self, the self of communal consciousness by which the new creation unfolds with new potential, is a radical break with the way we are "self-conscious," or constricted egos. We are called to unlearn the habitual consciousness of self-preservation and learn a new way of doing consciousness rather than being self-conscious. As Bruteau insightfully points out: "Our self-consciousness is not simply there, but we *perform it* as an act of living."[48] Performative consciousness is the creation of the self on the level of freedom and transcendence. Acting from a deeper inner center must be a union of our most vital energies, which do not flow freely if we are constrained by lower conscious levels of self-preservation.

---

46. Bruteau, *The Grand Option,* 173.
47. Bruteau, *The Grand Option,* 173.
48. Bruteau, *The Grand Option,* 158.

One who lives in Christ lives from the deepest center of the self, the God center, in which the freedom to express oneself is shown in the desire to love wildly and live in the adventure of the spirit. Every person has the potential to live the Christ life, but only a few arrive at this deepest reality. Many are caught in the traps of fear and distrust fostered by narrow religious convictions and a mindless culture. Only inner transformation can escape cosmic entropy and centrate energy on higher levels of complexity. Teilhard espoused a new type of Christian life that involves faith in the radicalization of God and faith in the evolution of ecological life. Living into wholeness is vital for the health of the planet and the direction of evolution toward Omega. Teilhard insisted that the human person is vitally related to the formation of the dynamic universe. One must train the mind, however, through meditation or contemplation, that is, forming a habitual practice of harnessing the levels of the mind and focusing on the centrality of love. When our minds and hearts expand in love, God is born in us and through us into the universe; the world moves ever closer toward Omega. We are God's becoming.

QUATERNIZATION AND THE OMEGA POINT

The new person reflects the newness of God and the newness of humanity. Like Jesus, the one who arrives at the level of Christ consciousness lives from a new center. God is active and alive in a new way as new potentials for wholeness are realized. God is not utter simplicity, Teilhard suggested. God complexifies in evolution, as consciousness attains higher levels. The more consciousness is unified, the more the world converges—but only love can unify. Unification is the coming together of mind, matter, and the power of love.

The process of pleromization or active fullness is symbolized by the Christic, the Fourth Person, the New Person. The triune God entangled with humanity is brought into a new union through consciousness. The Christic is both personal and collective; persons transformed by divine love personalize the world in love. This dynamic engagement is the emergence of quaternity. Quaternization is the fulfillment of Trinitarian life in evolution, that is, the rise of the Christic. Quaternization expresses the ongoing completion of God in evolution, which is the supremely personal cosmic life. This is what Teilhard envisioned as Omega. God is unfinished, and we are unfinished. In Teilhard's paradigm, pleromization *is* quaternization insofar as the process of trinitization is the openness of divine life to new life in a supremely personal way, the Christic, whereby the third nature—the conscious nature—completes divinity and humanity in a complexified whole.[49]

What would our world look like if we lived with awareness of an unfinished God? What would we do? How would we act? We have built a world of values based on finality when, in fact, every end is a new beginning. Our task is to become conscious of divinity within us and creatively advance in love toward the wholeness of life. God seeks to become God in us. It is not enough simply to believe in God, Teilhard said; rather, we are to incarnate God and to help God become God if we are to realize the potential of created existence.[50] As God emerges through higher levels of consciousness, the human evolves from an incomplete whole to a new level of completion.

We know today that we earthlings are part of one small planet in a universe of about two trillion galaxies and about one hundred billion planets in our Milky Way galaxy. God Omega extends far beyond terrestrial life. While Teilhard believed that evolution was teleologically oriented toward Omega, he never assumed that life on planet Earth could be its sole intelligent product. Just as the infinite universe stretches into new life by the

---

49. Teilhard spoke of a "third nature" of Christ. In his writings, he describes this nature as follows: "Between the Word on the one side and Man-Jesus on the other, a kind of 'third Christic nature' (if I may dare to say so) emerges...that of the total and totalizing Christ." He spoke of a third aspect of the theandric (divine-human) complex as "the cosmic nature" which, in his view, had not been sufficiently distinguished from the other two natures (divine and human). See Teilhard de Chardin, *Christianity and Evolution*, 179; Lyons, *The Cosmic Christ in Origen and Teilhard de Chardin*, 183–96.

50. Teilhard de Chardin, *Heart of Matter*, 53.

expansion and convergence of consciousness, so, too, God is not limited by Earth life but continues to seek fulfillment in all possible forms of intelligent life.

Conscious material life will continuously search for more life and consciousness wherever such life abounds; divinity seeks completion in all forms of intelligent life. In this respect, the Christian story is entirely too small and distorts the incomprehensible love of God. The universe will extend far into the future, to a point where consciousness and matter will unite in perfect unity throughout all galactic life and where the maximization of conscious material life will be divine. This will be the full flowering of the Omega point. Perhaps this will be the end of our Big Bang universe, but I am sure there will be others.

11

The Religion of Tomorrow

Teilhard de Chardin and Carl Jung realized that religious symbolic life is moribund and that the human person has become disconnected within and without. New developments in physics and biology, together with advances in neuroscience and psychology, led both thinkers to reconsider Christian faith in light of the new science. Teilhard stated that any religion that focuses only on individuals and heaven is insufficient; "people are looking for a religion of humankind and of the earth that gives meaning to human achievements; a place to enkindle cosmic and human evolution and a deep sense of commitment to the earth."[1] Jung thought that a reawakening of the symbolic life was needed if religion is to survive in the current age. The experience of God and the language in which such experience is articulated must find new forms of expression. Teilhard was convinced that the cosmos has become a cosmogenesis, and this fact alone "must lead to the

---

1. Ursula King, *The Spirit of One Earth: Reflections on Teilhard de Chardin and Global Spirituality* (New York: Paragon House, 1989), 109; Pierre Teilhard de Chardin, *Activation of Energy*, trans. René Hague (New York: Harcourt Brace Jovanovich, 1963), 240.

profound modification of the whole structure not only of our thoughts, but of our beliefs."[2] Human consciousness finds itself on the threshold of a new age, impelling religious systems to find new dimensions and values.

A NEW RELIGION OF THE EARTH

Teilhard spoke of two types of faith: faith in the world and faith in God. In his view, the emergence of a "new religion of evolution" must have a vertical dimension and a horizontal dimension: God above and God ahead. "Above" refers not to a spatiotemporal dimension but to a transcendence of the conceptual grasp; "above" is "below." One "ascends" by descending into the interior depth within. A true religion of progress, he thought, must integrate our faith in the development and perfectibility of this world as well as faith in God as the activating force of attraction which makes development possible.

He did not advocate for a new religion of humanity or a syncretistic substitute for old religions. Instead, he saw the need for a general convergence of the different religious traditions, each according to its capacity, to animate and nourish the evolutionary drive within human beings. The uniting force between and among the different religions must be dialogue and encounter, based on the various religions' perspectives of the human being. A new religious vision cannot develop in cultural isolation.

From Teilhard's perspective, such vision requires the coming together of experiences drawn from different religious traditions.[3] He saw the encounter of religions as full of promise for the future of religion and was anxious to encourage all efforts toward greater unity.[4] Ursula King notes that "a convergence of the historically diverse religious traditions appeared to Teilhard

---

2. Ursula King, *Teilhard de Chardin and Eastern Religions: Spirituality and Mysticism in an Evolutionary World* (Mahwah, NJ: Paulist Press, 2011), 160.

3. King, *Teilhard de Chardin and Eastern Religions*, 184.

4. King, *Teilhard de Chardin and Eastern Religions*, 193.

to be a structurally necessary requirement for the higher evolution of humankind itself."[5] "Convergence," she continues, "means the search for, or the movement towards, a common meeting point through which we can interrelate and create a unity that transcends our diverse particularities.... It includes the vision of a common meeting point or summit where different currents can converge."[6] Teilhard saw that each great tradition has centuries of experience that are indispensable to the integrity of a total terrestrial consciousness and that each tradition offers a way of contact with the "supreme inexpressible One" or Source of life. We can appreciate Teilhard's insights by saying that the world's religions have paths of spiritual wisdom, but such paths are not ends in themselves. There is no one doctrine or spiritual path that can exhaust the mystery of God; the mystery must remain open, both as a conceptual idea and as an unfathomable horizon of being.

The decisive test for evaluating traditional religions, Teilhard thought, has to do with the strength of their capacity to evolve, to lead humankind to greater unity. He wrote: "The biological function of religion is to give a form to the free psychic energy of the world,"[7] that is, to shape the mind in a particular way. Religion is the deepest energy of thought. No one religion has a monopoly on cosmic convergence; rather, all religions can contribute particular strands of wisdom that can lead to unity, "the supreme unification of the universe."[8] Religious convergence, therefore, should not manifest itself by way of doctrine but by what we hold together across languages, cultures, and religions, that is, the good of the planet and the welfare of our collective future. The evolutionary function of a religion, the "litmus test," so to speak, relates to whether religion can animate the spirit of evolution. All spiritual movements that draw human consciousness to higher levels of unitive consciousness, including secular movements of spirituality, help animate the spirit of evolution.

---

5. King, *Teilhard de Chardin and Eastern Religions*, 193.

6. King, *Teilhard de Chardin and Eastern Religions*, 120.

7. Pierre Teilhard de Chardin, *The Future of Man* (New York: Harper-Collins, 1964), 261.

8. Teilhard de Chardin, *Future of Man*, 261.

Although each religious tradition holds a wealth of spiritual wisdom, there is still a resistance, particularly in the West, to understanding God in a new way. In an essay on the "Zest for Living," Teilhard spoke of "unsatisfied theism" and on the need to rejuvenate what has been passed on:

> We are surrounded by a certain sort of pessimists who continually tell us that our world is foundering in atheism. But should we not rather say that what it is suffering from is *unsatisfied theism*? ... If the great spiritual concern of our times is a re-alignment and readjustment of old beliefs towards a new Godhead who has risen up at the anticipated pole of cosmic evolution—then why not simply slough off the old—why not, that is, regroup the whole of the earth's religious power directly and ... pay no attention to the ancient creeds? ... Why not have a completely fresh faith, rather than a rejuvenation and confluence of "old loves'"? ... The cosmic forces of complexification, it would seem, proceed not through individuals but through complete branches. What is carried along by the various currents of faith that are still active on the earth, working in their incommunicable core ... is experiences of contact with a supreme inexpressible which they preserve and pass on.[9]

What Teilhard, Jung, and Tillich help us realize is that the name "God" is the power of absolute life dwelling within us, although God is not exhausted by us. We are God in the flesh—the Christ. There is no God "up above," no sky God or supernatural Being. To the extent that we insist on an ontologically distinct God, we compromise the fate of the earth and the wholeness of life. Religion is not a special divine grace. It is integral to natural evolution and rises with the development of human consciousness. The only way to conceive of God is to begin with the evolution of consciousness, the experience of something deep within

---

9. Pierre Teilhard de Chardin, *Activation of Energy*, trans. René Hague (New York: Harcourt Brace Jovanovich, 1963), 240–42.

yet transcendent to an immediate grasp of knowledge. Without consciousness, God is not possible. Hence, as Jung and others realized, consciousness and divinity are correlated. The Eastern sages have known this for centuries: the practice of Yoga, for example, is based on the premise that God and mind are the same. Swami Vivekananda aptly describes the unified holism of mind and matter based on his own transcendental experience:

> The body is just the external crust of the mind. They are not two different things; they are just as the oyster and its shell, they are but two aspects of one thing; the internal substance of the oyster takes up matter from outside and manufactures the shell. In the same way, the internal fine forces which are called mind take up gross matter from outside, and from that manufacture this external shell, the body. We shall find how intimately the mind is connected with the body. When the mind is disturbed, the body also becomes disturbed. Just as a physicist, when he pushes his knowledge to its limits, finds it melting away into metaphysics, so a metaphysicist will find that what he calls mind and matter are but apparent distinctions, the reality being one.[10]

Sadly, the West rejected the spirituality of the East and argued for the existence of an ontologically transcendent God. The cost of having a supernatural sky God, however, has been detrimental to the welfare of the planet. Theologians are slowly catching up to the need for theological revision, but many still adhere to the philosophy of Aristotle, who seems more important to theologians than Einstein or Bohm. Teilhard maintained that Christianity is normative of evolution because of its faith in the incarnation: God is entangled with material life. "Christianity takes on its full value only when extended to cosmic dimensions," he wrote.[11]

---

10. Swami Jitatmananda, "Life and Immortality in Indian Thought," in *Discourses on Aging and Dying*, ed. Suhita Chopra Chatterjee, Priyadarshi Patnaik, et al. (New Delhi: Sage Publications Pvt. Ltd., 2008), 85.

11. Pierre Teilhard de Chardin, *Christianity and Evolution: Reflections on*

The myth of the entangled God in evolution impelled Teilhard to abandon the narrowness of Christian doctrine and advocate for a new Christian faith, a materially-entangled God: "Is it not evident that Christianity will be able to breathe freely and spread its wings to their full span only in the prospect that has at last been opened up for its spiritual potentialities by a true philosophy, not simply of the whole, but of a convergent whole?"[12] His theology is summed up in the phrase: faith in God *is* faith in the world. A true religion of evolution must be an integration of faith in the development of this world and faith in God as the activating force of attraction that makes development possible. A new religion of the earth, therefore, challenges us to bring about a new integration of spiritual and material dimensions, as well as sacred and secular energies, into a total global human energy. Only by gathering the energies of the sacred and the secular realms into a new whole will we evolve into more unified life. Teilhard's optimism rests on the fact that the universe is unfinished and anticipates more life up ahead; it moves toward the future. We need to trust this process of entangled life in evolution and find new ways to live in this reality. In one apt sentence he summarizes our challenge: "We will advance all together in a spiritual renovation of the earth, or not at all."[13]

CONSCIOUSNESS, CONTEMPLATION AND CREATIVE EVOLUTION

The religion of tomorrow is beyond the axial religions of yesterday. But what will be the myth of the new religion? This question may be too difficult to answer at this point because we are still too embedded in the culture and language of first axial religions. Jung was clear that Western axial religion has become a matter of the head and not of the total person. Jung's ideas on theogenesis

---

Science and Religion, trans. René Hague (New York: Harcourt Brace Jovanovich), 129.

12. Teilhard de Chardin, *Activation of Energy,* 226.

13. Pierre Teilhard de Chardin, *The Phenomenon of Man,* trans. Bernard Wall (New York: Harper and Row, 1959), 245.

are an argument for no religion in particular but for religion itself as an ineradicable function of the human psyche. He was concerned that symbolic life had withered, and that religions were stuck on a level of adolescent consciousness. His concept of natural grace rested on the experience of the unification of divine opposites in the individual, framed as the redemption of both divine and human agencies involved in a single organic process. God is redeemed as we are redeemed, in a co-redemptive process of individuation. History is the sole theater in which divinity and humanity complete each other, as the unconscious and its opposites are brought together in a suffering at once divine and human. This is a mature way of reading the Gospels and of interpreting Jesus of Nazareth as one who exemplified the difficult journey into complete God-consciousness. For Jung, the necessity of creation as the co-completion of divinity and humanity means that God creates in order to complete Godself in creation. Creation expresses God's need to be fully reconciled within and without, that is, to be perfected in love. Hence, the unconscious (in which God is ground) is driven to create consciousness in order to become increasingly conscious in it. A conscious God is the human person fully alive.

Paul Tillich saw this position of co-redemptive theogenesis affirmed in process philosophy but rejected it because it implied that God's well-being is conditioned by the historical outcome of creation.[14] He realized at the end of his *Systematic Theology,* however, that human maturation in history contributes to the being of God. In his last major address before his death, Tillich hinted at the Jungian wider embrace when he affirmed that the future course of religious studies need not assume the monotheistic claim to a final, exhaustive, and exclusive revelation. In this respect, Tillich shared Jung's conviction that religious consciousness is endemic to the human psyche, and so will be always with us. Monotheistic religion oversteps its boundaries when any of its variants claims exhaustive and exclusive finality.

---

14. Paul Tillich, *Systematic Theology*, vol. 1 (Chicago: University of Chicago Press, 1951), 24, 181.

Like Tillich, Teilhard was caught between institution and intuition. Like Jung, he espoused a theogenic process at the heart of evolution, but he also shared Tillich's skepticism of consigning God's fate to creation's outcome. Yet, this is exactly what his overall vision anticipates. The biblical promise of a new heaven and a new earth is exactly that, a promise. God cannot realize any new reality apart from materiality and the human consent to be part of the divine fulfillment. Teilhard emphasized the need for active engagement and immersion in the world; attachment to the world's becoming is necessary, and detachment from the world that opposes God is also necessary. To act on behalf of the evolutionary process requires us to overcome our inertia and apathy, our selfishness, our tendency toward individualism, egoism, and self-indulgence. To be attached to a world in process means that we must constantly leave behind what has already been achieved in order to move ahead to what is yet to be accomplished. It means to care about a world that is in formation.

To build the earth is to build human community, and to build community is to build the Godself. Beatrice Bruteau writes: "The "I" is God's creative activity...our very existence is God's creative activity."[15] However, it is God's creative activity only if we make the effort to actualize the creative potentials of divine life within us. Jung likewise said to the effect, I do not create myself; I happen to myself. The idea of co-creative personal formation was also expressed by Thomas Merton who wrote: "Our vocation is not simply to be but to work together with God in the creation of our own life, our own identity, our own destiny.... The secret of my full identity is hidden in Him."[16] No matter what path we travel, the mind that seeks to incarnate the God within is the mind that integrates the heart and its senses. One becomes a seeker of all things divine in all things material and lives in the beauty and joy of life's precious moments.

---

15. Beatrice Bruteau, *The Grand Option: Personal Transformation and a New Creation* (Notre Dame, IN: University of Notre Dame Press, 2007), 75.

16. Thomas Merton, *New Seeds of Contemplation* (Cambridge, MA: New Directions Book, 1961), 32–33.

MYSTICISM AND EVOLUTION

Teilhard realized the importance of the interior life in the God quest and developed his ideas along the lines of mysticism and evolution. To love God with all one's body, heart, and soul and with every fiber of the unifying universe is to be on the path of self-discovery. His mysticism is intellectually creative because it is the spirit of reason pursuing true knowledge. One begins with a world that is not understood and comes to know God at the point where experience lights up the fire of knowledge. That is, his mysticism sets *reason* at the center of the *mystical*. Mysticism is not a matter of contemplating a truth already established but *lies in the very act of discovery that creates a new truth;* the mind extends itself without. The mystical act involves the synthesizing work of the mind, a process of continuously probing into the unknown. The mystical knower is every person who searches for meaning. The mind—which includes the emotions, the imagination, and the senses—is oriented toward the mystical quest.

Scientists are mystics, educators are mystics, physicians are mystics, and politicians can be mystics if they see the *polis* as the arena of potentially new knowledge. Teilhard calls us to consider thinking as a spiritual act. The mind pushes through the boundaries of the unknown, probes the fields of the psyche, and experiments with the possibilities of what reality can be. In whatever area we pursue, forming a hypothesis is a supreme spiritual act. To discover and know is to become an artisan of the future. True knowledge creates new horizons of meaning and pulls us onward. Thinking extends the universe.

Karl Rahner had a deep sense of divinity at the heart of materiality and claimed that "the Christian of the future will be a mystic or will cease to exist at all."[17] He spoke of God as an ordinary experience because the human person is oriented by nature

---

17. Karl Rahner, "Christian Living Formerly and Today," *Theological Investigations Volume II*, trans. David Bourke (New York: Herder and Herder, 1971), 15.

toward mystery. Whereas in past ages, the mystic was the exceptional person, the one who lived on the edge of society, the mystic is now the ordinary person who is attentive to what we might call "deep grace." "There is nothing profane below here," Teilhard wrote, "for those who know how to see."[18] Grace is everywhere because God is everywhere. One has to learn to see the infinite possibilities of the present, but the inner eye must be opened for the outer eye to see clearly.

The human person is vital to the process of evolution: "Far from escaping the evolutionary structures of the world, the mystic refines those structures."[19] Spirit is the energy portion of matter, pulling matter in the direction of the mind. Teilhard spoke of religious experience as having evolutionary significance through the centration of the universe. Jung would agree with this idea. Evolution calls us into a new type of wholistic consciousness, where things are *first seen together* and then as distinct within this togetherness. Teilhard wrote: "Nothing holds together absolutely except through the Whole, and the Whole itself holds together only through its future fulfillment."[20] Wholeness is a function of maximized consciousness. The more one can enter into nondual consciousness, the more one lives by the life of the whole. Bruteau writes: "The more conscious the individual becomes, the more the individual becomes *person,* and each person is person only to the extent that the individual freely lives by the life of the Whole."[21] At the highest level of nondual consciousness, the outer world and the inner world are one unified whole or, as Rainer Maria Rilke puts it:

Through every being single space extends
Outer space within. Through us the birds

---

18. Pierre Teilhard de Chardin, *The Divine Milieu,* trans. William Collins (New York: Harper and Row, 1960), 66.

19. Martin Laird, "The Diaphanous Universe: Mysticism in the Thought of Pierre Teilhard de Chardin," *Studies in Spirituality* 4 (1994): 222.

20. Teilhard de Chardin, *Christianity and Evolution,* 71.

21. Bruteau, *The Grand Option,* 77.

Fly silently. Oh, I who'd grow,
I look outside and in me grows the tree.[22]

Teilhard thought that contemplation is necessary to maximize consciousness. Only inner transformation can escape cosmic entropy and centrate energy on higher levels of complexity. The maximization of consciousness is the expansion of love-energy, which is the energy of creativity and discovery; the energy of forgiveness, hope, compassion, peace, unity, and beauty; the energy that binds together because it is the energy of seeing together. Contemplation is the vision of depth and wonder, the vision that gets to the truth of reality, seeing matter in its divine reality bubbling over into the everyday stuff of life. The contemplative energetic, in the words of Martin Laird, is not necessarily the monk or the person of centering prayer; rather, the contemplative energetic is the explorer, the discoverer, the artist, the astronomer, the graphic designer, the mother, the widow, the kindergarten teacher, the car mechanic. Any person who allows the mind to expand into the deeper realms of the psyche and delights in exploring the unknown touches the hem of God. Such a person is a contemplative energetic—a mystic. Such a person who is willing to be an original lights the fire and creates something new, seeing the old in a new way by testing the possibilities of the normative rules. The one who explores reality in its endless depth contemplates God, forms the self, and changes the course of evolution. Higher levels of consciousness deepen cosmic personalization. The more one becomes individuated as God-person, the more one engages the world through the energies of love.

Contemplation is the wonder and awe of love, an awakening to all that exists, an aliveness that wells up from the infinite center of one's personhood: "Along the road of contemplation and prayer, we succeed in entering directly into receptive communication with the very source of all interior drive."[23] The contemplative

---

22. Cited in Etty Hillesum, *An Interrupted Life and Letters from Westerbork* (New York: Picador, 1996), 276.

23. Teilhard de Chardin, *Activation of Energy*, 242.

is one in whom the sap of the world flows; the one who embodies a zest for life. As the mystic goes about the world urging all things toward unity, she or he contributes to evolution through a process of mystical convergence, seeing *everything* bound in a luminous web of love. The more contemplation individuates the human person as a whole, the more the person creates and expands wholeness through the energies of love.

COSMIC PLANETIZATION AND NOOGENESIS

Teilhard expressed a vision of the entangled God-world moving toward the maximization of conscious matter—the Omega point. He coined different verbs to describe this movement, such as "planetization," "cosmic personalization," "pleromization," all of which underscore a dynamic movement toward a cosmotheandric unity. His ideas on theogenesis indicate that God is no longer the solitary One up above but the complexifying One who is not yet done being One. The One *is* the many unified by love. As Bruteau notes: "*We* are the New Creation in the active sense of being those who participate in the act of creating."[24] God is rising up in us, with us, for us, as us.

The religious holism of Teilhard and Jung reflects a new axial period of consciousness, a new awakening of being in evolution. The act of living is now on the interface between the present and the future, *not* between the present and the past. Life creates the next moment of life. According to Bruteau, "If we really accept creation as ever new, and if we ourselves are active participants in this ever new creating, then we are always facing the future."[25] The human being must be seen as a Christic fractal destined to complete oneself in a higher consciousness. The Christic refuses mediocrity, stagnation, domination, oppression, control, manipulation, and all factors that divide and conquer the human spirit and all that is living. She or he is part of the Christogenic process, a divine entanglement that orients life in the world's yearning for wholeness.

---

24. Bruteau, *The Grand Option*, 171.
25. Bruteau, *The Grand Option*, 171.

The key to Christic evolution is consciousness. Consciousness forms matter, and matter complexifies through energies of love. Bohm's model signifies that everything that is and will be in this cosmos is enfolded within this mind-matter implicate order. There is a special cosmic movement that carries forth the process of enfoldment and unfoldment into the explicate order. This process of cosmic movement, in endless feedback cycles, creates an infinite variety of manifest forms and mentality. Bohm speculated that a fundamental cosmic Intelligence is the "Player" in this process, a type of cosmic mind engaged in endless experimentation and creativity. The Player or Cosmic Mind is moving cyclically onward and onward toward an infinity of complexified being.

Both Teilhard and Bohm believed that there is an accumulation of a cosmic reflective nature in the human person who participates in the Whole and consequently gives it meaning. The human is a consequence of evolution but also a turning point in evolution, as the cosmic process culminates in self-reflective consciousness. Bohm compared the human person to the ultimate transformation of the atom into a power and chain reaction. Similarly, the individual who uses inner energy and intelligence can transform humankind. This power within us to be radically transformative is the divine presence. Jesus said, "if you have faith the size of a mustard seed, you will say to this mountain, 'move from here to there,' and it will move; and nothing will be impossible for you" (Matt 17:20).

To live consciously aware of divine presence and depth in every moment, every act, every touch of the hand, smell of the rose, taste of food, tear of sorrow, pain of wound is to know oneself as part of a cosmic whole. Teilhard suggested that the work we do throughout our lives to improve our world is the primary exercise of our faith. Our faith life, like our ethical life, is a productive activity. Since God is involved in evolution, our love for God requires cooperating with God in building up the world. Sanctification, for Teilhard, means freely participating in this stream of life that is ascending toward fullness. Fullness is a relational term; it means to be part of this theogenic, evolving world. As Teilhard wrote: "We are spiritualized by being carried along by the spiritualization of all things. We are united to Christ by entering into communion with all people. We will be saved by an option that has chosen the whole."[26] The whole is our greatest reality.

Meditation is one of the oldest paths of shaping the spiritual self and is practiced in both Eastern and Western religious traditions. Studies show today that meditation exercises the brain to establish the control of focused attention. Charlotte Tomaino writes: "An awakened brain and an awakened life means living from the inside vision of life desired, regardless of outside circumstances."[27] She calls this process of focusing the brain on desired choice "neural focusing," or developing a "Buddha brain."[28] Jesus, like Siddhartha, realized the transient nature of life and sought to expand the capacity of his mind: "Where your mind is, there your treasure lies," Jesus said.

Both Christianity and Buddhism advocate training the mind for higher ultimate reality. Prayer or meditation is a conscious opening to new depth of relationship with God or ultimate reality. It is a dynamic movement of the Spirit, a differentiation of being as one ascends through the stages of consciousness into the realms of the divine mystery. Growth and transformation of consciousness require vigilance, stability, and concentration of the mind as it enters into the infinite light within. Zen master Kosho Uchiyama states that when thoughts and fixation on the little "I" are transcended, an awakening to a universal, non-dual self occurs: "When we let go of thoughts and wake up to the reality of life that is working beyond them, we discover the Self that is living universal non-dual life (before the separation into two)

---

26. Pierre Teilhard de Chardin, *Science and Christ*, trans. René Hague (New York: Harper and Row, 1968), 77.

27. Charlotte A. Tomaino, *Awakening the Brain: The Neuropsychology of Grace* (New York: Atria Books, 2012), 52.

28. Tomaino, *Awakening the Brain*, 55–62.

that pervades all living creatures and all existence."[29] Thinking and thoughts must not confine us and blind us to true reality. The first objective of the Buddhist meditator is to become detached from the thinking process itself. To attain such a state is to reach *shamata* or "calm abiding."[30] This type of meditation calls for a willed self-emptying whereby the layers of ego—all of one's false identities—fall away and one arrives at the level of consciousness called *shunyata*, which is the level of the "unconditioned" or "emptiness."

Emptiness is not nothingness but, paradoxically, "all-ness" or "oneness." It is the deepest core of the self beyond thoughts, words, and concepts, the level at which there is no separate "I."[31] Only when we experience emptiness can our innate compassion arise. In Theravāda Buddhism, the cause of human existence and suffering is identified as craving, which carries with it various defilements, such as greed, hatred, and delusion. These are believed to be deeply rooted afflictions of the mind that create suffering and stress. To be free from suffering and stress is to be liberated from harmful attachments, permanently uprooting them by analyzing, experiencing, and understanding the true nature of such corruptions. The meditator is then led to realize the Four Noble Truths (the truth of suffering, the origins of suffering, the cessation of suffering, the path to overcome suffering) and attain Enlightenment and Nirvana.[32]

Tenzin Palmo, a British Buddhist nun, spent six years alone in a Himalayan cave, at an elevation of thirteen thousand feet, in a cell that was about six-by-six square feet. She came down once a year to meet her master teacher but otherwise dedicated herself to

---

29. Uchiyama Kosho, *Opening the Hand of Thought: Approach to Zen* (New York: Penguin Books, 1993), 98.

30. Dalai Lama, "Generating the Mind for Enlightenment," http://dalailama.com/teachings/training-the-mind/generating-the-mind-for-enlightenment.

31. Carol Flinders, *Enduring Lives: Living Portraits of Women and Faith in Action* (Maryknoll, NY: Orbis Books, 2013), 149.

32. Huston Smith and Philip Novak, *Buddhism: A Concise Introduction* (New York: HarperCollins, 2003); Richard Gombrich, *Theravāda Buddhism: A Social History from Ancient Benares to Modern Colombo* (New York: Routledge, 1988), 159.

meditation. Her example of monastic life shows us that one lives into the path of the Buddha by choosing against self-separateness, or the dissociated self, by meditation and disciplining the mind, by following the teachings of the Buddha through a master, and by putting the teachings into practice.[33] Similarly, one can think of Christian mystics who underwent ascetic disciplines, including extreme fasts and long hours of prayer and meditation in the pursuit of holiness. This type of transpersonal evolution, according to Ken Wilber, means discovering higher levels of being through an expansion and evolution of one's own consciousness. He writes: "Subconsciousness of matter and body gives way to the Self-consciousness of mind and ego, which in turn gives way to Super-consciousness of soul and spirit."[34] Consciousness expands from a self-centered self to self-in-God to God-self-in-world. "When inner reality is stronger than outer reality," Tomaino writes, "one can act from choice, creating one's own life."[35] Jung sees the transformation of person as the transformation of God. The formation of the God-self is the path to peace.

Systems have become fractured because we humans have become fractured. To build the inner self through meditation and contemplation is the basis of the ethical task of building the global human community and the earth itself. We must exercise our own creativity if God is to be complete; meditation is essential to training the potentially creative mind. Without the effort of human beings, God cannot realize God's vision. God uses and depends on our thoughts and affections in striving to build the earth. The will of God is co-created through the exercise of our own minds and hearts. God cannot make us whole without our own activity. God's relation to us is not only a real relation but also an entangled one; what we do makes a difference to God. Our unwillingness to cooperate with God is the meaning of sin. God is changed by the activities of ongoing creation; the tradi-

33. Vickie Mackenzie, *Cave in the Snow: Tenzin Palmo's Quest for Enlightenment* (New York: Bloomsbury, 1998), 113–14.

34. Ken Wilber, *Up From Eden: A Transpersonal View of Human Evolution* (Wheaton, IL: Quest Books), 11.

35. Tomaino, *Awakening the Brain*, 52.

tional doctrine of the immutability of God is no longer appropriate. Where relationships are seen to be a genuine perfection in love, God is maximally involved. If God could not be really related to what goes on in creation, God would be less than perfect. Our lives and our work fill out God's relational self.

The greatest significance of our work, therefore, is that it affects God's own relational life. When we contribute to the building of the world and to developing ourselves, we make a positive difference to God's life. Teilhard rightly notes that we should love humanity and the world because this is where God lives. This is the only dwelling place of God that we can adequately conceive. Hence, love of the world is love of God. We are responsible for the future of God and the future of the world. Our responsibility for evolution requires more than passing on a world no worse than the one we have inherited. Rather, a morality of entanglement and relational holism requires that we improve the world. Evolution has given us an ever-better world, and we are responsible for continuing that creative enhancement. Of course, worldly betterment will not consist in more things and more material resources, especially as our consumerist tendencies widen the gap between the rich and poor. Rather, improving the world means increasing our personal capacities for beauty, goodness, unity, and growth, greater religious devotion to the world's evolution in which God is being born, as well as closer cooperation among all peoples. Human life is a drama whose glory is acting out its completion. Even in the midst of terrible tragedy, Teilhard was ever hopeful.[36]

While the human species has collectively reached a new level of consciousness through progress and development, it does not quite have the energy to reach the whole, to put it all on fire. The collective consciousness may be one and indivisible, but it is the responsibility of each human person to contribute toward the building of the consciousness of humankind by "minding the mind," that is, by training the mind for higher reality. This is one

---

36. See Edward Vacek, "An Evolving Christian Morality," *From Teilhard to Omega: Co-Creating an Unfinished Universe*, ed. Ilia Delio (Maryknoll, NY: Orbis Books, 2014).

of the greatest challenges in our computer-addicted age when social media and gobs of information stream across our screens and capture our attention. Each individual has to seek and to recognize that which is alive and active within: the implicate must become explicate. In other words, the development of the outer noosphere depends on the evolution of the inner noosphere, first in the individual and then in the collective mind of the species. The mind is everything: what we think is what we become, and what we think together, we will become together.

CONTEMPLATION AND THE CONVERGENT MIND

The religion of tomorrow will be one that encourages the mind to grow by connecting with the collective unconscious and contemplating new truths. Religion awakens the self within, tethers the self to its divine ground, and enkindles the divine self to grow into personhood. Rituals that deepen the energies of love and enhance the divine radiance of matter will be part of the religion of tomorrow. Given the new reality of conscious evolution, it is not unusual that the fastest evolver today is computer technology. Since the twentieth century, there has been an urgent need to express the mind on deeper levels of consciousness because we have built a complex world of information. We need ways of making sense of human meaning and purpose in a world of complexity. In smaller worlds of the past, the world seemed more manageable, and axial religions functioned to provide connections to a transcendent God. Today, axial religions are much less effective because of outdated symbols and philosophies; hence, there is an urgent need to find new modes of conscious expansion whereby new meanings can emerge.

Computer technology appeared at the end of World War II. The imprisoned mind stifled by religious-cultural norms of gender, race, power, patriarchy, and all forms of exclusion was suffocating and about to explode. The development of a thinking machine was a liberation of the mind held captive by religious rules and political power. Cyberspace became the new cosmos of exploration and infinite potential. America proved fertile ground for the new marriage of technology and religion. The Calvinist ideals of asceticism, discipline, hard work, and progress provided a formula of preparation for a new apocalyptic mentality. According to religion scholar Robert Geraci, the Christian ideals of salvation and immortality were transferred to American technology as the new means of salvation.[37] The term "transhumanism" was first used in the 1950s by Julian Huxley who was a friend of Teilhard de Chardin. In his *Religion without Revelation*, Huxley wrote:

> The human species can, if it wishes, transcend itself—not just sporadically, an individual one way, an individual there in another way—but in its entirety, as humanity. We need a name for this new belief. Perhaps transhumanism will serve: man remaining man, but transcending himself, by realizing new possibilities of and *for his human nature*.[38]

Huxley saw transhumanism as a positive step for the whole of humankind rather than as individual perfection or enhancement. The human person is in process of becoming something new because humanity, like evolution itself, possesses a vital spirit unfolding through matter. Transhumanism is a philosophical and cultural movement that sees the possibilities of human betterment with technology. Suffering, disease, aging, and death all can be overcome with technology, so that humans can "wrest their biological destiny from evolution's blind process of random variation... using science and technology to overcome biological limitations."[39] Julian de la Mattrie maintains that: "If human beings are constituted by matter that obeys the same laws of physics operating outside us, then it should in principle be possible to

---

37. Robert Geraci, *Apocalyptic AI* (New York: Oxford University Press, 2010), 14–36.

38. Julian Huxley, *Religion without Revelation* (Westport, CT: Greenwood Press, 1979), 195.

39. Archimedes Carag Articulo, "Towards an Ethics of Technology: Re-Exploring Teilhard de Chardin's Theory of Technology and Evolution," SCRIBD (1998); cited in Nick Bostrom, "A History of Transhumanist Thought," *Journal of Evolution and Technology* 14, no. 1 (2005): 13–14.

learn to manipulate human nature in the same way that we manipulate external objects."[40] Kevin Kelly states that the future of
evolution is about "the marriage of the born and the made."[41]
F. M. Esfandiary, one of the early transhumanists who taught at
the New School for Social Research, defined the transhuman as

> a transitional human, someone who by virtue of their tech-
> nological usage, cultural values, and lifestyle constitutes
> an evolutionary link to the coming era of posthumanity.
> The signs as indicative of transhuman status include pros-
> theses, plastic surgery, intensive use of telecommunica-
> tions, a cosmopolitan outlook and a globetrotting lifestyle,
> androgyny, mediated reproduction (such as in vitro fertil-
> ization), absence of religious belief, and a rejection of tradi-
> tional family values.[42]

The singularity hypothesis refers to the idea that self-improving
artificial intelligence (AI) will at some point result in radical
changes within a very short time span. Vernor Vinge predicted
that "within thirty years, we will have the technological means to
create superhuman intelligence. Shortly after, the human era will
be ended."[43] His prediction was ambitious but the singularity is
still a future possibility. The futurist Ray Kurzweil anticipates an
increasingly virtual life in which the bodily presence of human
beings will become irrelevant. As we move beyond mortality
through computational technology, "our identity will be based on

---

40. Julian de La Mettrie, *Machine Man and Other Writings* (Cambridge:
Cambridge University Press, 1996); cited in Bostrom, "A History of Transhumanist Thought," 4.

41. Carter Phipps, *Evolutionaries: Unlocking the Spiritual and Cultural Potential of Science's Greatest Ideas* (New York: HarperCollins, 2012), 128.

42. F. M. Esfandiary, *Are You a Transhuman? Monitoring and Stimulating
Your Personal Rate of Growth in a Rapidly Changing World* (New York: Grand
Central Publications, 1989), 11; cited in Bostrom, "A History of Transhumanist
Thought," 14.

43. Vernor Vinge, *"The Coming Technological Singularity,"* *Whole Earth Review* (Winter, 1993); cited in Bostrom, "A History of Transhumanist Thought," 9.

our evolving mind file. We will be software not hardware."[44] Hans Moravec claims that we will be able to "wake up matter" by infusing it with intelligence and information.[45]

While the claims and aims of transhumanism may alarm us, we should take heed of their bold projections. These futurist thinkers continue to probe the infinite potential of the psyche. It is not surprising that the line between religion and technology blurs in their writings. Kurzweil speaks about becoming gods. Others have suggested that computer technology opens up the gates of heaven in a virtual way. Daniel Crevier argues that AI is consistent with the Christian belief in resurrection and immortality. Since some kind of support is required for the information and organization that constitutes our minds, Crevier suggests a material, mechanical replacement for the mortal body will suffice. Christ was resurrected in a new body; he states, why not a machine?[46] Antje Jackelén considers the possibility that AI technology has messianic dimensions. She notes that "when John the Baptist was in prison and heard what Jesus was doing, he sent his disciples to ask, 'Are you the one (the Messiah) to come, or are we to wait for another?' Jesus answered, 'Go and tell John what you hear and see: the blind receive their sight, the lame walk, the deaf hear, the dead are raised and the poor have the good news brought to them'" (Matt 11:2–5)."[47] This leads her to surmise that the development toward techno sapiens might well be regarded as a step toward the kingdom of God. "The requirements of the Gospel and the aims of technical development seem to be in perfect harmony."[48]

---

44. Robert Geraci, "Apocalyptic AI: Religion and the Promise of Artificial Intelligence," *Journal of the American Academy of Religion* 76, no. 1 (2008): 154.

45. Phipps, Evolutionaries, 142.

46. Daniel Crevier, *AI: The Tumultuous History of the Search for Artificial Intelligence* (New York: Basic Books, 1993), 278–80.

47. Antje Jackelén, "The Image of God as *Techno Sapiens*," *Zygon* 37, no. 2 (2002): 294.

48. Jackelén, "The Image of God as *Techno Sapiens*," 294.

COMPUTERS AND CONTEMPLATION

Philosophers today are wondering if technology is enabling us to become gods.[49] In some ways, it is. Cyberspace is the extended mind—the exogenous psyche—and thus the field of infinite potential. Cyberspace is the place where God is potentially alive and active. Philip Hefner suggests that technology is a mirror of our deepest desires. He writes: "What we want and who we are coalesce in this mirror."[50] Technology is part of the flow of evolutionary becoming; it expresses an awakening and growing cosmos. It is not outside the human person; rather, technology conveys the human longing to define "human" by rearranging the world, including the human paradoxical fear of death, and by desiring to know the unknown. In this respect, technology is like a mirror; it reflects back only what is given to it. The mirror image of technology and the mirrored image of the one who uses technology are the same. Without the "other" whom it mirrors, technology would cease to exist. Technology is developed to optimize and extend life and, in doing so, affects the life it aims to optimize. There is no such thing as neutral technology or passive technology. Technology finds its power in human consent. As it shapes human nature, it is shaped by humans. Without the intentional use and development of technology, we have a blind future.

Computer technology has developed too fast for us to adequately reflect on its philosophical and religious implications. The scattered mind evoked by computer technology is made visible in a world of confusion and information overload. We are searching online for that which is fully alive within. It is much easier to press a button and scan the web than to confront the unknown field of the psyche. In some ways, the computer is like an inverted

---

49. See Francesca Ferrando, "Are We Becoming God(s)?: Transhumanism, Posthumanism, Antihumanism, and the Divine," in *Religious Transhumanism and Its Critics*, ed. Arvin M. Gouw, Brian Patrick Green, and Ted Peters (Lanham, MD: Lexington Books, 2022).

50. Philip Hefner, *Technology and Human Becoming* (Minneapolis, MN: Augsburg Fortress Press, 2003), 41.

psyche. We explore the fields of potentials running across our screen, knowing how easily images can be constructed, edited, and reformed. How did we arrive at a machine that imitates the psyche and gives us the illusion of godly life? One possibility is that religion failed to align with contemporary science, creating a deep rift between the human psyche and the material world. Many Christian churches still treat matter as secondary to spirit, securing God in a heaven above. We live with divided minds: culturally in tune with a computer age and religiously locked into a medieval worldview. The search for God is readily fulfilled by the touch of a button.

Jung was convinced that religious consciousness is endemic to the human psyche. Teilhard shared Jung's abiding sense of the "within." Their religious holism offered a renewed religious ideal, namely, the vision of the divine approach to the human as initially wholly from within.[51] For Teilhard, this divine approach is the experience of the energy that has created consciousness by the very consciousness it has created. God is redeemed in a humanity that is itself redeemed through the unification of divine and human life. Transhumanists see the potential for Godly life with technology —and the lure of technology is powerful because it is efficient and rapid, unlike the slow work of individuation. We are at a crossroads in planetary life. Can we reclaim the depth of the human psyche? Can we direct technology toward an ethics of wholeness and love?

Teilhard was impressed by the computer as a thinking machine and saw the new possibilities of life on the level of noogenesis, a new level of mind. The noosphere is the natural culmination of biological evolution, an organic whole, now on the level of thought, destined for some type of superconvergence and unification.[52] Just as earth once covered itself with a film of interdependent living organisms which we call the biosphere, so humankind's combined achievements are forming a global network

---

51. Carl Jung, "The Relativity of the God-Concept in Meister Eckhart," *Collected Works* 6 (Princeton: Princeton University Press, 1921), para. 413.

52. W. Henry Kenny, *A Path Through Teilhard's Phenomenon* (Dayton, OH: Pflaum Press, 1970), 110.

of collective mind.[53] With the rise of technology, Teilhard saw a forward movement of spiritual energy, a maximization of consciousness, and a complexification of relationships. However, he realized that, without prayer and contemplation, technology can become misguided and misused and blindly lead us into a disastrous world. As he wrote, technology can extend the outreach of human activity, but it depends on a broader use of human activity, and how humans control psychic, spiritual energy, needs, and powers.[54]

THE RELIGION OF TOMORROW

We have in our midst the infinite potential to create a sustainable world, a world of shared life, a just distribution of resources, a new world connectivity to the whole, a new world soul. The power is within us. The human person is God-in-the-making. This is the religion of tomorrow, not one of finality, but of ongoing revelation of divine light. As Anthony Gittins notes:

> There will always be a tendency to reduce revelation to religion rather than to expand our own religion so that it better reflects God's revelation. . . . Religion seeks clear, bounded answers; it wants to quantify, reduce, set limits, and control. By contrast revelation is God's way of opening up for us unbounded possibilities; it expands our horizons and calls us beyond rules and law to love.[55]

God is not finished becoming God, and we are not finished becoming human. The Christic is the God-human in evolution.

---

53. Michael H. Murray, *The Thought of Teilhard de Chardin* (New York: Seabury, 1966), 20–21.

54. Joseph A. Grau, *Morality and the Human Future in the Thought of Teilhard de Chardin: A Critical Study* (Cranbury, NJ: Associated University Presses, Inc., 1976), 274.

55. C. A. J. Anthony Gittins, "Can We Get Beyond Religion? Revelation, Faith, and the Dignity of Difference," *New Theology Review* (April 15, 2013): 11.

God becomes more human as love expands and widens its embrace, and we become more God as we create through the energies of love. There is no one path to lead to this new reality of the new Person because God dwells in many mansions (John 14:2). Freeing religion from patriarchy, the ruling power of the male, is the beginning of a new earth: "The more humankind becomes conscious of the immensity and, even more, the organicity of the world around it, the more the necessity for a soul to make itself felt; that is, a soul capable of maintaining and directing the vast process of planetization in which we are involved."[56]

If God emerges through an intensity of consciousness that overcomes divisions, oppositions, fragments, and anything divisive, through a consciousness that unifies, expands, and liberates the mind to embrace the whole, then can we start to shape computer technology in this direction, as well? Marshall McLuhan, the brilliant media scholar and devout Catholic, saw the potential of computer technology to bring about a new earth community. In a 1960 interview with *Playboy* magazine, McLuhan shared his thoughts on computer technology:

> The total-field awareness engendered by electronic media is enabling us—indeed, compelling us—to grope toward a consciousness of the unconscious, toward a realization that technology is an extension of our own bodies. We live in the first age when change occurs sufficiently rapidly to make such pattern recognition possible for society at large. Until the present era, this awareness has always been reflected first by the artist, who has had the power— and courage—of the seer to read the language of the outer world and relate it to the inner world.[57]

McLuhan's insights highlight two significant ideas explored by both Jung and Teilhard, namely, that technology is a process of individuation in which the unconscious becomes increasingly

---

56. Teilhard de Chardin, *Activation of Energy*, 226.

57. Marshall McLuhan, "The Playboy Interview," *Playboy Magazine* (March 1969): 4

conscious, and that technology extends human bodies. He proposed that technology reshapes (or "massages") the human senses without humans being aware of this: "Most people, from truck drivers to the literary Brahmins, are still blissfully ignorant of what the media do to them...unaware that the medium is also the message...it literally works over and saturates and molds and transforms every sense ratio."[58] He realized that technology does affect us: it saturates our senses, overloads them, so that we are never really living in the present because we cannot grasp what is really happening. Because of this sensory overload, we are always living one step behind. McLuhan's insight addresses the cultural concerns of social critics of technology and offers a reason why we resist the changes brought about by technology, despite its attractive lure. We seek structures and paradigms that provide the illusion of stability. In McLuhan's words:

> Most people...still cling to what I call the rearview-mirror view of their world. By this I mean to say that because of the invisibility of any environment during the period of its innovation, man is only consciously aware of the environment that has preceded it; in other words, an environment becomes fully visible only when it has been superseded by a new environment; thus, we are always one step behind in our view of the world. Because we are benumbed by any new technology—which in turn creates a totally new environment—we tend to make the old environment more visible; we do so by turning it into an art form and by attaching ourselves to the objects and atmosphere that characterized it.[59]

McLuhan, like Teilhard and Bruteau, prophetically anticipated what our planet could become by "re-tribalizing" into a global community. Our planetary survival will depend on our capacity to converge and unify: "Something will explode if we persist in trying to squeeze into our old tumble-down huts the material and

58. McLuhan, "The Playboy Interview," 4.

59. McLuhan, "The Playboy Interview," 4–5.

spiritual forces that are henceforward on the scale of the world."[60]
Bruteau, too, offered powerful comments on the present moment:
"An entire attitude, mind-set, way of identifying self and others
and perceiving the world has to shift *first*, before any talk of economic, political, and social arrangements can be made. Anything
else is premature, useless, and possibly dangerous."[61] We can
build the world together only if we are becoming persons together. Technology expresses our desire to form a collective body
with a collective mind for the good of the whole. McLuhan was
also well aware of the problem of clinging to old ways, as new life
dawns through technology:

> Through radio, TV and the computer, we are already en-
> tering a global theater in which the entire world is a Hap-
> pening. Our whole cultural habitat, which we once
> viewed as a mere container of people, is being trans-
> formed by these media and by space satellites into a liv-
> ing organism, itself contained within a new macrocosm
> or connubium of a supraterrestrial nature. The day of the
> individualist, of privacy, of fragmented or "applied"
> knowledge, of "points of view" and specialist goals is
> being replaced by the over-all awareness of a mosaic
> world in which space and time are overcome by televi-
> sion, jets and computers—a simultaneous, "all-at-once"
> world in which everything resonates with everything else
> as in a total electrical field, a world in which energy is
> generated and perceived not by the traditional connec-
> tions that create linear, causative thought processes, but
> by the intervals, or gaps, which Linus Pauling grasps as
> the languages of cells, and which create synaesthetic dis-
> continuous integral consciousness.[62]

McLuhan could envision the new humanity in and through
the development of computer technology as super-conscious,

---

60. Teilhard de Chardin, *Activation of Energy*, 252–53.

61. Bruteau, *The Grand Option*, 171.

62. McLuhan, "The Playboy Interview," 15.

transpersonal cosmic being. His vision is optimistic, like that of Teilhard, for he saw the potential within the human for wholeness and unity:

> We must understand that a totally new society is coming into being, one that rejects all our old values, conditioned responses, attitudes and institutions. If you have difficulty envisioning something as trivial as the imminent end of elections, you'll be totally unprepared to cope with the prospect of the forthcoming demise of spoken language and its replacement by a global consciousness.... Tribal man is tightly sealed in an integral collective awareness that transcends conventional boundaries of time and space. As such, the new society will be one mythic integration, a resonating world akin to the old tribal echo chamber where magic will live again.[63]

McLuhan recognized human creativity and ingenuity as the heart of development, as the technological extension of human life into a collective sphere of information. Furthermore, he ultimately saw computer technology as the new Self and, like Jung, the realm of the divine, where the potential for God life could emerge through the highest integration of consciousness:

> The computer thus holds out the promise of a technologically engendered state of universal understanding and unity, a state of absorption in the logos that could knit mankind into one family and create a perpetuity of collective harmony and peace. This is the real use of the computer, not to expedite marketing or solve technical problems but to speed the process of discovery and orchestrate terrestrial—and eventually galactic—environments and energies. Psychic communal integration, made possible at last by the electronic media, could create the universality of consciousness foreseen by Dante when he predicted that men would continue as no more than broken fragments

---

63. McLuhan, "The Playboy Interview," 17.

until they were unified into an inclusive consciousness. In a Christian sense, this is merely a new interpretation of the mystical body of Christ; and Christ, after all, is the ultimate extension of man.[64]

Only a prophet of deep insight could envision the power of technology to knit humankind into one family, a cosmic body of unity. Teilhard had a similar insight and realized that the power forming the separate elements of cosmic human life into a conscious whole is the power of Omega. McLuhan would agree. Our old concepts of God cannot engage with the new revelation of technology and evolution. Matter has a divine ground and matter extended through technology brings the hidden God to light, expressed in the hyperpersonal person or the ultrahuman.

Technology is our deepest reality because it is the visible realm of the collective unconscious, the depth of which is God. As such, it invites us to reconsider the infinite potential of the human person to become a fully relational person, one who lives by the life of the whole. What constitutes the "good" is everything that brings the growth of consciousness to the world. What is best is what assures the highest development of consciousness and the spiritual growth of the earth. A new morality of growth is one that will foster and catalyze evolutionary change, a new formation of being, a deepening of what we are together in which care for one another humanizes us. The new collective energy needed to move the world toward greater wholeness must begin with updating divine reality—God 3.0—a reformatted religious consciousness at the heart of matter, including body matter, spirit matter, earth matter. Without religion, evolution is blind; without evolution, religion is dead. The new spiritual awakening must begin in the depths of our own minds as we journey into the Christ Self, the psyche, and conquer all that prevents us from embracing our divine reality.

The axial religions are coming to an end, and a new religious spirit is on the horizon. The Good News of relational holism, the entangled God, is essentially the message of Jesus of Nazareth.

---

64. McLuhan, "The Playboy Interview," 18.

We are the temples of the living God. It is time we begin to live as holy dwelling places of divinity by removing structures that divert our attention away from our divine reality, finding new rituals and stories that help us connect in a deeper way to our divine roots, rediscovering ourselves as the *Shenikah,* the glory of the divine presence fully alive. Each human person is the face of the living God.

Our troubles and sorrows, our disillusions and regrets, our anxieties and distrusts all speak to the frustration of divine life within. God is suffocating under the weight of our own dead matter. Divine reality is our root reality. The Self is potentially an explosive self in love, the love that can bring about a new world of justice, a new world of life for all, a new world that looks to the future. Love alone, Teilhard said, can bring us to another universe. That is why the words of the late Jesuit Pedro Arrupe could easily have been spoken by Jung and Teilhard, for they are words that vitalize the whole: "Fall in Love, stay in love, and it will decide everything."[65]

---

65. James Martin, *The Jesuit Guide to (Almost) Everything: A Spirituality for Real Life* (New York: HarperOne, 2010), 219.

Conclusion

As the twentieth century was drawing to a close, a number of spiritual books began to appear on mysticism and the spiritual journey. The *Classics of Western Spirituality*, developed by Paulist Press, revived the rich tradition of Christian mysticism among Catholic and Protestant writers. The Center for Action and Contemplation focused its mission on bringing contemplation and personal transformation into dialogue with social justice. The teachings of Richard Rohr, Jim Finley, and Cynthia Bourgeault have contributed to the renaissance of mysticism in the West. At the same time, many theological discussions continue to unwittingly mix medieval theology and modern questions. We are in a strange phenomenon of medieval mysticism made modern. Mysticism abounds, and mystics espousing pantheistic ideas are endearing. But, if one pays attention, one realizes that Christianity is a metaphysical mess. It is a syncretism of Thomistic theology, Eastern mysticism, and ecological concerns (among others) blended together like a theological smoothie. Lots of words are swirling around, but there is very little theological coherence or effort to develop a new myth. It is no wonder that the Catholic liturgy is often like a narcoleptic drug. Homilies on original sin and ecology, along with mustard seeds and farmers, are delivered each week by a male priest whose pivotal role demands utmost attention. The words of some preachers fall powerlessly from the pulpit, as Karl Rahner noted, "like birds frozen to death and falling from a winter sky."[1] One must leave the mind at the door of the Church before entering the pew.

Science underwent several significant shifts in the early twentieth century, including the development of quantum physics and the rise of systems biology. In his 1925 essay on "Religion and Science," Alfred North Whitehead wrote: "Religion will not regain its old power until it can face change in the same spirit as does science. Its principles may be eternal, but the expression of those principles requires continual development."[2] Despite the many conferences sponsored by the Vatican on themes in science and technology, the Catholic Church hesitates to bring science and theology into an integral relationship. Vatican II promised a new vision of the Church, one involved in a world of historical change; however, that vision has diminished over time and remains ambivalent. Historically, the Church faced headwinds in the late nineteenth century as evolution was introduced into theological discussion and modernism arose in response to shifts in culture and philosophy. Fundamentalism was born among Protestant scholars who vehemently opposed evolution and its seeming contradiction of scripture. The Catholic Church established a defensive border. In 1879, Pope Leo XIII issued the encyclical *Aeterni Patris* and made Thomas Aquinas the official theologian of the Church. Aquinas had a brilliant mind and would have supported the insights of relational holism. However, he worked with the intellectual tools of his own age; he brought together Christianity and Aristotle's philosophy, which was the leading philosophy of his day. Aristotle was to the Middle Ages what Einstein and Bohm are to the twenty-first century, natural philosophers. Thomas Christianized Aristotle, and the

---

1. Cited in Elizabeth A. Johnson, *Quest for the Living God: Mapping Frontiers in the Theology of God* (New York: Continuum, reprint edition, 2011), 30.

2. Alfred North Whitehead, "Religion and Science," *The Atlantic* (August 1925).

Church canonized Thomas. The Church continues to espouse a Christianized Aristotelianism.

To the everyday person, this may sound like a lot of abstract ideas or, as my mother used to say, "It all sounds jibberish." But theology based on medieval ideas in a world spinning out of control can no longer remain idle or unchecked. If we bracket science or treat it as a specialized discipline of study, then we fundamentally live with a split-brain syndrome. We are postmodern technocrats during the week, all glued to our computers, and sky-God believers on Sunday. No one wants to challenge the Church, and certainly no one wants to challenge God. Yet, if we understand the insights of Jung and Teilhard (and Tillich to some extent), challenging God is exactly what we should be doing. If one listens attentively, one can hear God saying, "Yes, please, challenge me!" To put this more eloquently, "faith seeks understanding," as Saint Anselm said. We must make every effort to understand God and God's relationship to the world, because we have become unplugged from the earth and unglued from one another. We are, effectively, a species out of control on a planet blindly hurling into the future.

CARL JUNG, THE SAINT?

Jung did for psychology what Teilhard did for science and theology; each thinker reconnected the mind and the body, severed by Cartesian dualism and the mechanistic paradigm. Their minds seemed to work in a field of morphic resonance or a synchronized field of energy. Both agreed that there is no God outside the material world. The depth of matter is the whole, and the whole is the transcendence of the psyche; the transcendent depth of the psyche is God. Matter reveals God—for those who have eyes to see.

The word "pantheism" is used in the writings of Jung and Teilhard because the openness of matter to the depth of God is an integral or entangled relationship. Although both Jung and Teilhard spoke in terms of pantheism, both thinkers eschewed reductionism and, in fact, did everything they could to avoid what Whitehead called a "fallacy of misplaced concreteness." The idea of pantheism is rejected by many theologians because it flattens God into matter: divine transcendence seems to collapse. This is true if we think that matter is stuff or substantive being and nothing more. Quantum physics tells us otherwise. Mind and matter are entangled; the depth of matter is mind, and the limits of mind are limitless. God simply cannot be considered apart from matter because, without matter, God-talk is impossible. This is the "hard problem" of God. We cannot think about God or relate to God apart from matter. God cannot be separated from matter because matter is the matrix of consciousness. Matter is formed by mind, and mind is the reflection of matter. Neither God nor matter can exist or change without affecting the other, as Teilhard reminds us. God and world form a relational whole.

The mind of matter allows for a renewed understanding of transcendence and immanence. To talk about an immanent God is to talk about the individuated psyche, and to talk about the unlimited horizon of the psyche is to talk about the transcendence of God: immanence is the basis of transcendence. If God is the ground and depth of matter, then the ground itself is an inexhaustible realm of potential life that draws the mind to contemplate that which is not yet realized. The limits of the psyche, the collective unconscious, are unlimited. We can go beyond ourselves precisely because there is an incomprehensible depth within ourselves or, in Augustine's words: "You were more inward to me than my most inward self."[3]

Jung probed the withinness of God in a deep and analytical manner. His *Answer to Job* is a personal confession of wrestling with God. His insights on the Trinity enlighten the God-human relationship in a way that theologians avoid. The Church regards the doctrine of the Trinity as inviolable, and many theologians have remarked on the social nature of the Trinity. But Jung was not writing within theological circles, and, therefore, he takes a new look at the triune God, not as the perfection of divine persons

---

3. Saint Augustine, *Confessions*, trans. Henry Chadwick (Oxford: Oxford University Press, 1991), Book 3, para. 11.

in relationship, but as an imbalanced, unreconciled God, who creates in order to complete Godself in a fourth, the human person. God has a shadow side that needs to be reconciled. This is the basis of Jung's Godself, the unreconciled God dwelling in the unreconciled person. He speaks of the reconciliation of opposites as both the completion of God and the completion of the human person. For God to be complete is to fully actualize divine love in that which is not God; and for the human person to be complete is to be fully reconciled with God and free to love at the level of Christ consciousness. In these acts of completion, both God and human become "new." God becomes new in the human person, and the human person becomes new in God. To speak of Christ in evolution is to speak of the newness of God and the newness of the human in a personal union of love: Christ *is* the New Person. Meister Eckhart exclaimed: "God is the newest thing there is, the youngest thing. When we are united to God, we become new again."[4] Evolution is God-in-the-making or Christogenesis.

Jesus of Nazareth is the exemplary human for Jung, the *verus homo*, the true human. Jesus brought the opposites of God and human together by accepting human suffering and trusting the power of God within him, drawing him into higher levels of consciousness. Jesus lived from the highest level of nondual or Christ consciousness, the level of ecstatic love. Jung did not see Christ as universal savior but as universal archetype, the model of what is possible for every human person.

Although Jung rejected Jesus as universal Savior, there is a way to see the Christ archetype as salvific. In the Gospel of Matthew, Jesus says: "Whoever wants to save one's life will lose it but whoever loses one's life for my sake will find it" (16:25). A literal reading of this passage would lead one to renounce all material possessions and join a monastery. But the passage is not meant for monks and nuns; it is a universal call. A Jungian reading of "Whoever wants to save one's life..." might be "Whoever wants to live on the level of adolescent consciousness and seek

---

4. Matthew Fox, *Meditations with Meister Eckhart* (Santa Fe, NM: Bear and Company, 1983), 32.

authority outside oneself, such a person never really grows into personhood and God remains thwarted and diminished on the level of the isolated ego." To live with a closed mind and a constricted ego is never to be born into freedom: "Unless one is born again, one cannot see the Kingdom of God" (John 3:3). However, if one "loses one's life for the sake of the Gospel," Jesus states, "one will be saved." This is the level of unitive consciousness where one faces the darkness within, wrestles with God, confronts the lures of Satan, and acts in faith, trusting the darkness. Such inner reconciliation eventually transforms the ego into higher levels of integrated consciousness and eventually toward the level of unitive consciousness or wholeness. Salvation is the path to wholeness, and Jesus's life is exemplary: "The one who follows me will have the light of life" (John 8:12).

According to Jung, the Gospels do not establish a new religion. The good news of Jesus Christ eradicated religion as tribal and opened up the mind as the basis of a new holism marked by the New Person, who sees the world from a new center. Christianity is not a new religion but the end of tribal religion, evoking a new type of person for a new type of world. The Church, in Jung's view, is to enkindle the human energies of growth into God consciousness, to nurture the Christic, the New Person; essentially, to nurture a new human community for a new earth. Teilhard agreed. The Church is to be the community that spearheads evolution toward Omega. The sacraments are to enkindle the work of evolution for those who seek the wholeness of Christic life by plunging them into the baptismal fire of wholemaking. Eucharist is the self-gift of one's life as one participates in the emergence of the conscious whole united in love.

TEILHARD DE CHARDIN, THE PROPHET

Teilhard was a mystic, prophet, and professional scientist whose theological insights complemented those of Jung. His broad, cosmic vision focused not on the human person as uniquely created by God but on the human person as a fact of nature. He looked for repeating patterns in nature in order to discern the direction of evolution. The pattern that Teilhard perceived was the rise of consciousness accompanying the rise of biological complexity. There is a tendency in matter to complexify as it evolves into multiple relationships whereby consciousness is increased. Like David Bohm and Carl Jung, Teilhard thought that matter and mind form an integral whole. He rejected Thomistic metaphysics and spoke of love as the core energy of the universe. Unlike Jung, Teilhard held to an explicit role for religion as the depth dimension of evolution. Religion and evolution belong together and are "destined to become one single, continuous organism in which their lives ... complete one another."[5] He confessed that he found the Absolute in that which changes—matter—and he found matter to be blessed and holy—enduring—because of God; God is entangled with matter. Like Jung, Teilhard said that the transcendent dimension of matter is God and the immanence of God is matter. Just as matter grows and changes, so too, God grows and changes. God, therefore, is neither immutable nor perfect; rather, God is self-surpassing perfection in evolution. God's perfection is up ahead, as God is completed through ongoing life in evolution.

Teilhard spoke of matter as two-fold, having withinness and withoutness, on every level of physical life. The withinness of matter (radial energy) is consciousness, and the withoutness of matter (tangential energy) is attraction. The human journey, within the flow of evolution, is one of matter's rising consciousness in order to unite more fully through the energies of love. Contemplation is the act of harnessing the mind to create and discover, to form new truths, not only awakening to divine light but also seeing the light in new ways. Contemplation is like scientific discovery, searching, seeking out the depths of matter until it reveals the divine mystery in a new way. The contemplative, therefore, like the scientist, is the artisan of the future. Teilhard's "Hymn to Matter" captures his deep insights in a poetic and lyrical fashion. He writes:

---

5. Ursula King, *Teilhard de Chardin and Eastern Religions: Spirituality and Mysticism in an Evolutionary World* (Mahwah, NJ: Paulist Press, 2011), 160.

The rising Sun was being born in the heart of the world. God was shining forth from the summit of that world of matter whose waves were carrying up to him the world of spirit....I bless you, matter, and you I acclaim: not as the pontiffs of science or the moralizing preachers depict you, debased, disfigured—a mass of brute forces and base appetites—but as you reveal yourself to me today, in your totality and your true nature. You I acclaim as the inexhaustible potentiality for existence and transformation. ...I acclaim you as the universal power which brings together and unites....I acclaim you as the divine milieu, charged with creative power, as the ocean stirred by the spirit, as the clay moulded and infused with life by the incarnate Word....If we are ever to reach you, matter, we must, having first established contact with the totality of all that lives and moves here below, come little by little to feel that the individual shapes of all we have laid hold on are melting away in our hands, until finally we are at grips with the single essence of all subsistencies and all unions....Raise me up then, matter, to those heights, through struggle and separation and death; raise me up until, at long last, it becomes possible for me in perfect chastity to embrace the universe.[6]

Teilhard contemplated matter throughout his career and discovered the hidden divine presence in every aspect of life, from the tip of his pen, to gazing outside the window. The whole field of experience is the *divine milieu*. Nothing is profane for those who know how to see. He rejected a metaphysics of being and described a metaphysics of union, a "hyperphysics." Something more is taking shape through creative union: God is being born from within. Like Jung, Teilhard thought that the static model of the Trinity is insufficient to describe the God-world relationship.

---

6. Pierre Teilhard de Chardin, *Hymn of the Universe*, trans. Gerald Vann, OP (New York: Harper and Row, 1965), 69–70.

Instead, he spoke of "trinitization" as a theogonic process, a dynamic engagement of God's enfolding life in evolution. His insights on the Christic are novel and insightful and correspond to Jung's notion of quaternity. The quaternity emerging in evolution is not a fourth person added to the Trinity (although Jung did have something like this in mind); Teilhard's quaternity is suggested by his ideas on the New Person, the Christic, whereby the Trinity, enfolded in matter through evolution, emerges as a new complex union of God and human. The Christic is the "ultrahuman," the newness of God and the newness of the human person, creatively united in higher levels of consciousness. Teilhard did not speak of Christ as universal savior but as universal power. Jung's notion of Christ as archetype is implicit in Teilhard's work. He clearly states that salvation takes place by an option for the whole cosmos: "We can only be saved through the universe and as a continuation of the universe."[7] The onus of salvation is on the human person in evolution.

Teilhard contributes to theogenic holism by recognizing the dynamic life of God Omega as the power of evolution. Omega is the entangled God open to completion up ahead. Since God and matter are entwined, God is becoming whole in us, as we are becoming whole in God. Whereas the ancients thought that God is the most simple and immutable, Teilhard posited that God is complexifying in evolution and hence changing as a result of attraction and union. He anticipated a full flowering of conscious material life up ahead, not only earthly life but all intelligent life throughout the galaxies and perhaps other universes.[8] The Pleroma far exceeds the limits of terrestrial life. All conscious matter has the potential for Christic life.

---

7. Pierre Teilhard de Chardin, *Christianity and Evolution: Reflections on Science and Religion*, trans. René Hague (New York: Harcourt Brace Jovanovich), 92.

8. Teilhard de Chardin, *Christianity and Evolution*, 231.

ESSENTIAL POINTS

There is more, much more to be said but, for now, it might be helpful to summarize the challenges raised by a new myth of relational holism or theohology:

— Science and Religion are complementary forms of knowledge, like a pair of eyeglasses, two lenses through which one sees the whole. We must move beyond the dialogue of Science and Religion to integrate these two disciplines into a paradigm of relational holism.

— There is no "sky God" or supernatural God. God is the ground of my life and your life. The openness of my life and your life to unitive consciousness is possible because God is the transcendence of the psyche, the endless depth of life's endless potentials—the Whole of the whole. The psyche is always more than the conscious mind can express.

— We cannot say anything about God apart from matter and consciousness; hence, the starting point for God is embodied conscious life.

— You are divine, as am I. You are God in the flesh and so am I. I do not exhaust the mystery of God, but the totality of God undergirds my life. I am divine and God is human, just as God is divine and I am human. To quote Catherine of Genoa: "My me is God."

— If my life and your life are God-lives, then why do we judge one another? To reject another human person is to reject God. You are divine, no matter the color of your skin, the gender of your identity, your place of origin, or the religion you do or do not practice. Perhaps I cannot accept that I am divine and that you are as well, but this reflects how disconnected I am within myself. I can remain at the level of mythic consciousness and seek out the rules of the Church to be saved. However, if I have any hope of salvation, I must take responsibility for my life as God's life. Jesus models the way, the truth, and the life. Not to acknowledge my life as God's life is not to know God or life because everything is God-life: trees, grass, water, sun, earthworms, and the fly on my wall. Faith is like matter itself, which hides the mind. Faith lives not by what is seen but by what is unseen.

– To have faith in myself, faith in God, faith in the earth, faith in one another, faith in the future, is to live on a higher level of consciousness. I must be willing to embrace my own weaknesses and those of others to make this journey. I must be willing to die over and over if I am to live on a higher level. Death is a vital part of life. I must be willing to travel through the narrow gate and resist the power of the constricted ego if I seek the glorious road of abundant life, where God is the brilliance of all possibilities. Higher conscious life is unencumbered by egoic demands. Ego gods are little idols who demand utmost power and control; the living God is alive simply by being. Just to be is a blessing, Rabbi Abraham Heschel wrote, just to live is holy. To be, to really be, in the freedom of life's astounding beauty, is to breathe in the deep peace of the moment, to love. Love puts matter into motion for the one who is inwardly free. I must make every effort to move beyond a level of narrow consciousness, trying to protect my small ego from small wounds, and strive for an expansive Christ consciousness, where true freedom and love impel me to go beyond myself, into the unknown where God is bubbling up with life. Albert Einstein made this journey, so too did Rosa Parks, Helen Keller, and Steve Jobs, among countless others.

– As a posthuman, I know that I am a fractal of a whole and that the beauty of my life complements the beauty of your life. We are an entangled whole and cannot live without each other. For there really is no other reality, including God, than the deepest reality of the Whole.

— God is incomplete and desires to become complete in you and me. I am the Christ in formation; so too are you. As we become whole in God and God becomes whole in us, the earth becomes whole because we love it as our own God-lives.

— We will save ourselves by saving God from oblivion and irrelevance. If we begin to save ourselves, we will save the earth from utter destruction, because we are earthlings and what happens to the human, happens to the earth. The earth is our living whole, our lifeline: God is the heart of matter.

— Axial religions have run their course and will eventually mutate into a new type of religious expression. Second axial religion is emerging as the religion of tomorrow, a multiplicity of spiritual paths and rituals that expand consciousness and create wholeness. The Church of the planet will include all those committed to healing and wholeness, that is, all who are committed to shaping their God-lives toward unity, goodness, truth, and beauty. Focal communities will form around shared values and desires. The axial religions will be helpful to the religion of tomorrow by sharing from their wisdom and spiritual treasures, but they can no longer claim finality of revelation in an unfolding universe, where God is open to completion.

— Western religions must reunite with Eastern religions because what was separated is now being united on a new level of holism. Can we find new ground together on the level of mysticism and action? Harnessing our spiritual energies and our wisdom traditions for the sake of the global community will help heal the earth.

– We need a new myth of relational wholeness in evolution, new ways of reading the Gospels as stories of
wholeness, new rituals, and new symbols of relational
wholeness.

– To pray is to acknowledge a deep current of love-energy
within us, connecting and empowering us. Prayer can
free the mind to explore the deeper God-self. God
grounds our capacity for courage to face challenges, support one another, and risk doing new things. Where there
is God, there is the invitation to create and act. Divine life
is a high-flying adventure of the spirit.

– Finally, nothing is outside the concern of God. A God-
life is one that is unafraid to be original: to discover,
create, invent, push boundaries, face criticism, suffer
rejection without defeat, and dream of the future. A
Godly life lives as fully human, and a reconciled
human life lives as fully divine. The key to God-matter
entanglement is creativity. We have the capacity within
us—infinite potential love-energy—to become a new
person, a new human community, a new planet of life.
God is being born through all our efforts to focus our
minds, center them on the deepest self, let go into the
realm of infinite possibilities (imagine, dream, think)
and trust in the power of Omega. The one who is at
home with oneself discovers God in new ways. God
can break through our narrow minds when we live
each moment as an opportunity of choice, decision,
risk, and adventure. God delights in the ever newness
of love.

In addition to the points above, Danah Zohar provides a set
of values that can be helpful in shaping the New Person:[9]

---

9. Danah Zohar, *Spiritual Intelligence: the Ultimate Intelligence* (New York:
Bloomsbury, 2001).

Self-Awareness: Knowing what I believe in and value, and what deeply motivates me

Spontaneity: Living in and being responsive to the moment

Being Vision and Value-led: Acting from principles and deep beliefs and living accordingly

Holism: Seeing larger patterns, relationships, and connections; having a sense of belonging

Compassion: Having the quality of "feeling-with" and deep empathy

Celebration of Diversity: Valuing other people for their differences, not despite them

Field Independence: Standing against the crowd and having one's own convictions

Humility: Having the sense of being a player in a larger drama, of one's true place in the world

Ability to Reframe: Standing back from a situation/problem and seeing the bigger picture; seeing problems in a wider context

Positive Use of Adversity: Learning and growing from mistakes, setbacks, and suffering

Sense of Vocation: Listening to the inner call to serve. To know that each person has a special role in the formation of the world.

Living into Tomorrow

The Christian story of a perfect God in heaven—a God unaffected by earth's dysfunction—and a fallen human race in need of a savior has fractured the earth like a heavy hammer on a piece of glass. It is time to tell a new story, the myth of the relational whole, the story of a living God in relationship with a living earth. God is incomplete, not-yet, and we are incomplete, not-yet. We are only really alive if we fall in love with matter over and over. Otherwise, the illusion of an other-worldly God and a mundane world leads us to pulverize ourselves into fragments of disconnected individuals. As love draws God and self together into a unitive conscious life, God is born: the self becomes God and God becomes the self. Self and God are completed in a union of love, born in spacetime and destined for eternal creative union. Faith, hope, and trust in the power of matter are needed to engage this new reality. We are the New Person in evolution, the Christic, a new person for a new planet, the birth of God life for the wholeness (and holiness) of all life.

Jesus of Nazareth laid out a path to unitive God consciousness, the way to wholeness, the truth of reality; so too did Sri Aurobondo, Raimon Panikkar, and others. Clinging to our isolated, fearful selves, temperamental and easily wounded, leaves us cut off from one another and from earth life. Our consumer habits, honed by our addiction to technology, is blindly causing the death of the whole. The rise of mysticism and contemplative practices in our own time, along with the surge of computer technology, are all telling us something.

The human mind is desperate to find the whole with which it is connected. Jung and Teilhard were hopeful realists. Something new and wonderful is in our midst—it is potentially alive but must be awakened and made actual. The light of divine love is shining through all matter. This light seeks to be reflected in the human person. God is longing to be born from within. To give birth to God is to be fully alive.

The God-life we are to give birth to begins with coming home to ourselves. We are to give birth to our fully integrated selves—

to become Christic, New Persons co-creating a transpersonal cosmos. We can do so because the divine energy of love is already within, calling us to unite. To give birth to God is to give birth to the freedom of our identity, a birth that takes a lifetime and endures eternally. We are God in the flesh, and to the extent that we enact Godly lives, we will live resurrected lives. If I live in love, then I am always investing myself in the future of another. While I am alive, the other is me—my many selves that I am becoming; after I am dead, that other is you with whom I am entangled. My growing never ceases.[10] Death is the sum of our loves, and we live on to the extent that we love. The process of my becoming continues on in the many loves I enact. All that I am is all that you are and together we will always be part and parcel of all that is to come. It is important to grasp the present moment as the revelation of God, the reason to be and what we here for. Mary, the mother of Jesus, said "Yes," as she beheld the light within her. We, too, must see what we are and what we are created for, mothers of the divine mystery. For the question of God is our question, the human question and no other. We are the mystery of God.

---

10. Danah Zohar, *The Quantum Self: Human Nature and Consciousness Defined by the New Physics* (New York: William Morrow, 1990), 149–52.

The Christic

I am looking at a tree, but I see such astounding beauty and
graciousness, the tree must be You, O God,
I look at the wild weeds playing across the fields, and their
wild joyful freedom speaks to me of You, O God.
Yesterday, I saw a child crying alone on a busy corner, and
the tears were real, and I thought, you must be crying, O God.
God, you are the mystery within every leaf and grain of sand,
in every face, young and old, you are the light and beauty
of every person.
You are Love itself.
Will we ever learn our true meaning, our true identity?
Will we ever really know that we humans are created for
love?
For it is love alone that moves the sun and stars
and everything in between.

We are trying too hard to find You, but You are already here,
We are seeking life without You, but You are already within,
Our heads are in the sand, our eyes are blinded by darkness,
our minds are disoriented in our desperate search
for meaning.
Because You are not what we think You are:
You are mystery.
You are here and You are not,
You are me and You are not,
You are now and You are not,
You are what we will become.
You are the in-between mystery
The infinite potential of infinite love,
And it is not yet clear what You shall be,
For we shall become something new together.

Index